# GENERAL PSYCHOLOGY



HANS RAJ BHATIA

Oxford & IBH Publishing Co. Pvt. Ltd.
New Delhi

CBS

(A Unit of CBS Publishers & Distributors Pvt Ltd)

New Delhi • Bengaluru • Chennai • Kochi • Kolkata • Mumbai
Hyderabad • Jharkhand • Nagpur • Patna • Pune • Uttarakhand

Last Reprint 2017
ISBN 81-204-0149-2

**CBS Publishers & Distributors Pvt Ltd**
**204 FIE, Patparganj Industrial Area, Delhi-110 092**
**E-mail: delhi@cbspd.com, cbspubs@airtelmail.in**

19-Y17-06

# PREFACE

This book has been specially prepared to meet the requirements of students offering General Psychology as a part of the course in psychology, philosophy and education in the B.A. examination of the Indian universities besides offering in a brief and simple manner an introduction to a number of important psychological concepts and an insight into the basic principles and methods of scientific psychology for the use of the general reader. There is a plethora of popular books on psychology which the lay reader is eager to read but he can make the best use of this growing literature only if he has acquired a basic background in the subject which this book is designed to provide. The professional student of psychology in the Indian universities finds it difficult to follow some of the excellent books on the subject recently published in both England and America, and needs a simple but comprehensive book dealing with different topics of study included in the syllabus. But this is not all the reason for writing this book. For some time past the author who has written some very popular books on the various branches of psychology has been receiving advice and suggestions from kind friends in colleges and universities that a book on general psychology will prove helpful, and he has succumbed to their advice in the hope that this too will prove useful to the student community.

The order in which the various chapters appear in the book is my own and I feel that it will facilitate a better understanding of the subject. A number of minor topics are dealt with at many places but this repetition is justified as it will help a compact approach to the main subject of study. A number of illustrations have been added to make the study more interesting and to enable students to acquire a practical approach to the subject. It is really no use knowing a subject and not being able to see its bearing on life and its problems. Psychology is a fascinating subject, it is a recent addition to the galaxy of sciences, the number of students offering this subject at the degree and post-graduate level in Indian universities is on the increase, and even laymen are keen to know what psychology is about. Therefore the author has taken pains that the interest of the readers should be kept up, both by including topics of practical interest and by treating even routine topics from a new angle and in a simple language.

Questions are added to each chapter to enable students and readers to check up on what they have studied, and a brief list of books recommended for further study is added at the end of the book. Readers are urged to study them for a more detailed knowledge of the subject.

There is a vast amount of literature on psychological research and investigation, and the author has deliberately avoided referring to it as such references are more likely to confuse than enlighten the beginner. However important studies recently made on some of the important topics have been briefly touched upon.

The author wishes to express his gratitude to teachers who have been urging upon him to do this book and have been making very helpful suggestions. I venture to hope that they will continue to send advice and suggestions for the improvement of this book.

HANS RAJ BHATIA

286, Adarsh Nagar
JAIPUR-4
15 November, 1967

## CONTENTS

## Chapter I

# DEFINITION AND SCOPE OF PSYCHOLOGY

### A definition of psychology

Psychology is the study of human behaviour, of how people behave and why they behave in just the way they do. Its chief purpose is to know more about human nature and human activity. In the past psychology was defined as the science of soul or mind but it is not possible to have any direct knowledge of the soul or mind. While behaviour is objective and can be observed, both soul and mind are just assumptions, and even if we agree that they are justifiable assumptions, they cannot be observed and are not a proper object of scientific study. Later psychology was defined as the science of consciousness or conscious experience, but nobody has been able to say what makes us conscious of things and people around us, and in any case there are a number of things an individual does without being aware of them. Many people bite their nails or mop their heads and are surprised when their attention is drawn to these acts. They perform them unconsciously. Besides anybody's experience is his own private and personal world into which others cannot enter. It is known directly only to him who has that experience. But a person's behaviour is open to everybody to observe, it can be directly studied and it is better to confine the study of psychology to behaviour alone, to those activities of the individual which can be observed, compared and analysed by all. It is a systematic study of all that man does in response to his world of things and persons.

It is a matter of common experience that people differ from each other in many ways. They differ in likes and dislikes, tastes and temperaments, needs and interests, habits and skills, talents and abilities, ideals and values. What makes them so different? How do such differences arise? Why do people behave differently even under similar circumstances or with similar goals and purposes

Answers to such questions are given by the science of psychology Psychology helps us to understand the behaviour of people around us to find out how and why they behave differently and what influences have worked to make them so different, and to study human nature and the manifold ways in which it expresses itself in the life of different individuals.

Behaviour may be simple as learning a skill, forgetting or solving a problem or it may be complex and varied as educating young children, managing thousands of labourers in an industrial concern, advising people about suitable jobs, curing people afflicted with acute anxiety, controlling a rowdy mob or making people buy and use a particular brand of soap. This means that there are several areas of psychological work and study, that psychology bears on numerous and varied areas of life and work and that specialists in different branches of psychology are engaged in tackling problems of behaviour in different areas. Let us take a few samples of their work :

*Learning a skill.* If you have to learn a skill the question often arises whether you should take continuous practice over a long period of time, say six to seven hours daily, till you have learned it or whether you should have short periods of daily practice and spread it to several weeks. A number of experiments have been made to decide the issue and they show that distributed practice is more efficient than massed practice. In such experiments two groups of similar subjects are taken, one is asked to make persistent and continuous effort to learn and the other is allowed to distribute effort and take rest in between periods of practice. Generally it has been found that the second group learns better, showing that teacher's insistence on more and more practice and effort is not always very wise. It means that the student who studies ten hours the night before a final examination will not learn as well as the student who studies one hour daily for ten days.

*Why do we forget?* People usually attribute forgetting to bad memory and there is no doubt that the capacity to remember is inborn and varies with individuals. But a well-known psychologist gave a very interesting reason for forgetting. People forget things which are unpleasant—we forget to pay our bills, to post letters which we did not relish writing, to keep engagements which are disagreeable or to make purchases for the family which we do not approve. This means that we forget because we want to do so.

*Thumb-sucking*. Many infants develop the habit of sucking their thumb and mothers are unable to check or explain this "bad" behaviour. Psychologists have made detailed studies of infants found sucking their thumb and concluded that thumb-sucking was mainly due to the infant's dissatisfaction with the amount of sucking he was getting from the breast or the bottle, that infants who finished their bottles in the shortest periods of time were more apt to suck their thumb than those who took longer, and that infants who had infrequent feedings were more apt to suck their thumb than those who were fed more frequently. When thumb-sucking persists longer it does not serve the child to satisfy the need for sucking but is a means of fighting fatigue, boredom or frustration. Parents themselves are responsible for it and should provide more recreation, playthings and playmates.

*Changing eating habits*. In times of food scarcity leaders advise people to change their food habits as they are doing now in India. But psychologists move methodically to change this type of behaviover. Kurt Lewin, an American psychologist, made some interesting studies in this direction during the Second World War. He was director of the Research Centre for Group Dynamics and decided to approach housewives whose role in controlling food habits is obviously very important. He selected those who were deeply interested in war work and could be relied upon to undertake such programme as will help the war effort. He divided them into six groups. Three groups were given carefully prepared lectures on the merits of less popular foods. These lectures were given by women who themselves had tried and found good the foods they were now recommending. The other groups were given similar information but in the form of discussion in which they all took part. Such discussion usually ended by asking how many housewives were prepared to try those foods during the next week. Women took great interest in the movement but later observation showed that while only three per cent women of the first three groups who only heard lectures really tried those foods, in the other three groups the percentage was as high as thirty-three thereby proving that the second method of persuading was much more effective. Thus psychology showed that in dealing with social problems the technique of group discussion is superior to lecturing.

*Selecting people for jobs.* Reaction-time experiments are very common in psychology. In a simple experiment an individual is asked to raise his finger as soon as he sees red light or hears a sound and the interval between light or sound and his finger movement is measured. This is reaction-time and a study made in a large town revealed that road accidents were made by drivers whose reaction-time was longer and who were thus slow to react to things on the road or by those whose reaction-time was shorter, who were too quick to respond to changes on the road and whose over-confidence made them take chances. Drivers with medium reaction-time were safer. Reaction-time experiments also helped to select telephone switchboard operators whose speed and accuracy of reaction helps them to do better in their job.

These samples of psychological study of behaviour show how useful a systematic study of behaviour can be in practical life. In view of the fact that human behaviour is capable of innumerable and complex variations it is not surprising that the new science of human behaviour, psychology, has split into a number of branches to facilitate detailed and accurate research and study by specialists in different areas of life and work. Even otherwise scientific knowledge and understanding of human activities and behaviour is fascinating and valuable in itself.

So we may define psychology as the science of behaviour and the two terms *science* and ***behaviour*** need further explanation.

**Is psychology a science ?**

The term science is used for any systematically organized body of verified knowledge about a certain class of facts and events. We know how some of the natural sciences like physics, chemistry and biology deal with definite subject-matter, they are systems of knowledge about a specific field in which bits of information find their respective place and are connected with other facts. Physics deals with energy, with facts about heat, sound, light and electricity; chemistry deals with matter, how material things are composed and decomposed; and biology deals with living things, plants and animals, how they grow and develop; and psychology deals with human behaviour, with such activities as knowing, feeling, thinking, remembering and striving, how people grow and develop into what they are today. Thus each science is concerned with a group of facts and principles related to each other.

Secondly, the body of facts or the subject-matter dealt with by each science must be obtained through carefully controlled observation. Truly scientific knowledge can be attained only through accurate observation of nature. Now accurate observation is not easy, it must be carried on by trained observers who have learned to distinguish between what they observe and what they merely imagine.

Thirdly, each science has to formulate general principles or laws which govern facts and events included in the field of study. These general principles are very necessary for without them it is not possible to understand new facts, to explain them by relating them to already known facts, to foresee their recurrence and control it. These are not axioms like those laid down in geometry, they are verified general statements regarding relations which exist among observed facts and events. That is why scientific knowledge is described as universal, its goal is generalization.

Fourthly all knowledge called scientific must be definite, accurate, reliable and verifiable.

Lastly science is quantitative and the scientist is for ever measuring, calculating and weighing. Scientific inquiry and research is concerned mostly with the relationship of intensities of two phenomena.

Psychology as a science concerns itself with facts of behaviour. Its specific subject-matter consists of facts about individual organism's activities in relation to environment. Human activity is a vast field ranging from simple acts of satisfying hunger or thirst to highly complicated and prolonged striving for power and prestige. Psychology classifies such activities, traces their growth and development and describes how a person has grown and developed into what he or she is. Every one acquires facts about behaviour, about his own behaviour and about the behaviour of others but such knowledge is not scientific because facts by themselves have no meaning. They make sense only when they are related to other facts, when they are organized into a system and when they are collected with some plan or purpose in view. Such a purpose may be purely theoretical to gain knowledge and understanding of human behaviour for its own sake or practical to acquire understanding with a view to control it as it is done in education or advertising. This is done by discovering relations among facts so that some general statements about their occurrence and recurrence may safely be made. These are the laws or principles of psychology which tell us in broad outline the nature and course of human activity, and they help us not only to understand human behaviour but also to predict and control it.

Psychology as a science is empirical, that is, based on facts of experience. Such facts are obtained through carefully planned observation. Of course every science argues about facts and there is room for reasoning and opinion but the ultimate foundation of all sciences are facts of observation. If we have opinions and draw inferences they must be judged by reference to facts. Psychology, therefore, does not take notice of opinions unless they are supported by facts. We often hear people say "Women are safe drivers", "Tall people are frank and honest". "Bald heads are steady and sober". These opinions may be true, partially true or wholly false. A psychlogist will not accept them till he has facts to support them, till he has verified them. This is a great difference between common sense and psychology. Common sense may give us a true picture of behaviour but often it is based on ideas which have not been tested. There is a good deal of guess work, superstition or fancy in our common-sense view, but psychology as a science must go beyond common sense and check up the correctness or otherwise of opinions by resorting to careful and systematic observation. Common sense is not free from prejudice or bias but a science has to be objective and critical. Psychology has therefore to dispel many wrong notions about human behaviour in its pursuit of truth, and this it seeks to do through methods of careful observation and investigation.

Psychology as a science has devised several tools for measurement. There are intelligence tests, tests of interests and aptitudes, tests measuring attitudes and attainments, and with their help it is possible to place people in a series of increasing ability or any trait of personality. Of course human behaviour cannot be as accurately measured as water, heat or electricity, but what reasonable amount of accuracy can be achieved in comparing individuals with regard to these qualities of behaviour has been achieved as we shall see in the course of our study in this book.

Human activity may be studied in two ways. We usually try to judge it as right or wrong, good or bad, in terms of some standard of worth or value. Sciences which follow this appreciative approach are called *normative*. Ethics is a normative science of behaviour and logic is that of thinking. Another method of studying human activity is to describe it as it is observed in different stages, aspects or phases without any regard to its moral worth. Right or commendable behaviour is as interesting and important as unworthy or bad behaviour. Such sciences are descriptive or *positive*. They describe facts as they are, not as they ought to be. Psychology is a positive science. It is concerned not with how we ought to behave but with how we actually do. It seeks only to describe behaviour as it is observed in the life of an adult, a child, a lunatic or a genius Behaviour in all its aspects is of interest to a psychologist and questions of worth do not enter into his methods of observation and study.

**The nature of behaviour**

The term behaviour is used in a very broad sense. It includes not only motor activities like walking, playing, digging or pulling but also such activities as give us knowledge as perceiving, remembering, imagining or reasoning, and emotional activities like feeling happy, sad or angry. They are all activities of the individual, his life depends on them and it is difficult to think what the individual would be without them. They all are included in the term behaviour. "Any manifestation of life is activity" says Woodworth and behaviour is a collective name for all such manifestations. Whatever an individual does from the most passive state of sitting still and looking at the wall to the most active striving after a goal like training for a job or writing an article, is included in behaviour. Movements of limbs and acts of hearing, smelling or seeing are as much behaviour as thinking, remembering or feeling frightened. Behaviour expresses the entire life of the individual.

The individual is both a body and a mind. It is a psychophysical organism whose life is an integrated unity of mental and bodily activity. Though for purposes of study and description we distinguish between mental processes and bodily changes, between thoughts, emotions and memories on the one hand, and movements and actions of hands and feet on the other, in actual experience there is no mental activity separate and isolated from physical activity. Life is one single continuous flow of activity and its mental and bodily aspects though distinguishable are not really separable. Behaviour is both mental and bodily.

All behaviour has its roots in two reciprocal sources : the organism acting on the environment and the environment acting on the organism. Behaviour is the activity of the individual organism in relation to its environment and when we say that psychology helps in understanding and predicting behaviour, we mean that an individual's activities are to be studied in response to definite situations or environment. Walking on the road a child sees a big dog rushing toward him, is frightened and thinks of running away and hiding himself. His behaviour cannot be understood apart from the situation in which it has been aroused. Now the influence which the environment exercises on the organism and rouses it to activity is called the *stimulus* and the activity that is so aroused is called the *response*. A very bright light makes me close my eyes. The bright light is the stimulus and closing the eyes is the response. A noise makes me turn my head, the noise is the stimulus and turning my head is the response. All forms of behaviour are responses or reactions to stimuli.

Stimuli may be conditions within the body. Instead of the dog frightening the child the thought of his father's anger at his misbehaviour in the school may cause fright. There may be nothing wrong in the external environment but some condition within the individual may cause behaviour. Depression of mind may be caused by missing the train, by memory of a recent loss or by bad liver. Thus stimuli may be inside the organism, and for our purpose whatever provokes an organism to act is called a stimulus. Some psychologists have made it the keystone of their view of behaviour. To understand behaviour, they say, we must find the stimulus, and the goal of psychology, according to them, is to find relations that exist between stimuli and responses so that given a stimulus they can predict the response and given the response they can point out the stimulus. Their view of behaviour may be expressed in the following formula :

S—O—R

S stands for the stimulus, O for the organism and R for the response.

The environment in which the behaviour takes place need not necessarily be material or physical. It may consist of other organisms and their behaviour. The stimulus may not be a dog or a noise but a question, a taunt or a smile from another person. The reply to that question or the behaviour aroused by that smile or taunt will be the response. Man not only eats, puts on clothes or has a hair-cut but he does them in a manner approved and commended by other individuals who are members of his group or society. Customs, fashions and etiquette influences our behaviour and are a part of our social environment. Our likes and dislikes, loves and hates are largely influenced by people of our group. Social environment is a powerful stimulus of our behaviour.

Behaviour is also described as *adjustment to environment.* The organism acts to meet the needs of a situation. He blinks his eyes in dazzling light, puts kerchief on his nose when there is bad smell, wraps his body in cold and unbuttons his shirt in severe heat. In very cold water his blood rushes towards the outer skin to make it warm and in hot water it rushes inward to make it cool. While walking against a very strong wind the individual bends his body. He smiles to greet a friend but frowns to slight an enemy. He behaves and changes his behaviour to suit his physical and social environment But this does not mean that he always submits to or accepts what his environment demands of him. Often he does not like things around him and he makes changes in them. In fact making changes in his environment is keynote of man's behaviour and the vast edifice of civilization that he has built in the course of history is a testimony to his creative and constructive genius. Thus adjustment is not merely passive but also active and creative.

But whatever view we take of behaviour the individual does not come into behaviour all at once. It has been a matter of slow growth and development from the early years of infancy to maturity and old age. Behaviour grows through maturation of the body, through learning skills, through development of mental functions like memory, thinking and feeling. What a grown-up person is able to do today is the result of a number of changes which have come about in his physical and mental life. His limbs have grown, his sense organs have matured and his abilities have become more definite and perfect. In fact life is growth and behaviour changes with different stages of life like infancy, childhood, adolescence and youth. Psychology studies the growth and development of behaviour as a whole as also in its distinguishable aspects like preception, thinking, feeling and striving.

**Behaviour and consciousness**

There was a time when an individual was distinguished into mind and body. Psychology was able to deal with mind and physiology with body. The most important activity of the mind was consciousness—sensations, perceptions, imagination, memory feelings, emotions, thoughts and volitions, and it had nothing to do with bodily movements. It was not realized that there could be no mind or consciousness without a body and consciousness can be known through behaviour. If there is no behaviour there is no consciousness. The two sides of life are so closely mixed up that no sharp line can be drawn between them. We now talk of an individual rather than a mind or a body just to stress that the two are only distinguishable and not really separable.

As has been pointed out above your consciousness or conscious experience is known only to you and cannot be shared by others. I may have the same pain in the tooth as you have but your pain is felt and experienced by you and mine by me. Our experiences are similar but not identical. I can never share your pain nor can you share my pain. Our experiences are our own private property, they are personally and intimately known only to us. But we can know about other people's conscious experience through their behaviour, from their facial expressions and movements. If a person shouts and shrieks, gets excited and red, and flourishes his arms as if to strike we infer that he is angry. You can find out from a person's laughter whether he is full of joy mocking at others or just sneering. Behaviour expresses and gives a clue to conscious experience.

And there is behaviour of which the individual is not conscious. Witnesses to a traffic accident give conflicting reports of what actually happened. They are distorting facts without being aware of it. Psychologists have tested this phenomenon many times. We consider human behaviour to be rational but most of us have strong wishes, prejudices and notions of which we are not at all aware and which determine what we shall see, hear or think. We have already considered the case of forgetting important things because they are unpleasant and we remain happily unconscious of them. Our slips of tongue and pen reveal that our behaviour is being determined by forces over which we have no control and of which we are not even conscious.

Psychology deals with both conscious and unconscious behaviour.

**Explaining, predicting and controlling behaviour**

All science seeks to explain events by finding out their causes, to establish laws regarding causal relations, to predict events on the basis of such laws and then control events by controlling their causes. In this process sciences make certain assumptions, that is, they assume that all events are caused and the same cause produces or leads to the same effect. Psychology too makes such assumptions. All behaviour is caused and can be traced to certain factors which determine it; human beings are capable of observing, analysing, classifying and measuring such causes; and generalizations based on this study and analysis enable them to predict behaviour. True to this scientific tradition psychology since the latter part of the nineteenth century has been trying to develop principles which make it possible to predict the behaviour of individuals under certain conditions. In this field of scientific inquiry psychology is relatively a new entrant and the subject-matter of psychology is most difficult to study and the problem of making predictions about the behaviour of individual organisms is full of difficulties. Yet the success which psychology has achieved in this short period of time has been quite remarkable.

For example, psychology has from time to time put forward certain universal determinants of behaviour like instincts, motives, needs or drives and traced all human behaviour to one or more of them. Factors determining concentration of attention, learning, remembering, problem-solving have been analysed and through such factors these activities have been predicted and controlled. Intelligence tests have revealed the ability of students to benefit by education,, and their scores are being used to predict how far an individual student will go in achieving academic success.

Most of us readily accept predictions of physical sciences regarding, for example, the lunar eclipse, the health of a patient, the speed of an aeroplane, the action of a chemical compound but when it comes to predicting an individual organism's behaviour, very few people are ready to accept the claims of psychology. Yet all of us make predictions about other people's behaviour every day. We are prepared to swear that the booking clerk will be at the window by ten in the morning, that he who does not attend to his study will fail, that women take long to get ready to go shopping and the like. Predictions which psychology makes are less concerned with the activities of individuals or specific events in the lives of people. They are concerned mostly with studying, analysing and measuring factors which can be used to predict the behaviour of people in general. To what kinds of stimuli people attend readily, under what conditions should we take practice to learn more readily and effectively, what minimum score in intelligence tests is essential for success in any course of training, what attitudes are harmful for cordial relations among colleagues and the like are questions to which psychology has provided very definite answers. By analysing such factors and conditions and formulating general laws and principles about their working a psychologist is able to predict about behaviour in general.

It is no doubt true that predictions made by psychology are not as firm as those made by natural sciences. Its reason is not far to seek. The number of factors involved in any physical change is small and it is possible to keep in view all those factors which will interfere with our prediction of events. But in the case of human behaviour the number of possible factors interfering with our predictions is large and it is not possible to keep all of them under observation. In boiling water or in melting iron the process is very simple and it is possible to foretell at what temperature water will boil or iron will melt. But in the case of predicting brilliant success for a very highly intelligent student there are numerous factors which may interfere with his performance. He may not be really interested in his success, during the examination he may be very much worried about the illness of a relative or the financial difficulties of the family, he may have developed a love affair just before the examination and his mind may be torn between two interests or just too much work the night before the examination may have upset him. There are thus very many factors which may interfere with our firm prediction of his behaviour. Therefore predictions in psychology can be made firmly only at the general level or for a group. We can predict only in a general way that students with a high degree of intelligence will score brilliant success.

We are now in a position to offer a complete definition of psychology. *Psychology is a science which seeks to understand, describe, predict and control behaviour.*

## Other definitions of psychology

It would be interesting to know other definitions of psychology which have been given up for one reason or the other. The earliest psychologists defined psychology as the science of the soul or the psyche. By soul was meant a being residing inside the body and directing its activities as a sailor directs a boat. Recently it has been described as an active principle animating each human body and giving its activities a direction which it otherwise would lack. But the term soul is theological in its bearings and psychology made no progress so long as it was given that defintion. The soul is beyond experience and knowledge.

Later psychology was defined as the science of mind but attempts to describe mind intelligently did not succeed. Some said it was an immaterial substance, others described it as the sum-total of our mental states and processes or a bundle of sensations, perceptions and ideas. But how this sum-total or bundle was made up, how its units of ideas and perceptions were related and under what principle of organization they followed each other, was not explained.

Others defined it as the science of consciousness. Conscious life is likened to a stream, conscious experiences flow in a never ending river and mental processes and activities like pains, ideas, memories, perceptions can be known directly only by the individual to whom they belong. But the definition does not work. There are a number of activities which are conscious to begin with but which on being performed a number of times become automatic and are continued without awareness. Riding a cycle requires concentrated attention in the beginning but later it is carried on without attention. One may talk, think or sing while cycling. Again some unpleasant experiences or unfulfilled wishes are banished from consciousness and forgotten but they continue to influence our daily behaviour and experience even though we are no longer conscious of them. We are told they lie in the field of the unconscious. Thus it would not be correct to define psychology as the science of consciousness for it would leave out a large part of our activity which has become automatic or which has its source in the unconscious.

The definition of psychology set forth in this book is more recent and popular. It is broad and covers all the relevant facts. It helps psychology to achieve the position of an exact positive and objective science employing methods of observation and experiment. Both mental and bodily facts receive their due consideration and the knowledge obtained can be fruitfully applied to other fields for the simple reason that it relates to the entire life and behaviour of individuals.

## Branches of psychology

*General psychology*, with which we are primarily concerned, deals with general conditions under which normal human adult beings act, think and feel. It is concerned with universal characteristics of behaviour and, as has been pointed out, seeks not only to describe them but also to relate and explain them by reference to some general laws. But due to tremendous recent growth in psychological knowledge the field of general psychology has grown so vast that it has become necessary to mark out the subject-matter into special fields or branches. It helps specialization and makes for rapid progress in knowledge. Some of these branches are simply different approaches to the subject, taking a slightly different point of view in studying behaviour, and others are applications of general psychology to special departments of life. General psychology draws from, and in turn contributes to, these special branches and sub-divisions. It is the trunk from which the various branches of psychology have grown.

*Physiological psychology* studies the physiological processes which directly or indirectly affect behaviour. It is the study of physiological processes in relation to mental life. Since behaviour is both bodily and mental this branch of psychology is very valuable in throwing light on how we act, see, hear or smell. By revealing differences in the physical constitution of persons it helps to explain individual differences. Recently it has thrown a flood of light on how gland activity affects behaviour, particularly emotions. A person, for example, may be highly excitable due to excessive activity of his thyroid gland.

*Comparative psychology* is a study of the differences and similarities of behaviour between men and also between men and animals. The first is individual psychology and is implicit in all our judgments. We cannot describe a man as intelligent without in some form or another implying that he is more intelligent than some and less intelligent than others. This branch gives us detailed knowledge of individual dfferences. The second by its experiments on animals has shown how the nervous system functions and what are the conditions of learning. Comparing the developed mind of man with the lower manifestations of behaviour among animals brings out the nature of simpler forms of behaviour.

*Genetic psycholcgy* studies growth and development, and inquires into what we inherit and what we acquire, and the several ways in which our inheritance is modified in childhood and youth. How do we become what we are, what changes take place in thought and behaviour at different stages of life are the main concern of genetic psychology. It studies the growth and development of not only individuals but also of specific activities, habits and attitudes. Genetic psychology revealing what factors determine personality, character and intelligence in children helps their right education.

*Abnormal psychology* studies behaviour which is unusual and different from the normal. Such abnormalities of behaviour may be due to defect, disease or disorder of mind. For example, some peo e are haunted by fears of disease or death, some imagine themselves to be some great person, some lose memory or some go mad. They are a great problem for society, and abnormal psychology investigates into the nature, causes, prevention and cure of mental disorders and abnormal behaviour. These types of abnormal behaviour are exaggerations of normal activity and their study gives us insight into our thoughts, fears and actions. Genetic psychology deals with growth, the maturation and development of personality, abnormal psychology is concerned with breakdowns, degenerations and serious difficulties in personality organization.

*Applied psychology* is the use we make of general psychology in different areas of life and work. Thus *social psychology* deals with behaviour resulting from social interaction between individuals and groups, *educational psychology* deals with the processes of growth and learning and how they can be influenced to mould life, character and personality of young people, *child psychology* is concerned with the several phases of the growth and development of children. *industrial psychology* is interested in problems of human relations and behaviour in business and industry, and we have psychology of religion, psychology of advertising, psychology of study and efficiency and the like. The names indicate clearly the sphere in which general psychology is sought to be applied.

## Schools of psychology

When a science is making rapid progress through the investigations of a large number of scholars differences of approach are bound to arise. Modern psychology has grown out of several different approaches to the study of human behaviour, and though these points of view are gradually merging, their knowledge and study by students will help to make the picture of psychology fuller and clearer. Let us describe them briefly.

*Structuralism* stresses the need and importance of studying only conscious experience. Obviously its sole method would be looking inward into the working of one's own mind, that is, *introspection*. A person exists because he is conscious, and therefore, the main problem of psychology is to explain complex mental processes in terms of simpler processes of sensations, images and feelings. Its approach is analytical: what parts of the body give sensations of warmth, cold or pain, how does looking at one colour affect what we see when we look at another colour and the like problems analyse our mental processes to discover how complex structures of mind are built up. But we know today that many items of behaviour cannot be explained by merely looking into what is taking place in our minds, conscious experience is not all, and there are processes affecting our behaviour of which we are not even aware, and which cannot be reached through introspection.

*Behaviourism* holds that psychology should study not consciousness but behaviour, what people do. J.B. Watson was the chief exponent of this school. He insisted that bodily behaviour is all that psychology can and should study through objective observation Only then psychology can become a natural science. He refused to consider mental states and processes as making any difference to behaviour. But how are we to understand the difference between a person running to catch a train, a person running to escape an enemy or a person running for physical exercise? Watson cannot answer. For a complete explanation of behaviour some reference to mental processes and states is necessary.

*The Gestalt School* holds that to explain any behaviour we must know the whole situation in which that behaviour takes place The figure 6 has different meanings in 6, in 60, in .06 or in 0 6, and the meaning is determined by its relations to other factors. The meaning of what we see, feel or do is determined by the whole situation or the complex set of relations involved in behaviour. Therefore behaviour should not be studied piecemeal but in wholes before we try to explain it.

*Functionalism* stresses study of activity of the organism and activities are both mental and bodily. It is interested in such problems: how can we remember more effectively, how do we solve problems, how can we get rid of bad habits. In the study of mental life functionalism seeks to explain activities rather states of mind.

*The psychoanalytic school* beginning with the study of abnormal behaviour and mental disorders stresses that all of our behaviour cannot be explained in terms of conscious states or processes and that hidden motives and wishes of which we are not even conscious influence it nor are all physical disorders and diseases due to purely physical causes, and their origin has to be sought in such hidden motives and ideas. Freud and his followers developed the psychoanalytical method by which such hidden motives, wishes and ideas could be brought into the light of consciousness and they believed that the patient would be cured of abnormal behaviour and mental disorder by merely reviving in memory the old forgotten and repressed thoughts and wishes.

All these approaches have helped to make our knowledge of human nature and activity fuller and more exact and reliable.

### The Value of Psychology

Psychology is a new science but already it has made a universal appeal. People in all walks of life are eager to acquire some knowledge of psychology and in the western countries general courses in psychology for laymen are very popular. All young students beginning a course of psychology will be helped if we briefly consider the values that should result from the study of psychology.

Psychology gives knowledge of human nature and should help students to understand themselves and others better. Understanding ourselves we can make the most of our abilities and opportunities and make a success of our lives. Some people like a well regulated life, they have understanding and knowledge, keep their emotions in balance and poise and act thoughtfully. Others are creatures of impulse and give themselves away at the slightest provocation. They have no stability in their lives. Understanding what makes for poise and balance one can make his life happy and successful.

Understanding others, their variety of interests and abilities, their weak points and good points, one is able to get over his prejudices and adjust himself to people with whom one works and lives. There is a proverb that to understand all is to forgive all, and it is true in daily living that most of our difficulties with people at home and outside are due to our failure to understand them. Knowledge and understanding makes for better social relations.

Psychology helps us to solve our personal problems and difficulties and thus achieve better mental health and efficiency. Many people have too high an opinion about themselves and go about expecting others to treat them as such, and many people have too low an idea about their capacities and suffer from feelings of inferiority. Both types suffer from anxiety and tension. But those who have a correct estimate of their strong and weak points act accordingly, making the most of their strong points and reducing the handicap of weak points.

In the fields of education, medicine, industry, social affairs and in all areas of life and work where human beings work together our concern is to influence and change the behaviour of people in definite directions for the purpose of attaining specific ends and a knowledge of psychology is very helpful. That there are branches of applied psychology in respect of all such fields shows that psychology is being used by them to solve their problems. In education psychology tells us how learning can be made more effective, how students' attention can be secured in the class, how discipline can be maintained and the study of psychology is necessary for teachers in training colleges. To sociologists and social reformers psychology provides principles and methods of changing attitudes and thereby affecting social changes. In fact all areas of life and work the knowledge of human nature and behaviour which psychology provides is of great help.

---

## QUESTIONS

1. Define psychology and explain your definition.

2. Is psychology a science? How far can it predict and control behaviour?

3. Comment on the following definitions of psychology :

   (a) Psychology is the science of mind.

   (b) Psychology is the science of conscious experience.

   (c) Psychology is the science of behaviour.

4. What is a "school of psychology"? What are the distinguishing characteristics of the following schools :

   (a) structuralism, (b) functionalism, (c) behaviourism, (d) the Gestalt school, (e) psychoanalysis.

5. Write short notes on the following :

   (1) genetic psychology, (2) comparative psychology, (3) physiological psychology, (4) abnormal psychology.

6. What is the value of psychology? What advantages does the study of psychology bring ?

CHAPTER II

# METHODS OF SCIENTIFIC PSYCHOLOGY

## Growth of Scientific Psychology

People have always been interested in the study of their own and other people's behaviour and psychology is as old as any other science. But scientific psychology of the type envisaged here is only a hundred years old. Three German psychologists may be said to have laid its foundation. Wilhelm Wundt set up the first psychological laboratory in 1879 at the university of Leipzig. He was greatly influenced by the work of E. H. Weber, a physiologist, and G.T. Fechner, a physicist. Weber studied the relation between external stimuli and sensory experience and put forward the result of his investigations in the form of a law known as the Weber's law It was: "How much must intensities of stimuli differ before such differences can be noticed?" For example in a lighted room what proportion of the existing light intensity must be increased or decreased before it can be noticed? He found that just noticeable increase or decrease must be one hundredth part of the existing light. In the case of weight it must be one-thirtieth part of the weight lifted. Fechner carried the investigations of Weber further to make his conclusions more precise. These studies showed that experience could be measured and that psychology could develop into a science.

Wundt used the apparatus and methods of these two pioneers in his laboratory. His aim was to analyse conscious experience, more exactly *perceptions*, and to know the underlying biological structures and functions. Attempts were also made to measure emotional feelings and motor reactions. He held that there is one-to-one correspondence between the excitation of the cerebral cortex and the various forms of experience. He made extensive use of introspection and trained workers in his laboratory to analyse conscious experience in the process rather than after it had occurred.

Wundt's experiemental work dealt mostly with the psychology and physiology of vision and reaction-time. He did not make new experiments but verified and extended the work of his predecessors. However he widened the scope of psychology and extended the use of of what he called the method of experimental introspection.

A German philosopher H. Ebbinghaus did some experimental work on memory. He studied such questions as how we remember, why we forget and what are the best methods of memorizing. He memorized lines of poetry and meaningless groups of letters to see how well the learner could repeat what he had memorized. Such studies had great bearing for educational psychology and shifted the point of view of psychology from analysis of conscious experience to description of behaviour.

Memory is verbal learning and the research on memory opened a vast field of the subject of learning, motor learning and learning of skill as in typing or playing a musical instrument. Results of such studies were made use of in industry.

An Englishman Francis Galton studied individual differences and began to measure them in bodily terms. His primary concern was to trace such differences to hereditary factors. An American student of Wundt, J. M. Cattell studied individual differences in vision, hearing, memory and reaction-time. He paved the way for statistical analysis of individual differences.

In the beginning of the present century tests of intelligence were devised by a French psychologist Alfred Binet to see whether a child had sufficient mental development to benefit by ordinary schooling.

Darwin's theory of evolution by natural selection played an important part in the development of psychology as a science of behaviour. If human life and behaviour is a continuation of animal life and behaviour the original and elementary forms of complex human behaviour must be sought in animal behaviour. Animal psychology threw much light on unlearned behaviour, processes of learning, and sensory and learning ability. How intelligent animals are, how much do they respond to environment, have they any consciousness, how are brain processes related to behaviour, how does the brain structure of animals differ from that of men, how do secretions of glands influence sexual and other aspects of behaviour, and the like, were some of the questions raised and answered by animal psychology, and such investigations helped to understand our own complex learning processes and to see the psychological importance of our own physiological structures and functions.

Though educationists like Rousseau and Pestalozzi stressed the importance of studying children and providing them facilities for developing their natural capacities as early as the eighteenth century it was only in the latter half of the nineteenth century that the first systematic study of child mind and behaviour was made by a German physiologist Preyer in his book *The Mind of the Child*. He made careful observation of children's reflexes and how their behaviour grows more complex in successive stages. Sully and Hall led the movement, the "recapitulation theory" of the latter by which it is meant that the child passes through a series of stages similar to the stages in the life and history of the group caught the public imagination and scholars and educators began to seek historical epochs in the early activities of the child. But this tendency soon took a correct turn and educators and psychologists began to study processes of child development in their several aspects and to ask what reactions are normal and usual at any stage of child development. Such search for normal reactions was first confined to memory and intelligence and led to Binet's work on intelligence tests. Later on, growth and development of motor activity, imagination, perception, emotional and social behaviour received the attention and study they deserved.

An Austrian doctor Sigmund Freud (1856-1939) and his followers stressed that early childhood experiences largely determine the nature of adult personality. Such experiences according to Freud were connected with sex but his followers attached greater importance to frustration and insecurity in childhood. These psychoanalysts did great service to psychology in focussing attention on early experiences of children and parent-child relationships and thus paved the way for a scientific recognition of child study in education.

**Freud's contribution**

Freud saw very early that some behaviour cannot be easily explained and may be due to early experiences which have been forgotten and of which the individual is not conscious at present. Such experiences were painful and the individual very conveniently pushed them out of his consciousness and memory into the field of the unconscious. From there they continue to influence the conscious behaviour of the individual and the individual is unable to understand why he behaves in that manner. Freud held that through the method of psychoanalysis such repressed experiences can be brought back to memory and when that is done the individual is able both to understand his behaviour and to control it.

In his clinical practice Freud had to deal with a number of people who were mentally ill and whose behaviour was abnormal, unusual and socially unacceptable. He sought explanation of such behaviour in previous "repressed" experiences and effected cures by reviving the memory of such experiences. His studies brought out the distinction between normal and abnormal, between milder simple mental ailments we call *neuroses* and serious mental diseases we call *psychoses* and paved the way for close co-operation between medicine and psychological treatment or *psychiatry* in the treatment of behaviour disorders. Hysteria is an important neurotic disorder and French doctors had found before Freud that its symptoms could be induced by putting an individual in a sleep-like trance we call *hypnosis*. Hypnosis was also used to produce anaesthesia and many people underwent painless operations under its influence. Charcot, a French neurologist, used hypnosis in studying hysteria and his pupil Freud used it in curing neurotic disorders. In a hypnotic state people recalled past experiences, fears and desires which they never recognized as their own in waking life. They had no knowledge or memory of them during their normal life before and after the hypnotic trance. Freud believed that these unconscious experiences, desires and fears accounted for the neurotic behaviour.

Freud's view that there is a realm of the unconscious which introspection cannot reach and which influences our daily conscious life has revolutionized not only psychology but also our entire social thinking. Though people felt that he attached undue importance to sex and its repression they acknowledged his great contribution to our understanding of the working of human personality in different life situations and of the nature of abnormal behaviour. Abnormal psychology has been developed by a number of pioneers in the field in both Europe and America, and now psychiatrists and clinical psychologists are working in all progressive countries for the treatment and prevention of mental disorders.

During and after the first World War the movement for mental testing gained ground. Not only numerous types of tests were devised and applied but it led to the growth of educational psychology as an independent applied field in which teachers saw a way of helping children by making teaching more effective. Examples of such applications have been given in the last chapter and they show how useful psychology is making itself in various fields.

The study of psychology is growing more and more popular because man's interest in his fellow-men over-rides all other interests. Readers have known in the last chapter about its various branches. These branches are growing fast and they are both contributing to, and drawing from, the advances made in general psychology.

### Methods of scientific psychology

How does psychology obtain its facts? What are the methods by which psychologists are constantly increasing and improving their knowledge of human nature and activity? We shall now turn to those methods of investigation by which psychologists are trying to extend their knowledge of human behaviour. They are observation, experimentation, statistical analysis, comparative method, genetic method, clinical procedures and psychoanalysis. Because of the peculiar nature of mental activity that goes on inside our mind without being observed by others psychological observation takes the form of introspection when such activities have to be studied. We shall deal with these methods in detail.

## Observation

All sciences use observation to obtain facts. But simple observation is not enough because we observe a large number of things and a good many of our observations may be either useless or unnecessary for the purpose of a particular science. Again the tendency to see what we want to see is strong when we make observations and our cherished beliefs or prejudices affect our observation. Therefore it seems very necessary that the work of observation is entrusted to trained observers.

A psychologist has one great advantage over other scientists. He can observe the phenomenon of his interest both from within and without. He may watch other people's behaviour and he may also look into his own behaviour from inside or ask other people to report about their behaviour as they observe it. A botanist observes the growth of a plant from outside but cannot ask the plant to give information about its growth.

There are thus two kinds of observation. Observation which can be verified by others as well as by the subject is called naturalistic or *objective observation*. Anybody can see how fast or accurately I type, walk or play cricket and such observation is objective. But while doing these acts I may be feeling pain, fatigue or hunger and may be conscious of them. When we study this consciousness or awareness of these mental activities our observation is *subjective*. Our behaviour can be observed in its bodily aspect, movements of the body or changes inside the organism and it may be observed in its mental aspect, that is, thoughts, feelings, wishes, purposes or memories which accompany bodily movements or changes. Both kinds of observation are needed in psychology for every act of behaviour has both mental and bodily aspects. Buying a piece of cloth is understood not merely by referring to the kind, price and length of cloth but also by the need and purpose of the buyer, the feelings of joy or sorrow which accompany the act.

## Introspection

When observation of mental states or activities is careful and detailed it is called *introspection*. If the doctor asks you how you feel and you say that you feel tired, you are making a report on your mental state and it is subjective observation. But if he continues and asks you how it feels to be tired, that is, if he asks you to attend carefully to the sensation involved in fatigue and to make the state of fatigue itself the object of your observation and analysis, it would be *introspection*.

Introspection is to look into the workings of our own minds, to observe and report the contents of conscious experiences. It is not merely self-reflection or self-examination but attending to and describing experiences under known external and internal conditions. One phase of psychology has been studied effectively through introspection and that is sensation. It is practically the only way of determining what sensations are.

But introspection is not easy. If you ask a person why he gets irritated when questioned about his relations with his boss he may feel confused. We need courage to make our introspections accurate.

Secondly introspection destroys the very object it seeks to observe. It has to record experiences going on in our minds but the more successfully we introspect the more readily the thing we want to introspect is missed. There are three factors in every experience, the person, the object and the relation between the two, that is, the awareness of the object by the person. The psychologist wants to observe this awareness but the moment he does so, the awareness disappears because attention is withdrawn from the object of awareness. The awareness cannot be attended to without attending to the object and the attention of the person engaged in introspection is divided between the object and its awareness. This is more so when introspection has to deal with emotions. If when you are angry you say that you are a psychologist and must analyse the mental process or activity of anger, your anger at once disappears. By concentrating attention on the mental process we withdraw it from the object of that process and so arrest the process itself.

It is argued that introspection can remedy this defect by *retrospection*, that is, by recalling the process in memory when it has passed. But then introspection is not observing any mental state but a memory of it. This objection has considerable weight.

Thirdly judged from its results introspection is unscientific. The divergence and lack of unanimity in its findings speaks for its unscientific character. Individual investigators differ in their results in almost all science and such discrepancies are not peculiar to psychology.

A fourth difficulty is that introspection is purely a subjective method. It can reveal to us the mental processes of a single individual only and will not enable us to arrive at universal knowledge which is the object of scientific psychology. But it is possible to compare the results of several observers and on the basis of our knowledge of individual minds arrive at a knowledge of people in general.

Lastly the use of the method of introspection would require a very keen power of abstraction because we are dealing not with things but processes and mental processes at that which are difficult to grasp. Thus introspection needs great practice, training and the habit of alterness in attending to mental processes as they occur.

There are certain classes of people with whom introspection cannot be used. Children, insane persons and animals cannot be studied by this method. For them we have to fall back on objective observation.

**Experimentation**

To observe is to find a fact, to experiment is to make one. Experiment is observation under conditions which we can control and vary. One advantage of this control is that we can repeat our observations as often as we like and obtain better, fuller and more accurate results. We have already given examples of psychological experiments in the beginning of this book and we may now outline some of the main steps in the process of experimentation, and scientific investigation.

The first step is the formation of a *hypothesis*. Through insight and on the basis of previous knowledge and research you hit upon a provisional explanation of the relation of certain facts. It is essential that this provisional explanation or hypothesis should be sensible and plausible, and the interest of science can be promoted if the verification of that hypothesis leads to an advance in our knowledge. The second step is to *deduce consequences* from that hypothesis which can be experimented upon. The third step is to arrange an experiment to test and see if those consequences can be verified or not. If they are verified the hypothesis is strengthened and may be accepted for the time being. If the experiment gives negative result the hypothesis stands disproved and will be rejected. Then we will have to frame another hypothesis. Finally efforts will have to be made to see that the verified hypothesis is tested again and again to make sure of its truth and ultimately change it into a law or a general proposition expressing causal relation. Thus the scientific method of experimentation is basically a method of testing some hypothesis or guess about the possible causes of an event.

Suppose the teacher finds that in his class some students do better than others and wanting that all should do better insists that those who achieve less should work harder. He is working on the assumption that success depends entirely on hard work. A psychologist rejects this hypothesis straightaway as he finds that quite a number of students work very hard and yet do not learn much. He frames the hypothesis that this must be due to differences in methods of work and study. So he arranges an experiment in which he takes two sets of students who are known to be of equal intelligence and whose score in previous examinations is nearly the same. He makes them work under similar conditions, gives them, for example, the same poem to commit to memory. One set of students is asked to spend six hours at a stretch in memorizing the poem and the other is asked to spend one hour at a time, take rest for an hour and then return to the task for another hour completing six hours in six instalments even if their work is stretched to another day. Then their achievement was compared and it was found that the second set did better. Thus it was proved that the methods of study make a difference and that spaced learning is more effective than massed learning.

Let us now describe some of the essential features of an experiment.

In the first place an experiment is an observation which we can repeat and repeat as often we like. The above experiment can be repeated. The advantages of repetition are clear. It will remove all possible doubt. If we are able to repeat an observation over and over again we may be reasonably sure that our results are valid and reliable. In experiment we do not have to wait for an opportunity for right observation and arrange for it ourselves, and check it up by repeating it. It saves a lot of time that otherwise would be wasted in looking out for right opportunities.

We cannot generalize without such repetition. If every time you frighten a child the latter has a stomach upset, you may be reasonably sure that fear is the cause of his trouble. The more often it has happened the firmer is your conclusion and the more general is the causal relation between the two.

Secondly for sound generalizations repeated observations must be made under similar conditions, that is, conditions must be controlled. If conditions are allowed to change the results may not be the same. Now it is very difficult to keep all the conditions similar and under control but we have to see that all the relevant and important conditions remain unchanged. For example to say that all the later experiments must be made on Monday because the first one was made on that day is not relevant.

Suppose we have to inquire if a particular drug like caffiene has any effect on the alertness of a person. Many factors would be involved but it is possible that a person might be influenced by the fact that caffiene is being tried on him. In order to control this factor two groups of people are taken, they resemble in age, sex and intelligence and two kinds of pills are prepared, one packet containing caffiene and the other similar in appearance but not containing caffiene. The latter pills are called *placebos*. The group taking the caffiene group is called the *experimental group* and the group taking the placebos is called the *control group*. The latter resembles the former in every respect except that it is given placebos instead of caffiene. By comparing the behaviour of the two groups we can find out the effect of caffiene, if any.

Many experiments in psychology are of this type as will be found in this book.

Thirdly every experiment must have *variables*. A variable is any characteristic that may appear in changed amount or quality in different instances. In any experiment we must have two variables. In the above example caffiene and alertness are the two variables. Caffiene is called an *independent variable* because we can change its amount independently of the other. Alertness, on the other hand, is a *dependent variable* because we are trying to see if it depends on caffiene. It is possible that there may be more than one dependent varible. Caffiene may lead to liveliness besides alertness.

The experimental method is not without its limitations and a student of any science must have them in mind. In the first place, as must have been already clear, an experiment is an artificially arranged observation and the psychologist has to select what he wants to control and observe. In this selection he may have to work on unchecked suppositions and his conclusion may have a very limited validity. Another great disadvantage of the experimental method is that we cannot use it wherever we like. We cannot make experiments with human beings or even animals as we like or as is possible with material things. People have wishes and feelings, there are social codes and they may prevent making experiments with marriage, education, personal relations and the like. Mental activities and behaviour are a vital part of human personality and making experiments with them we may do them irreparable damage. Thirdly psychological experiments are sure to interfere with the very thing they aim at studying. Natural sciences are able to isolate the object of their observation but such isolation is not possible in psychology. People on whom experiments are made are highly sensitive and the mere knowledge that their behaviour is being studied will make them behave differently.

There are a good many people who talk of making experiments in education and social organization by introducing new curricula or bringing in a minor reform in social living. There can be no experiment without such control of factors as have been described above. They are only trials.

**Genetic method**

An important characteristic of behaviour is that it grows and develops. From infancy to old age human behaviour is always changing, growing and maturing and it is clearly the responsibility of psychology to study this growth and development methodically. The genetic method seeks to study the part played by several factors in such growth and development. How heredity and environment interact, what are the several stages through which human life passes what is the influence of social and economic conditions on personality and behaviour, what kind of home and school environment is most helpful to such growth, are questions which are studied by this genetic method. It is not so much a method or a technique as an approach. The whole question of tracing the process of child development is being seriously studied by psychologists but they cannot make experiments on children. In the developmental method the observer is on the spot and just watches the process as it occurs. But often he has to deal with children which are not quite normal. There is a very bright child with a genius for doing things, a very much spoilt child who does just the opposite of what he is told, a criminal child, a child given to very anti-social habits and the psychologist has to find out how that child has come to be what he is. He tries to reconstruct the history of that child by making him and his relations and friends recall the incidents of his early life. All information about the present and past life of the child is collected and on the basis of record prepared an attempt is made to explain his present behaviour. This is *case history method* within the genetic method. It is not quite scientific as memory is not very reliable but then under the circumstances this is all that can be done to answer the questions raised.

Uptil now case histories have been prepared only of mental patients with a view to find out where their development went wrong or what factors brought about their illness but very useful purpose will be served by preparing case histories of successful eminent people with a view to find out what influences in their lives contributed to their success so that similar influences may be made available to other young people. Such case histories are definitely not available. One obstacle to such a study is that successful people may not like that others should probe into their past or may present a biassed picture of their early life in order to gain prestige but we could spot superior normal children early and a record could be kept of their life and achievements.

The genetic method is also used with groups of children. We may study the same children from the kindergarten stage to the college, giving them a variety of tests, observing their behaviour in a variety of social situations and comparing their activities and performances at different stages to trace the pattern of growth and development. This approach is called *longitudinal*. It takes a lot of time as it has to be spread over a number of years and is very expensive. Or we may select sample groups of children at each age level and study changes in development by comparing their performance from one age level to the next. This approach is called *cross-sectional* as a cross-section of children is studied at each age level. This approach suffers from a serious drawback that children selected at each age level may be drawn from different social groups. For example one may belong to a rural community and the other to an urban area.

But the genetic method does not deal with the individual alone. It also helps us to trace the growth and development of complex forms of behaviour from their simple elementary beginnings. How complex habits, sentiments and beliefs are formed, how from simple sensations perceptions of time and space are developed, how complex skills are learned and the like are studied by the genetic method.

## Clinical procedures

These are employed by psychologists to understand, diagnose and treat people with problems and ailments, through tests of intelligence, aptitudes, interests. Many children in outbursts of rage throw themselves on the ground, refuse to eat or steal things. Many husbands and wives cannot get along with each other. Some have needless worries, others meaningless fears. When they approach a psychologist for treatment he gets their case history prepared obtaining all necessary information from their families, friends and associates, he may seek the help of a medical man, often a clinical psychologist is himself a medical man, and after psychological and medical tests a course of treatment is suggested. During the World War army men suffering from "shell shock" were given both psychological and medical treatment in hospitals. Such treatment is called *psychotherapy*. An important part of the clinical method is interviewing the patient and his associates so as to get from them the most important details about his past history. Often social workers are called upon to help with information about the social background and environment of the patient. Treatment will vary with individuals. What we are concerned with here is that such methods add to our knowledge of human nature and activity and are helpful to psychology.

## Survey methods

In the study of social problems we cannot control and manipulate people or perform experiments on them. We observe them under controlled conditions. Suppose we have to study the causes of successful and unsuccessful marriages. We cannot experiment with marriage and therefore we observe married people from several fields. We take some married people from the educated classes and some from the uneducated class, some married early in their teens and some married in their thirties, from different professions and classes of society, both rich and poor, caste-bound and free from caste. In this survey we study successful marriages and try to arrive at certain conclusions. The control we exercise is not in the organization of facts but in their selection. This metl psychology has learned from the social sciences and has been found useful in the study of attitudes, social relations and personality.

### Comparative method

It seeks to study the comparison of the behaviour of different animals and of the behaviour of animals with that of men. It is not possible to place children into non-human environment but an animal can be reared in human environment to see how far it can be taught to behave like man within the limitations of his nervous system. Experiments with animals have added to our knowledge of the working of the human nervous system.

### Statistical method

In every science measurement of quantitative relations between facts is believed to make our knowledge more accurate. Statistics manipulate facts in such a manner as to express them in a numerical form, and to find out how frequently a certain phenomenon occurs. For this purpose three techniques are used. The first is to find out the *average*, that is, the central point where the largest number of individuals are grouped. Not all individuals group around this central tendency. Many deviate from it and they represent *variability*. Mental patients deviate from the average and they are said to possess traits or variables dispersed from the normal. If we are interested in finding out what factors go with such mental disorder, we may, for example, find lack of intelligence frequently going with it and speak of this association as *correlation*. We say that mental disorder and lack of intelligence are correlated. Correlation is a method for measuring the degree of relationship between two sets of facts and if the relationship is strong it may become a law.

### Method of psychoanalysis

Psychoanalysis is a method devised by Freud to help a mental patient achieve a deep understanding of his own behaviour and thereby enable him to solve his own basic problem. Freud held that most mental ailments are due to the repression of unfulfilled wishes, desires, and ideas of the patient and merely reviving their memory and bringing them to consciousness will cure the individual. The psychoanalyst tells the patient about the aims and purposes of the treatment, the long time recovery will take and the course of treatment to be followed. The patient lies down on a coach, relaxes and then says whatever comes into his mind regardless of how irrelevant and objectionable it may be. This talking out technique Frued called *free association.* He found this superior to hypnosis because the patient remained in an active, cooperative state while coping with his difficulty.

This method is designed primarily for the treatment of neuroses but can be used with a large variety of disorders. It is very time-consuming as the treatment has to go on for several months and even years the patient taking a one-hour sitting every day. For that reason it suits people in great trouble but with plenty of money and time to spend.

Psychology has acquired great knowledge of the unconscious sources of behaviour through this method.

### Conclusion

It must have become clear to the reader that the use of a particular method will depend on the type of problem he has to face. In searching for an underlying cause or motive of behaviour often he will have to employ a number of methods and analyse a variety of types of behaviour. The feeling of inferiority may be indicated in a number of ways and many types of behaviour may have to be studied before we conclude that the individual is suffering from inferiority complex. He may shy away from tasks, withdraw from social gatherings, or boast about his great power, ability or wealth. Discovery of a single principle working in a number of obvious different situations adds to our understanding of behaviour and makes prediction and control easier.

---

## QUESTIONS

1. Trace the early beginning of scientific psychology and show how psychology came to be a science.

2. Describe the scientific method and bring out the essential characteristics of experimentation as well as its drawbacks.
3. Show the difference between objective and subjective observation, and discuss in detail the value and difficulties of introspection as the sole method of studying psychology.
4. What is genetic method? In what fields of psychology is it most useful? Discuss the value of case histories.
5. Describe briefly the statistical method, psychoanalysis, survey and clinical methods showing the special fields of their use and application.
6. Is psychology a natural science? Discuss its methods.

CHAPTER III

# PHYSIOLOGICAL BASIS OF BEHAVIOUR

## Body and Mind

Mind and body are very closely inter-related and all our activities and behaviour depend in an intimate manner on the nervous system. This is supported by the following facts :—

(1) Bodily health depends on mental health and mental health depends on the health of the body. Anxiety and fear upset the digestive system and may lead to headache, palpitation and physical weakness. And disturbances of the liver make a person peevish and irritable. Bodily fatigue causes mental fatigue and when we are tired of reading we are not inclined to do any manual work either. Drugs like alcohol which deaden the nervous system make an important difference to man's mental activities and states of consciousness as well. Very high fever affects both body and mind. Diseases, like paresis, which involve degeneration of the nervous system bring about general decay of mental life. The individual affected by this disease is unable to judge for himself and manage his own affairs. He may suffer from delusions that he is a very rich or powerful person. Mental and bodily depression go together and drugs stimulating the body stimulate the mind as well.

(2) All our knowledge comes basically from sensations and without sense organs like eyes, ears and their nerve connections there would be no sensations. We close our eyes to avoid seeing disagreeable sights or hold our nose to keep from smelling bad odour. In surgical operations the doctor deadens the parts of the nervous system nearby and thereby he deadens the pain as well. If an individual were deprived of all sensations, that is, if he were to lose all sense organs there would be little mental life left and practically no knowledge of the external world would be present.

(3) The complexity and range of behaviour increases with the complexity and size of the nervous system. A fish has a very simple nervous system and its behaviour too is very simple. Mammals have much more elaborate and organized system of nerves and nerve centers, and their behaviour is therefore most complicated, that is, the variety of responses they make is very large and the possibilities of adjustment they make in response to their environment is far more numerous. Of all mammals man's nervous system is the most complex and naturally his responses and adjustments are far more numerous and complicated than those of any other animal.

Psychologists and philosophers have deliberated a great deal as to the nature of this relation between mind and body. Some say that the two act upon each other, the mind acts on the body as the desire to light a cigarette makes the arm take out a packet from the pocket, and the body acts on the mind as pangs of hunger make us think as to how to get food and where to eat it. This is a commonsense view and is known as *interactionism.* Others hold that mind is immaterial and cannot act on the physical body and the body cannot act on the mind, and the two only run parallel to each other so that every mental activity and change is matched by a corresponding activity and change in the body. The two series of activities and changes never meet or intersect each other. This is known as *paralellism. Behaviourism* denies the need of any relation by attempting to explain all mental activities and behaviour in physical and chemical terms. According to this view mental states and processes are not real and do not exist. All that man does, thinks or feels is traced to internal bodily changes, to activities of muscles and glands. Therefore for behaviourism the problem of mind-body relationship does not exist. But as we have already seen the mental aspect of behaviour cannot be ignored for how can we otherwise distinguish between running to catch a train, running to escape a mad dog or running to get exercise. Modern psychology is concerned with behaviour which has both mental and bodily aspects, it looks upon the individual as one integrated whole in which mind and body are distinguishable but not separable, and therefore the question of the relationship between mind and body is of no moment to modern psychology.

**The human nervous system**

The nervous system works like a well-organized corporation with a number of departments and sections. It has a high degree of unity and each department, section or part performs certain specific tasks. One part of the brain takes charge of seeing, another of hearing. One part of the nervous system is in charge of the vital processes of breathing, circulation and digestion and another is concerned with memory, thinking and speaking. Thus different units of the highly organized machine have their own parts to play and yet there is great co-ordination and unity in their functioning for a common end.

It is capable of a large variety of functions and movements. It has not only to keep life going but also to adjust the organism to the numerous changes taking place in the environment, first by understanding and later by adaptive movements. Man's nervous system is capable of infinite modifications and during the period of growth from infancy to maturity, responses to environment have to be so numerous and various that there takes place a delicate differentiation of function among the various parts. In fact the greater and finer the differences in the nature of the external stimuli, the greater and finer the differences in the functions of the responding organism. During growth the several parts of the nervous system develop distinctive functions and are able to discriminate between finer differences in the stimuli.

The range of human responses and the variety of patterns of behaviour is so large that only a very complicated system can cope with them. That is why the human nervous system is much more complex than that of any other animal. Like a complex organization some functions are performed by lower departments but some important functions have to be referred to the central part, the brain, whose function is to direct and co-ordinate the functions of the various parts of the organism.

It is difficult to describe the whole nervous system in detail in an introductory book on psychology but a simple description of the various parts will help students to understand the physiological basis of behaviour. For purposes of study it is convenient to divide the nervous system into three parts :—

1. The peripheral nervous system.
2. The central nervous system.
3. The autonomic nervous system.

Let us describe the structure and function of each part in outline.

**The peripheral nervous system**

All human activity has been described as responses to stimuli received from the external environment and the peripheral part of the nervous system consists of nerves which receive stimuli and make responses These nerves are bundles of small fibres. Those which receive impressions from the outside world and carry them to the brain are called *sensory* nerves. As their function is to take messages from the outside world inside to the brain they are called in-going or *afferent* nerves. The nerves which bring from the brain an order for movement or action are called motor nerves. As the message they carry goes outward they are called out-going or *efferent* nerves. Sensory or afferent nerves bring in knowledge and information, motor or efferent nerves take out impulses for action. Impulses travel only one way so specialized is their function.

An individual makes adjustment to environment only after receiving impressions from outside or inside his body. The special bodily apparatus designed to receive such impressions are the sense-organs. They are also called *receptors*. Eyes, ears, nose, tongue and skin are the main receptors through which impressions are reeceived. Each sense organ is equipped to receive a special kind of stimuli which are called the appropriate or adequate stimuli. Eyes respond only to light, ears to sound, nose to smells and so on. Receptors carry impressions to the brain which alone perceives them. Most of these receptors or sense organs are located at the surface of the body and sensory nerves connected with them carry messages to the brain.

Simple acts like pushing a chair or holding a spoon are done by hands, our limbs are said to be organs of action and movement. These limbs would not act or move except for *muscles* and muscles are moved by nerves bringing messages from the brain. Although we are not aware of changes in muscles, motor nerves or brain yet when we act or move it is entirely due to such changes. These muscles are known as *effectors* because they effect changes in the environment. The only other effectors possessed by human beings are certain glands such as the salivary gland which moistens food in the mouth, tear glands or sweat glands.

The muscles are of three kinds. The *smooth* or unstriped muscle cell is found in the walls of the intestine. It is very simple and undeveloped. The *striped* muscle cell is more elaborate in form. They are found in legs and arms and spread or contract as we wish. Their fibres are longer and differentiated into two substances, one darker than the other giving it an appearance of striped muscle. The *cardiac* muscle in the heart and its fibres branch and unite with each other in a network.

The nervous system, like the rest of the body is made up of a large number of cells. A nerve cell with all its branches is called a *neurone*. This is the structural and functional unit of the nervous system, and its branches are really part of the cell. The nerve cell called neurone is of microscopic diameter and of great variation in length. Each neurone consists of a *cell body*, and *axon* and *dendrites*. It has a single axon and many dendrites. The axon is smooth and slender and may be many feet in length. The dendrites are short and look like the branches of a tree. They are thin and hair-like. The nervous system is made up of numerous such neurones and impulses or messages are carried on from one neurone to another.

The dendrites are the receiving stations which pick up such messages and axons pass them on to other neurones through dendrites. Their work is their own and they do not change function. The point at which the dendrites of one neurone come in functional contact with the axone of another neurone and receive impulses is called the *synapse.* The synapse has only one-way traffic and impulses are carried only in one direction. The impulses come to the synapse over the axone of one neurone and are taken up by the dendrites of another.

The nervous impulses travel only one way and the connections formed between sensory neurones and the motor neurones endure so that the nervous impulses tend to travel the way they did in the past. The synapse resists their going any other way. Thus actions are easier the way they were done before.

Interaction between neurones is possible at synapses and here the impulses of several neurones may combine to check or help further movement of the impulse. Synapses are centres where movement of impulses is slowed down and often completely blocked.

Nature has equipped each organism with such an apparatus which helps him to make useful reactions and successful adjustments to environment and promote survival in the struggle for existence. When a specific stimulus is presented, a certain fixed and predictable response is made. When anything irritates the nostril we sneeze, when bright light suddenly appears we blink. These are reflex actions, they are automatic, occur in a fixed mechanical way, and when a particular stimulus is presented, must take place for the good and safety of the organism. It is because certain connections between the sensory and the muscular neurones are fixed from birth. The whole path covered by the impulse from the sensory neurone in the region of a receptor or sense organ to the muscular neurone is called the *reflex arc.* A reflex arc is an essential neural mechanism involved in a reflex action ; it starts with a receptor, a sensory neurone and goes on to a motor neurone and an effector.

Reflex actions are simple, prompt and involuntary movements which are useful for the wellbeing of the organism. In human behaviour there is a large variety of such reflex acts. The reflex arc is of special interest to the psychologist because reflex action

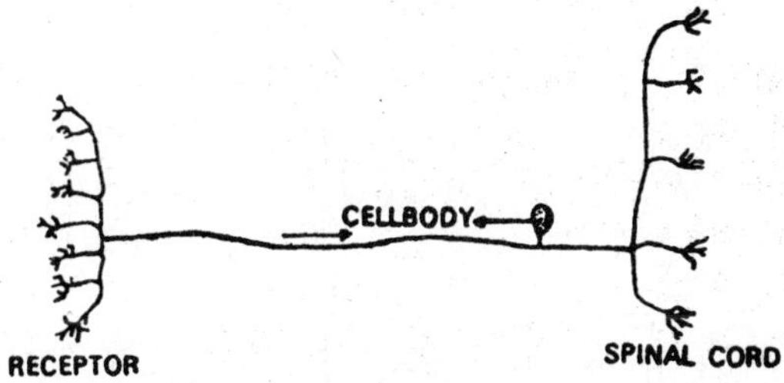


Fig. 1. Typical sensory neuron

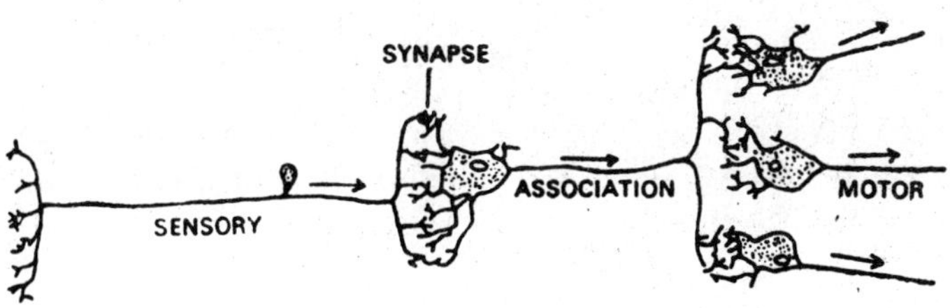


Fig. 2. Neurons and junctions

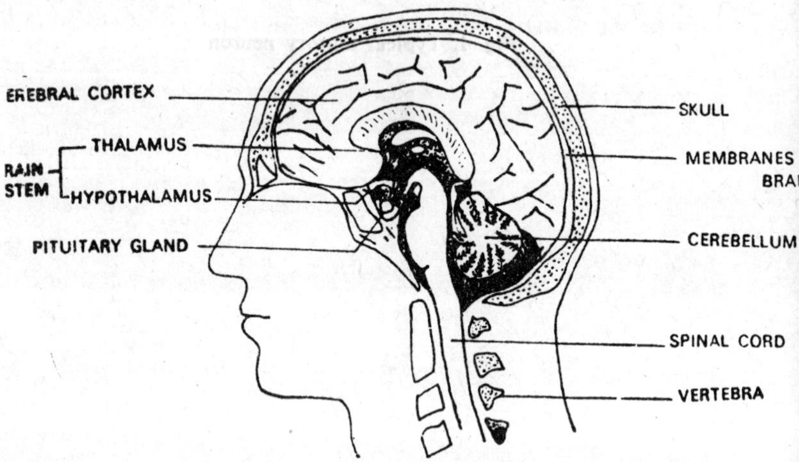


**Fig. 3. The human brain**

play a significant role in much of everyday behaviour. Reflex actions are found in many parts of the nervous system. In bright light there is dilation of the pupil, the mouth waters when we chew food, the dog pricks up ears when it hears a strange sound, the leg pulls itself up when the foot is pricked, if liquid gets into the mouth of an infant, its muscles immediately respond and the liquid is swallowed, the new-born begins to breathe immediately on birth as a reflex response to lack of oxygen.

In simple reflex actions the reflex arc is short and only a few neurones take part, but in some complex reflex actions there may be many more neurones working together and then their function is co-ordinated by the brain and the impulse travels a much longer path. When we have to check, control or change a reflex action it is not done automatically but involves reference to brain.

**The central nervous system**

The central nervous system consists of the spinal cord and the brain. Both of them are designed to effect adjustments of the organism to its environment and to co-ordinate the several activities of the body.

The spinal cord is that part of the nervous system which lies within the backbone, enclosed in the bony case of the vertebral column. It consists of a bundle of nerve fibres. Its function is two-fold. In the first place it is connected with receptors and effectors by more than thirty pairs of spinal peripheral nerves and directly converts impulses received from the sensory areas into motor impulses. Secondly, through it nervous impulses travel to and from the higher brain centres. When a message is sent to the brain, it sends back impulses to the cells in the spinal cord and they, in turn, transmit motor impulses to muscles. Thus the spinal cord works as the relaying centre for all behaviour involving reference to the brain. It connects the brain with the peripheral part of the nervous system.

The spinal cord also controls activity connected with the organic sensations and with sensations arising from the skin. Reflex actions which involve a direct connection between sensory and motor areas are also controlled by the spinal cord. Mechanical automatic activity like walking, running, sitting, spinning, riding a cycle is also to a large extent controlled by the spinal cord. It means that it directs most of our daily routine which consists of mechanical movements.

*Brain.* The brain is the highly developed and enlarged portion of the central nervous system contained within the skull. It is the chief centre for inter-connecting the outgoing and incoming impulses, for co-ordinating the receptive and the reactive, the sensory and the motor, activities of the organism. It is a very complex system of nerve centres and communication tracks. It is fully protected by the bony structure of the skull. As is well known the brain plays the central part in all complex behaviour like motivation, learning, perception, thinking.

The brain is a gray mass of semi-jellylike material. It is roughly divided into four main parts not completely separated from one another but connected by large cables of nerve fibres. It includes the central part or the *cerebrum*, the *mid-brain*, the hind-brain or the *cerebellum*, the *thalamus* and the *medulla oblongata*.

The medulla is made up of a number of nerve fibres connecting spinal system below with the higher brain centres above and is the path way for impulses passing between the brain and the cord. It is an adjustment centre in its own right and plays an important part in the control of certain bodily functions like breathing, heart beat and circulation of blood.

The thalamus is like a complex switchboard consisting of a large mass of special connecting centres. Its chief function is to route incoming sensory impulses to appropriate regions of the brain. Impulses arising in ears are taken to one part of the brain and those arising in the skin to another part. It is a sort of relay centre. Underneath the thalamus is the *hypothalamus* containing centres which control emotional behaviour and wakefulness.

The cerebrum is the upper part of the brain structure. It consists of two hemispheres with a layer or rind of grey matter.

This layer is called the *cerebral cortex* and in function is an important part of the cerebrum. The cortex is like a rumpled piece of cloth which encloses almost all the fore-brain and the mid-brain. In this cortex are the nerve centres controlling by far the greater part of behaviour and all our higher psychological processes. It is believed that the two hemispheres are mapped out into areas, each area dealing with a special mental function, but all parts also work together.

The hind-brain or *cerebellum* is a center for motor co-ordination and helps to make our movements smooth and accurate. It also helps to maintain the equilibrium of the body and posture. When it is removed the organism is unable to maintain its balance. Much is known about this part but much more has to be found out about the function of hind-brain. The mid-brain is a sort of bridge connecting the fore-brain with the hind-brain and regulates complex movements such as are involved in locomotion and which do not require any reference to the higher powers of the cerebral cortex.

**Localization of the brain function**

The brain is divided by a groove or fissure which runs from front to back dividing it almost into two halves. The groove is called the central fissure and the two parts into which it divides the brain are called hemispheres. These hemispheres are further sub-divided by other fissures.

The two hemispheres are distinguished into right and left halves. The right hemisphere is connected for the most part with organs and limbs on the left side of the body, and the left hemisphere is connected with organs and limbs on the right side of the body. The purpose of this relation is not yet known.

The brain is mapped out into *lobes*. Though they appear to be separate they are continuous underneath. The *frontal lobe* is inside the forehead and behind it is the *parietal lobe.* The frontal lobe is concerned with motor function and the area for the muscle and skin sense is located in the parietal lobe. The *occipetal* lobe at the rear of the brain is the seat of visual sense and the *temporal* lobe has the auditory area in its upper margin. Thus it is believed that important psychological functions are localized in the brain and this belief is the result of a long process of investigation by numerous research scientists. The following methods were used in studying brain localization :—

1. By tracing nerve fibres from one part of the nervous system to another. For example, when nerve cells in the eye are destroyed the attached fibres degenerate and so do the corresponding centres in the brain and the occipital lobe.

2. When certain parts of the brain are destroyed in animals it is found that functions associated with them are also destroyed. This is the method of extirpation.

3. When disturbed function in sense organs or other areas is observed in human beings due to accident, later surgical operation has revealed that definite parts of the brain connected with that function were injured. Localized brain injury found with certain disturbance of mental functions establishes the connection between the two.

4. Weak electrical stimulation is given to animals and men to see what effect it has, if any, on brain processes.

Detailed analysis of visual perceptions and the changes which are observed in the occipetal lobe confirm the fact of localization. There are areas in the brain which interpret visual sensations and produce recognition and if they are injured the individual may see but fail to recognise. Similarly an individual may hear sound but not be able to reply as the brain injury has affected the connection between hearing and speech. Even if localization is proved in all cases under investigation it should not be assumed that these parts of the brain function in an isolated manner. Brain activity is highly co-ordinated and integrated.

**The autonomic nervous system**

As the name itself suggests the autonomic nervous system is self-adjusting and semi-independent. It consists of numerous nerve centres called *ganglia* which are located alongside the spinal cord

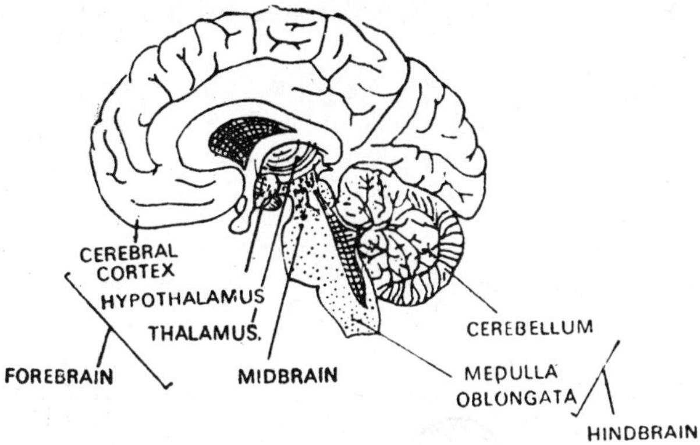


Fig. 4. The principal parts of the human brain

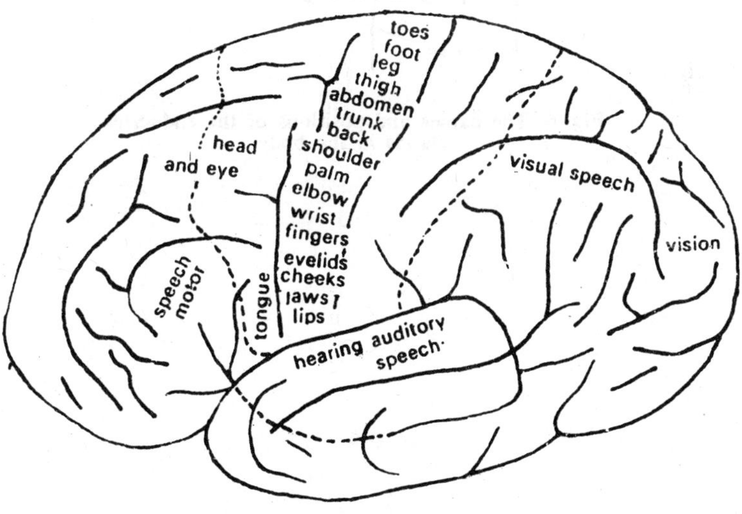


Fig. 5. Diagram showing some of the main sensor and motor centres in the brain

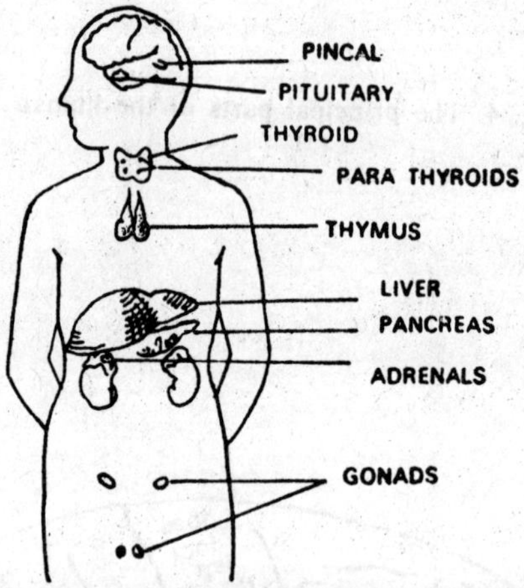


**Fig. 6. The names and positions of the endocrine glands in the body**

as well as in other parts of the body. Most of the ganglia of the autonomic system are located in the head and along the spinal column are called the cranical system, the part in the chest and abdomen is called the sympathetic section and the part located in the hips and pelvic region is called the sacral section. Their function is to regulate involuntary processes, circulation of blood, digestion and action of the glands.

The glands of the body are cell structures which secrete different substances. They are of two kinds. In the first place there are duct glands which secrete their fluids through ducts or channels to the body surface or into the alimentary canal such as tear glands, sweat glands, salivary glands. Secondly there are ductless glands which do not have such channels and pour their secretion known as *hormones* into the blood stream. They are also known as endocrine glands and are active in emotional behaviour. In fear and anxiety the salivary glands fail to secrete and the frightened or excited person has dry lips. Worry, fear and anger have a very harmful effect on digestive functions as they upset working of the stomach glands, and good company, cheerful experiences, hope and zest stimulate the digestive process.

Endocrine glands or glands that secrete within, have much greater influence on behaviour and deserve close study. The most important of them are the *thyroid*, the *pituitary*, the *suprarenal* and the *gonads*. If these glands are over-active or under-active, it makes a difference not only to the growth and development of the individual but also to his temperament and outlook on life.

*The thyroid gland.* The thyroid lies at the base of the neck in front of the wind-pipe. It secretes a chemical known as thyroxin in which the principal ingredient is iodine. When the gland is destroyed by disease the individual loses his former vigour and altertness and becomes more sluggish and dull. He is slow, stupid and forgetful and cannot concentrate effectively on any task. The skin is puffy and the muscles and brain are inert. This is known as myxoedema. If the gland is defective from birth and the defect is not corrected in early infancy, growth is blocked and intelligence does not develop. The individual remains a dwarf, calm and quiet but an imbecile. Such individuals are called "cretins". One of the remarkable discoveries made in this direction is that simply feeding sheep's thyroid quickly restored the normal condition, and this condition is maintained if an adequate dose of the extract of this gland is regularly given. Even the cretins can be helped if they are treated early in infancy.

Thyroid deficiency is common in regions where iodine is scarce and has to be made good by a adding iodine to table salt.

When this gland is over-active, the individual is tense, restless, irritable and worried. If he is in the growing stage his growth is very rapid and he is generally too tall for his age.

Feeblemindedness in children is often due to thyroid deficiency.

Lying close to the thyroid are the four tiny *parathyroids.* If they are removed the patient is restless, over-excited and tense, he may have pain in his muscles. This condition can be cured by giving him extracts of parathyroid. Their over-activity makes the person too quiet and flabby.

*The pituitary gland.* This gland is situated at the base of the brain and exercises great influence on other glands as well. Without it other glands do not develop and function normally. That is why it is called the "master gland". It secretes a number of hormones that stimulate or inhibit secretion in other glands.

If this gland is over-active it affects the growth of the body as a whole. Its over-activity in childhood leads to an abnormal size of the body as seen in early giants. When it becoms over-active in later life the bones of the face, hands and feet grow very large. But the gland becomes exhausted after a period of over-activity and such abnormal giants die young. When the gland is under-active in childhood, it produces midgets who are different from cretins in being more sociable and intelligent. If midgets are given pituitary extracts when they are still young, their growth is increased. These midgets are, however, lacking in aggressiveness, give up easily and cry readily.

*The pancreatic gland.* The pancreas is located along the lower wall of the stomach. It delivers secretions to the digestive area thus helping digestion. Besides it manufactures a hormone, insulin, which it pours directly into the blood. This hormone is concerned primarily with the use of sugar by the tissues of the body. When insulin secretion is low, as it is in diabetes, blood sugar does not get into the tissues but remains in the blood at a high level. This means that muscles do not get fuel, that is, to burn or oxidize sugar. This affects the organisms activity and feelings. An excess of insulin makes him feel very hungry, tired, nervous and anxious, and a still greater excess may cause mental distress, even delirium and unconsciousness. Sugar in the blood is used as fuel by the brain and muscles, brain uses it almost exclusively. That is why pancreas is very important to the brain.

*The adrenal glands.* These glands are close to the kidneys Each adrenal consists of two parts, the cortex producing the hormone *cortin* and the medulla producing *adrenalin.* Adrenalin is a powerful hormone. Its activity is closely connected with emotional behaviour. If the pancreas are removed death occurs within three days during which the individual become very weak, temperature drops and the heart beats become very slow. Over-activity of the glands make a man very aggressive and virile, and their over-activity in women makes them develop masculine characters such as the growth of moustaches and a deepening of voice. These glands are closely related to sex glands.

*The gonads.* They are sex glands and lie in the sex organs. Their activity leads to secondary sex characters and they determine human sex development, both physically and psychologically. Hormones secreted by the gonads, testes in males and ovaries in females, are responsible for sexual behaviour. The male sex hormone is androgens and if its source is cut off before puberty due to castration there is no sex drive. The female sex hormone is called estrogens and if by the removal of ovaries its secretion is stopped female characters fail to appear. The sex hormones are not very active in children. They come into play at puberty and are responsible for marked changes which take place in boys and girls like growth of breasts in girls and growth of beard in boys. They also determine personality characteristics of men and women.

Effects of the over-activity and under-activity of these glands have been shown above to bring out the importance of these glands. The endocrine glands do not have any direct effect on personality. They only initiate physiological changes, the final results of which are complicated by habits and experience.

These glands do not function in isolation; they interact. A normal person is he in whom these glands work in a proper balance. More disturbances in personality and behaviour are caused by the lack of this balance than by the deficiency in any one gland. Therefore it is useless for any one to try to analyse his personality in terms of endocrine glands or to try to improve it by glandular treatment. Of course we all need the hormones to feel the glow of life, vigour and health, and quacks have not been slow to exploit this general desire among people, but it should not be overlooked that differences among individuals are not entirely due to those of balance in gland functioning. There may be other biological and social factors. All that can be safely affirmed is that these ductless endocrine glands are the basic biological factors of personality.

**Reflex actions**

Reflex actions are the simplest type of human behaviour, and as has been pointed out above, a reflex action or reflex is a constant, uniform, definite and direct response to a given stimulus and is caused by an inborn natural connection in the nervous system between the sense organ which receives the stimulus and the muscle which makes the response. If anything irritates the nose, sneezing immediately follows. If a bright light is thrown on our eyes, the pupils contract. These responses are quick and occur always and as soon as the stimulus is presented. They are involuntary and often we are not conscious of them. They are not learned, they are always ready for action and they are local movements limited to a particular part of the body.

We do not attend to reflex actions unless the stimulus is very strong or we wish to control them. They cannot be modified and they serve the welfare of the organism. Some reflex actions cannot be controlled. If you stand behind a window with glass panes and let somebody throw a bucketful of water suddenly and violently at the window, you will not help wincing even though you know full well that the glass stands between you and the water. Reflex actions are primary, natural, automatic, universal and useful to the organism.

---

## Questions

1. How is the mind related to the body? Discuss some of the views put forward and illustrate your answer by giving instances of the interaction of mental states and bodily processes.
2. What do you understand by behaviourism? Can it explain all facts of behaviour?
3. Describe the human nervous system in broad outline.
4. Describe the main features of

   (a) the peripheral nervous system

   (b) the central nervous system

   (c) the autonomic nervous system.
5. What are the principal endocrine glands? How do they influence behaviour and personality?
6. Write explanatory notes on :—

   1. Reflex arc
   2. Neurone
   3. Localization of brain function
   4. Glandular balance

## CHAPTER IV

# DYNAMICS OF BEHAVIOUR

### Homeostasis

We have seen that any understanding of the individual and his behaviour must include a knowledge of the physiological structure and the biochemical processes which enable it to work. This structure maintains itself with definite amounts of oxygen, calcium, sugar, temperature, acidity, water and the like. Life goes on in an organism only so long as a certain minimum of these conditions are fulfilled. If any of these conditions vary beyond limits life ends. Thus every organism if it is to survive must try to achieve the maximum equilibrium of internal conditions. This is called *homeostasis*. This means that in order to maintain itself every organism must have a kind of balance so that essential bodily processes continue and keep constant. Homeostasis is a state of balance of internal conditions and processes so that adequate bodily temperature, water supply, sugar, blood, oxygen and the like are ensured. For example, when temperature falls we shiver and the activity of the muscles warms us; when the temperature goes up, we perspire and are cooled by the evaporation of the liquid. This state or process of keeping internal conditions constant and in a balance or equilibrium in our physiological system is homeostasis.

In some cases the organism makes internal adjustments to bring about this state of balance, in others the individual seeks the help of outside conditions to maintain this balance. When temperature outside is low we may put on more clothes or light a fire to keep warm. When it is very hot the body perspires to keep cool but we may also use a fan or iced water to keep cool. Such behaviour serves bodily needs and to restore homeostatic balance.

### Characteristics of behaviour

The individual is a centre of internal energy, he acts from within. He is an active creature constantly interacting with his environment. His life and behaviour is his interplay with things and persons around him. He makes changes in his environment and is himself changed in the process.

Like drives motives are many and varied. They lead to activity in relation to environment. Those modes of activity which give satisfaction in reducing tension and meeting needs tend to be repeated and those which fail to do so are dropped. All behaviour is directed toward a goal and when the goal is achieved the need, drive or motive is satisfied.

**Classification of motives**

Many psychologists classify motives according to the degree of complexity. At one end they place most rudimentary biological and primitive motives and complex, learned and social motives at the other. The former consist of drives which help to maintain bodily processes and the latter of attitudes to oneself and others. Other psychologists classify motives into *primary* and *secondary*. Primary motives or drives are mainly physiological and satisfy tissue needs for nourishment, water, air and sex. Secondary motives or drives are learned through social experience. One author speaks of biological needs and psychological needs for security, sex, social recognition and adventure or new experience.

Y.I. Thomas lays stress on four 'fundamental wishes' to include the above psychological needs and holds that for the development of a well-adjusted person these wishes must be adequately satisfied. Recently A.H. Maslow has given us a list of basic needs one leading to the other in order of satisfaction and development, and this list has gained popularity. They are:—

1. Physiological needs—hunger, thirst, sex and physical activity.
2. Safety needs—security from physical and mental loss.
3. Need for belongingness and affection.
4. Esteem needs—the need for self-respect, recognition and prestige.

5. The need for self-actualization, the need to realize the best one is capable of, for self-expression and self-realization.

We shall discuss here some important physiological drives and social motives.

**Hunger**

We all know what it feels like to be hungry, but what are the physiological activities whithin our bodies that stimulate this feeling. When deprived of food for a long time human beings report pain or gnawing experiences known as hunger pangs. These are said to be due to strong contractions of the muscles of the stomach wall. Scientists have studied the stomach activity before and after meals and compared stomach movements of individuals with their subjective statements about their hunger. They used two techniques: X-ray observation and direct measurement of stomach motions recorded by swallowed baloon connected with a recording device. It was found that hunger was felt when the stomach was contracting. In another experiment stomach walls were removed or deprived of the contraction processes but animals behaved as they would do after being deprived of food for some time. This shows that there are other factors also which lead to hunger. In another experiment a dog who was given its fill started eating again when the blood of a starving dog was injected into it showing that complex chemical processes are also a part of the hunger state.

Again how much a hen will eat depends on the size of the pile of food. It eats less from a smaller pile and more from a larger one. Again after it has stopped eating it will start eating again if more hungry hens come in. Similarly, hunger among men depends on physical and social surrounding. How carefully and attractively the table has been set, with what great affection and love food is served, how formal or informal is the meal or how sweet and mirthful is the company are some of the factors which determine our reactions to food. Thus the physiological need for food has been modified by social learning, perception, cultural influences and social relations.

Again the range of likes and dislikes in food is very wide. Each individual learns to like certain foods. A Bengali relishes fish and rice, a Panjabi prefers bread and curry. The biological need does not determine what an individual would like to eat but the social and cultural environment decides it. Again we may be very hugry for spiced foods but disgusted with the thought of sweets.

## Thirst

It is very remarkable that our bodies maintain a constant water balance even though we lose a good deal through perspiration, respiration and elimination and gain a good deal of it by drinking various liquids from time to time. Often in a social gathering we take a lot of hot and cold drinks and as often we forget to drink any liquid when we are engaged in an interesting task for a long period of time. Generally we are led to drink because our mouth and throats are dry. In an experiment sufficient quantity of water was placed directly in the stomach bypassing the throat and the mouth, and after some time there was no feeling of thirst. This shows that water in order to be effective in removing thirst must get into the tissues sufficiently to remove the dryness of mouth and throat. On the other hand merely wetting the mouth and throat reduces thirst. While fasting many people take a gulp of water, move it in mouth, gargle to remove dryness of thirst and spit it out. Thirst may be induced by bodily changes quite remote from mouth and throat as in diabetes. But the most important condition is the dryness of body cells which may be stimulating glands to regulate water needs.

## The need for air

Our needs for food and water are those of which we are frequently aware because the body is frequently in a state of deficiency. But we are not generally aware of our need for air unless we are deprived of it even for a short time. Air is plentiful and few of us get into situations in which there is a risk of suffocating. However this is obviously a very vital need. Many interpret the need for air as the need for oxygen but there is no drive associated with our need for oxygen. A person may be deprived of the need for oxygen without being aware of it as often happens to pilots flying at high altitudes. If the carbon dioxide level rises as happens when we are running fast, a portion of the brain becomes more active and breathing becomes very fast to increase the intake of oxygen. Thus the proportion of oxygen to carbon dioxide in the blood is kept at a constant level.

### Sex drive

The sex drive seems to be stimulated by three kinds of events: the presence of sex hormones, external objects and cerebral processes of imagination, memory and the like Possibly glands other than gonads also produce sex hormones. But this drive is so much influenced by social customs and prejudices that its expression in marriage varies from one society to another.

### Sleep

The drive for sleep is no less important. People cannot do without sleep as they cannot do without food. How much sleep any individual needs, what sort of bed, hard or soft, he needs for sleep, when he sleeps, depends on habits. Some take a nap during the day, others sleep less than six hours, some need cold water before sleep; others want hot milk, some sleep in a dark room others need light. Such differences are very wide. But this is true that during sleep the individual is not bodily active or mentally conscious of what goes on around him though our autonomic activities continue, brain waves change and thinking goes on in the form of dreams. The physiological basis for sleep is not fully known nor are we quite clear about the chemical changes occurring in sleep. But there is evidence that hypothalamus has centres for sleep and wakefulness. We can exercise some control over sleep and stay awake but there are people who can sleep even in dazzling light or very loud sound.

Let us now consider the psychological drives, which are acquired in the course of experience. But once aroused even biological drives have psychological consequences. Prisoners on hunger strike go without food for several days, and their main concern is the social cause they uphold. People do not wish to quench their thirst with a glass of water but seek aerated drinks or even liquor in a restaurant in the company of friends, and they may put off quenching their thirst till these conditions are fulfilled. Others may put off drinking till their task is finished just as students put off sleep near their examination.

### The desire for security

Everybody wishes to feel secure and safe. Pain, want, discomfort and loneliness make us feel unhappy, and so does the fear of these things or even the thought of them. To *feel* safe and secure is even more important than to *be* safe and secure.

There is more than one kind of security. Physical security means that we should feel confident that our bodily needs would be satisfied, that we will get food in time, will be protected from pain, disease and injury, and will have shelter when it is too hot or too cold. Economic security means that we will have enough money and material to satisfy our needs and we will not suffer from want or loss. Psychological security means that our adjustments to things and people around us is healthy, happy and harmonious, and we are free from anxiety and worry. It is obvious that these types of security are dependent on each other. Too many people today are in hot pursuit of wealth, they want to earn more and more as they think that money will make them safe and secure, all their needs will be met and they will have no worry.

This drive has its beginning in infancy when the new-born clings to the breast of its mother. The mother provides not only feeding but also protection from pain and injury, and the infant often feels safe when on being frightened or injured it is put to the mother's breast. How even grown-ups cry for mother when they are in trouble or danger shows how safe and secure mother's protecting hand was. Every child feels safe and satisfied in the presence of his mother, and anxious and restless in her absence. Orphans who lose their mothers very early in life continue feeling insecure all their lives.

The desire for security is universal whether people have lived safe or insecure. It is because of this drive that grown-up children seek the company of friends and are eager to be accepted in several groups. Primitive people cling to tribes and castes because they feel safe and secure in their membership. In modern society people join clubs, trade unions and associations, they pay taxes and large amounts to insurance companies against death, theft or accident, they work hard to train and qualify for a job and do even many unpleasant jobs for the security they promise. People who resent all change and reform are anxious to make their way of life safe and secure.

There is a great hunger for security in the modern world. Two world wars have made people anxious that there should be no more wars and the United Nations' Organization is a symbol of humanity's quest and desire for security. When an epidemic breaks out, when there are riots, invasions or earthquakes, or when water and power supply breaks down, the state is very anxious that people should not lose faith in the capacity of the government to deal with them and leaders and officials try their best to make people feel safe and secure.

The drive for security does not call for any specific pattern of behaviour as other drives do. Any threat to the satisfaction of any need, bodily or social, is a threat to one's security. Any kind of loss of food, affection, property, social status or prestige results in a feeling of insecurity. Security means that all is going well and human beings are for ever trying to remove all those factors which are likely to make their world and life uncertain

**The desire for affection**

We all wish to love and be loved, to belong to others and be tied to them by relations of affection. Giving and receiving affection in the family parents and children feel that they are wanted and liked for themselves.

In the beginning the child only receives affection. His parents try to satisfy all his needs, he depends on them in every way and they also love him as their own. Thus he is able to get over his feeling of helplessness. Fondness and kindness on the part of adults rouse similar feelings in children, and young people too begin to love those around them. Indeed parents take so much trouble to bring up their children and make sacrifices of their own comfort and happiness for their sake is all out of their affection for their children. Parents and children need each other for the great satisfaction and pleasure which mutual affection produces and history is full of examples of people who sacrificed their power, kingdom and wealth for the sake of some person they loved, thus showing that the need for love is more powerful than any other need.

All people seek companionship with others, they need a partner, a friend, a lover, a husband or wife because they need to be liked, wanted, desired and loved; to feel accepted, welcomed and approved, to be needed, to be of importance to others. That is why even in most matter-of-fact organizations like government department or business office the need for personal contacts and relations is being stressed.

### The desire for recognition

Every person has a strong desire that he should be recognized and noticed, that others should praise him for his work and that people should accept him as an equal or even a superior person. Many psychologists hold that here are few people who do not have this desire in a very strong degree. Every child wants that members of his family should watch and praise all that he does and says, and when he grows up the hunger for praise and prizes grows. There are many honours in society and all wish to get them. Mention in the honours list of the state, in *Who's Who* or in a daily paper gives us great pleasure. An honorary degree given to an already famous leader does give pleasure. Even the highest of people have had daydreams of their greatness. It is all due to the powerful and universal desire to win the esteem of their fellowmen. The footballer, the wrestler, the skilled surgeon or the army general may be hating his job but he does it for the recognition he gets from the public. Many people embrace death to earn the respect and recognition of their countrymen.

**The desire for new experience**

All human beings get bored with things and experiences which are repeated again and again. The best foods, the sweetest songs, the most enjoyable game or the most jovial company does not always please and we soon feel fed up with them. So human beings are for ever searching new ways of behaving and acting. If they meet with obstacles they persist in trying to overcome them. The child is daily getting into one mischief or the other, he explores his house and garden for new discoveries, he tries to do things in new ways and even though parents try to check him he continues to satisfy his curiosity by changing his ways of doing and knowing things. Often his desire for variety and novelty lands him in trouble but he does not stop. Our vast civilization with its science and technology has been built up by men and women who sought new experiences. Explorers and travellers, scientists and engineers, statesmen and economists, businessmen and social reformers are always trying new experiences, to get out of the rut and the routine and chalk out new ways, and thereby have enriched human life and culture.

**The desire for self-expression**

Every man and woman feels an urge to do particular things and is satisfied only when he or she is able to get suitable opportunities for it. The child feels like pulling the tail of his sister and cannot suppress his desire to do so. Young people play, draw, sing, dance because they are expressing an urgent desire to do so. These activities are not fulfilling any bodily need but only meeting their urge to express themselves freely. When people grow up they choose jobs which are less paying but in which they think they are able to express and show their ability better, they say they are not able to do justice to their ability, taste or aptitude even in a job with a higher salary and they are not developing what is best in them. Many people give up very paying work, they say that they feel suffocated or the atmosphere is not congenial and they seek jobs which give them opportunities for developing what they consider to be their special talents and abilities. These needs are very difficult to find out and judge, but there is no doubt that they are there and are the highest needs of man.

**Other social motives**

Besides these major drives there are several minor ones which influence human behaviour. The desire to collect and amass things and goods in life is common enough. Childern collect all sorts of things from nails, insects, pebbles to coins and stamps. In many homes and schools collection is encouraged as a hobby and stamp collecting is undertaken by both young and old. Grown-up people collect all sorts of pans and pots, furniture and luxuries in the home, misers collect wealth and property, scientists collect specimens of plants and insects. Others collect pictures, books and what not.

The desire for mastery is fairly widespread and human beings long to gain power and mastery over their fellowmen, to make them do what they want and gain strength and popularity. Many wish to be famous only because fame will bring them power. In modern life in every sphere there is keen struggle and people show a strong desire to dominate people and things. It is the "master motive" or self-assertion and leads to aggresive behaviour. Even very small children start crying and screaming to express their resentment against restrictions placed on their movements. Temper tantrums throwing oneself down on the floor and kicking in rage, negativism– doing just the opposite of what they are told, refusing food and other forms of protests are born of urge to mastery or self-assertion. Unnecessary argument, trying to speak ill of others, complaining, fault-finding and the like are expressions of a desire to assert oneself. This drive is greatly stimulated in the modern struggle for success and pays in business and official transactions.

**Mixed motives**

These needs and motives depend on each other and in any act of behaviour more than one need or motive may be satisfied. Human beings so organize their behaviour as to obtain maximum satisfaction from it, that is, to satisfy as many needs as they posibly can. Man eats to satisfy his hunger, but he may eat in the company of his wife and children and satisfy his need for affection as well, he may give a dinner and invite his colleagues to show off and satisfy his need for mastery as well or he may invite a foreigner as an adventure for new experience. Thus he is fulfilling several needs at the same time. Motives mix and depend on each other.

**The cycle or activity**

We are now in a position to describe the course or activity from the first experience of the need to its satisfaction. The first stage is the experience of the basic need arising from physiological and psychological tension. Secondly the individual seeks those stimuli and situations which will reduce this tension and satisfy this drive. Thirdly, there is the state of satisfaction which the organism ultimately achieves. Tension is removed and there is a feeling of rest.

Obyiously these cycles of activity may be of short or long duration. In some cases the time between the need and its satisfaction is very short, we feel thirsty and help ourselves to a glass of water. But sometimes it is very long stretching into a whole lifetime as an individual may take long to become a big officer, a doctor or a principal.

Often motives have to be blocked due to social conditions. We all learn to wait for our meals and do not start eating till other people have been served in a party.

**Social facors in motivation**

Our biological needs are rooted in our physiological organism but the mode of their satisfaction is influenced by the social environment in which the individual lives. These needs are universal but they are largely influenced by social factors. We all eat to satisfy our hunger but we eat in a manner common to our society. A Hindu eats vegetarian food followed by a glass of water, eats with his fingers and washes his hands before and after meals. A European eats with knife and fork and finishes with a cup of coffee, tea or liquor. He does not wash his hands. A Japanese uses chop-sticks to eat rice. Thus while the motive is the same the forms of behaviour are different.

Again experience affects motives. Children go out to play; if they are happy and satisfied with their experience in the playground they go again, but if their experience is unhappy they do not go again. Thus experiences also modify our motives.

In our age great stress is laid on competition. Children are encouraged to do better than their fellows and are awarded prizes when they do so. The system of marks and prizes has taught children to consider their own good and welfare better than that of their fellows, and there is less of co-operation, humility and service. Social patterns influence our motives.

### Emotions as motives

Emotions are the prime movers of behaviour and their power to function as motives is readily recognized. Anger, fear, anxiety and hatred also produce tension to remove which the individual is driven to action. We have found that every motive has a goal and so have emotions. Anger makes the individual fight against the source of irritation, in fear the goal is to remove or run away from the object or situation which is the cause of fear, in hatred the goal is to destroy or do harm to the person whom we hate, and in anxiety the goal is to seek those responses which will give us relief. Emotions persist till the goal is achieved, and they are spread over the whole organism so that the entire behaviour is organized and directed toward the attainment of specific goals. When a person is extremely angry he forgets everything and directs all his energy against the object or person which has provoked him. His sleep too is disturbed and he does not rest till he has expressed and satisfied his anger against that person. Thus emotions not only function as motives but also help to strengthen other motives.

### Ideas as motives

In every age and society there are certain ideas and ideals which direct the behaviour of people and act as strong motives. 'Obey your parents', 'do not steal', justice, honesty, social service and the like prompt people to behave in a definite manner. Among superstitious people in India small pox is due to the wrath of a goddess and they would much rather worship and give offerings in her temple than get their children vaccinated. In modern enlightened communities the ideas of cleanliness are so strong as to compel them to wash their hands with carbolic soap every time they touch anything which will carry infection, to get themselves vaccinated, to take injections for the prevention of diseases like typhoid or cholera and to wash fruits and vegetables with disinfectants before using them. Such ideas function as strong motives which influence people's behaviour patterns.

### Instincts as motives

Some behaviour is due to urges which are partly inborn and partly learned and they function as strong drives to action. In the past it was believed that they are solely inherited, are present in all members of any one species and are implanted in the organism by nature to serve the ends of survival. They are instincts. All human beings tend to collect things, to be curious about strange and new things, to care for their children, to build houses, to save themselves from danger and the like. They do so because they have instincts which prompt them to behave in this manner. As the term instinct was very popular for a long time and was widely used to explain behaviour the subject is being dealt with in detail in the next section.

### McDougall's theory of instincts

In 1908 William McDougall published his book *Social Psychology* in which he developed a comprehensive theory of instincts. He defined instinct as an inherited tendency to perceive and pay attention to certain objects, to experience an emotional excitement upon perceiving such an object, and to act in regard to it in a particular manner. Thus every instinct has three aspects—knowing (cognition), feeling (affection) and acting (conation). According to McDougall, instincts are the equipment by whcih man perceives certain stimuli, experiences certain emotions and acts in particular ways. These innate tendencies are the prime movers of all human behaviour and activity. Every train of thought and every bodily activity owes its origin and progress to some instinct.

According to McDougall each instinct has an emotion as is its core so that when an instinct is aroused its characteristic emotion is also aroused. When threatened by danger man tries to run and escape and this instinctive tendency is accomponied by the emotion of fear. It is fear that sustains the act of running and escaping. Intelligence, reason, will and ability to learn work within instincts.

McDougall put forward the following list of instincts and held that they have an important bearing in life.

1. Escape (fear)
2. Repulsion (disgust)
3. Curiosity (wonder)
4. Pugnacity (anger)
5. Self-assertion (elation or display)
6. Self-abasement (negative self-feeling)
7. Parental instincts (tender emotion)
8. Sex (lust)
9. Gregariousness
10. Food
11. Acquisitiveness
12. Constructiveness characteristic emotion associated with each instinct is given in brackets

Collecting, hoarding and capitalism are traced to the acquisitive instinct; seeking company, social approval, migration to cities to the gregarious instinct; acquisition of knowledge, research, discoveries and explorations to the instinct of curiosity. Law courts, army and police are traced to the instincts of pugnacity and self-preservation. The institution of family is based on sex, parental instincts and acquisition. The desire for gaining power in political and social life, for controlling educational institutions, for making name in any area of life, is traced to the instinct for self-assertion.

Along with these specific tendencies McDougall put forward some general tendencies which are also inborn and universal. They are imitation, suggestion, sympathy, play, forming habits.

For a time McDougall's theory was very popular and many psychologists used the term instinct to describe and explain human behaviour. But soon some of them found out that the term was just a class name, that many of the responses which are described as instinctive are learned, and that the so-called instinctive behaviour differs from person to person. Even the same individual does not behave in the same manner on different occasions under the same instinct of escape for example. Much of what goes by the name of instinctive behaviour is a matter of habit. So the term instinct fell into disuse. Instead the term physiological drive or motive is considered more suitable. As we have seen a physiological drive is inherited and meets an organic need but its expression is partly determined by the environment of the individual.

**Freud's theory of instinct and motives**

Freud's approach is biological. He bases all motives on instincts like sex, hunger, thirst and aggressiveness. Most important is the sex instinct which he calls the *libido*. Libido is best described as a drive energy, striving and pulsating force which is largely sexual, and all social and emotional life and experience of man is rooted in it. Sex is at work from infancy though we are not conscious of it. All acts, all thoughts, all dreams are caused by the unconscious sex urge.

To explain human behaviour Freud also put forward two principles, ***pleasure and pain principle,*** and ***reality principle.*** We all know that we do what is pleasant and agreeable, and avoid what is unpleasant and disagreeable. Rising early, going for a walk and taking exercise are unpleasant and young people avoid them. But soon they realize that to maintain health and efficiency they must undertake such activities. They avoided them on the pleasure—pain principle and later undertake them on the reality principle. In the course of human progress man has always been giving up the pleasure—pain principle for the reality principle.

**Autonomy of motives**

It has been said earlier that all our motives are rooted in our basic needs. A person writes books to earn money and support himself, a merchant earns profits to make himself secure, a labourer drinks wine to quench his thirst. But in course of time they continue these activities independently of these needs. Even if the person has earned enough from his books to make his living safe he continues to write out of sheer joy. This motive is no longer tied to the basic need and has become independent. It is working by itself and for itself, it is functioning in an autonomous manner. Similarly the merchant continues to make profits even after having amassed fabulous wealth or the labourer continues to drink long after he has quenched his thirst. Secondary goals like books, profits and wine have become primary goals. They were originally values because they satisfied our basic needs but are now ends in themselves. This is called *the functional autonomy of motives.*

**Unconscious motives**

Unconscious motives of behaviour are those of which we are not aware and which we do not recognize as causing our behaviour. We may have little difficulty in explaining why we behave in the way we do but our explanations do not take into account all the factors involved in our behaviour. When we explain our behaviour we generally try to offer what will be acceptable or reasonable but not what really is the motive behind it. Professor Keshav has genuine difficulty in accompanying his wife to a shopping trip. Not that he grudges her money, nor that she is extravagant, nor that he does not like it. He wishes to but he feels upset and embarrassed. He does not know why though he offers excuses like fatigue, indisposition or some urgent reading to do. But the real motive may be that he feels inferior in making or advising purchases, is neglected by shopmen or feels useless during shopping, but he is not aware of these motives, and does not recognise them as his own. Freud laid great strees that a man's behaviour can be completely understood only when his unconscious motives are laid bare.

Slips of the tongue, forgetting of unplesant experences, invol untary acts nd gestures, and dreams result from unconscious motives One President of Austrian House of Deputies in opening a session said "I declare the session closed" to the merriment of the house and his own embarrassment, but the really wished it were *closed* instead of *opened.* We forget where we placed the book which we do not like lending but blame it on memory. We urge a visitor to stay but unknowingly leave our seat to bid him good-bye. At the conscious level we wanted him to leave. The mother does not really wish the child to have another helping of sweets but in trying to pass the dish on to him drops it on the floor. Such errors and unwitting movements have motives of which we are not aware or which we do not recognise. If they were revealed to us we would not readily accept them as our own. Unconscious motives are very often known as *unrecognised motives.*

These motives can be brought to light by the methods of free association which has been described in the first chapter and projective techniques which will be discussed later in the chapter on personality.

**Habits as motive.**

A good part of our behaviour can be traced to habits which we have acquired in the course of past experience. A Hindu takes off his shoes before entering the kitchen, an English man eats with fork and knife, a priest raises his hand to say grace and the like are actions which are done automatically in particular situations. The force of habit made a retired soldier working as a butler to drop dishes and stand erect and still when some naughty boy shouted "attention" from behind. Often people are not conscious of their habitual behaviour. If we consider some bad habits like smoking, drinking we will know about the great impelling power of habits in inducing behaviour. Habits as motives are persistent and demand certain kinds of activity to continue.

To sum up: motive are springs of behaviour, they are rooted in basic drives and needs, they have goals and make behaviour purposive. Often more than one motive is served by a single activity. Such motives are inter-dependent. We are not always conscious of our motive, some of them are unconscious, some of them are rooted in emotions, habits and ideas. Motives are greatly overlaid by social influences and the behaviour patterns in which they are expressed is determined by social environment. Often they themselves become goals and work independently. A complete knowledge of human behaviour is not possible without understanding all motives, conscious and unconscious, inherited and learned.

Instincts also function as motives but the behaviour patterns in which they are expressed varies from individual to individual, even in the same individual at different times, and it is not always possible to distinguish between the inherited and learned parts of instinctive behaviour.

---

## QUESTIONS

1. Distinguish between a need, a drive and a motive. Are these terms contradictory? Give an example to illustrate the cycle of activity involved.
2. Discuss the important biological and psychological motives and bring out the essential nature of the latter.
3. Can instincts function as motives? Discuss the views of McDougall and Freud about instincts critically.
4. What do you understand by the autonomy of motives? Give examples.
5. What are unconscious motives? How do we know about them?
6. Describe how emotions, habits and ideas work as motives in human behaviour.
7. Explain:—Security needs, need for self-expression, homeostasis and need for recognition
8. Discuss in a general way the role of psychological needs in adult behaviour.

CHAPTER V

# SENSATIONS

## General nature

Human behaviour has been described as responses to environment. Stimuli from the outside world impinge upon the human nervous system and arouse responses. The simplest of such responses are sensations, they are the most elementary form of mental activity and they arise only when a particular sense organ has been stimulated. We have already seen how receptors receive impressions from the outside world and carry messages to the brain through ingoing nerves. Sensations are our primary knowledge of the world. They are both physiological and psychological. Sometimes one sense organ or receptor is active and dominant, and sometimes another, but most often impressions are gained through more than one pathway. When we see a rose, eyes tell us that it is pink, fingers through touch reveal that it is soft, eyes give us its shape and size, the nose gives us its sweet smell. Thus several sense organs may work at the same time to give us knowledge of the sense qualities of outside objects and a large variety of sense impressions are being experienced by all of us when we look around, go out for shopping or sit down to lunch. Our sense organs are the gateways of knowledge; colours and brightness are known through eyes, sounds through ears, taste through tongue and smell through the nose; and watching film on the screen, listening to the radio or tasting tea we are using mainly one sense-organ though our other sense organs are not altogether inactive.

## Sensation and stimulus

Commonly we refer only to five senses *seeing*, *hearing*, *smelling*, *tasting* and *feeling* or *touching*. But a little analysis will show that we have sensations of *warmth*, *cold* and *pain* which are given to us by skin, and we have sensations of hunger, thirst and the like coming to us through our internal body. We shall deal with them later. Here we will study the relation of sense organs and stimuli.

We get a sensation only when some sense organ is stimulated. A sensation is a response or a reaction aroused in us by a stimulus. It is the stimulus that comes to us and the sensation is our own act aroused by the stimulus. A stimulus is any change in outside energy that arouses a sense organ and its receptors. It is a stimulus only when it stimulates. Light is not a stimulus to a blind man nor is sound to a deaf person. A sensation is an act of the sense organ which when stimulated sends nerve currents to the sensory centres of the brain, and the first response of the brain is sensation. Without this brain response there would be no sensation. The activity of nerve cells at the sense organ by itself does not constitute a sensation.

There are some common impressions about sensations which should be corrected here. In the first place many people think that in sensations we are not active and passively receive impressions from outside stimuli. We do not act but are acted upon. In watching a show we just look on, in listening to music we just sit still. This is not quite correct, for we have already seen that sensations depend on the activity of the nerve cells and the brain and we cannot be said to be entirely passive or inactive. Secondly the stimulus is not always external in the sense of existing outside and independent of our organism. Many of our organic sensations like hunger and thirst are not stimulated from without but are aroused from within. Thus the stimulus is not always external to the nervous system. To be exact it is external in the sense of being other than, and independent of, the sensations it is capable of arousing.

Again it is not to every type of stimulation that a sense organ will respond. Every sense organ is so constituted that it will react to a definite kind of stimulus. Eyes will never respond to sounds, tastes or smells but only to bright or coloured objects. The nose will never see colours, the ear will not taste sugar. The reception of stimuli from the outside world is very selective and every sense organ is adapted to respond only to specific types of stimuli. This is termed the *appropriate stimulus.*

**Sense organs and stimuli**

The nature and kind of sensations depends on the structure and stimulation of a sense organ. That is why the classification of sensations is based on the one hand on sense organs and on the other hand on stimuli. Since all stimulation is determined by receptors the number of sense organs ultimately rests on the nature and kinds of receptors which give rise to sensations. The receptors which are found in the various sense organs are of three kinds. The *exteroceptors* are located at the surface of the body to receive stimuli from the external environment and are found in eyes, ears, nose, tongue and skin. The *proprioceptors* are found in the bodily substance itself and their purpose is to give information to the organism about itself. They are found in the sensory cells of muscles and joints. The *introceptors* are found in the lining of the digestive tract and intestines. These receptors receive stimuli and send nerve currents along sensorry nerves attached to the sense organ to the brain where they are understood and interpreted and then directions are sent along motor nerves for making suitable movements and adjustments required by the environment.

Similarly we may clasify stimuli into *mechanic l, thermal, accoustic, chemical* and *photic*. We know where we are hit in the dark, where a fly has sat on our skin, that my mouth and throat are dry because of thirst, in what posture we are standing or bending. All these are examples of *mechanical* stimulation. Thermal stiumuli affect the body temperature which must be kept constant for life and health. If the stimuli give us too much or too little heat we may fall ill or even die. When it is very cold we wrap ourselves in heavy clothes and when it is too warm we switch on the fan. These are *thermal* stimuli. Living in air and water men and animals hear sounds. The absence of sound would take away half the life from this world. How people long to be in a quiet place and equally strong is their desire to escape from quiet places into the world of sound, speech, music and communication. These stimuli are *accoustic*. Sensations of taste and smell are due to chemical stimuli. Only those things which dissolve in the mouth are capable of giving us taste and only those things which mix with air can give us smell.

Taste is a liquid sense as smell is gaseous sense. These stimuli which give taste and smell are *chemical*. Lastly the eyes see because of light. Light is the most important stimulus which makes our knowledge of the external world accurate and complete. Vision is the response to *photic* stimulus of light.

### Attributes of sensations

Sensations change and differ in many ways and we can understand and describe them better if we indicate some of the possible dimensions in which they change and differ. These possible dimensions constitute the characteristics or atributes of sensations. Pinkness and softness of a rose are two different ***kinds*** of sensations. We say they differ in ***quality***. One rose may be deep pink and another only light pink, these differences are of ***intensity***. Sensations may last for a short or long time. We say for two hours in the noon the sun was very hot, this is the *duration* of the sensation. My friend may just tap my shoulder with a finger or grip it with his hand. The two sensations of touch differ in *extensity*, the latter is more extensive than the former. Let us discuss these attributes in detail.

*Quality*. Sensations are said to differ in quality, kind or modality when they cannot be regarded as belonging to the same wider class. Sounds and sights cannot be placed in the same class and therefore differ in quality, they are not sub-classes of a particular kind of sensation. They have nothing in common, no affinity except that they are sensations. On the other hand sensations of bitter and sweet do not differ in quality because both can be classified as belonging to a class of taste sensations, they can also be mixed to form a new sensation or in different proportions can give different kinds of tastes. Sensations of different qualities do not fuse or blend. They remain distinct even when they are given together.

Differences in quality are not merely differences of sense organs as may be readily assumed because certain sense organs give us more than one kind of sensation, for example, ears give us sensations of sound as well as giddiness or the tongue gives us sensations of taste as well as pain or temperature. Again more than one sense organ gives us the same kind of sensations, for example, skin and tongue give us pain and temperature sensations. Thus we may guard ourselves against the temptation of identifying differences of quality with those of sense organs.

Nor should we confuse the attribute of quality belonging to sensations with the primary qualities of objects. External objects are said to possess qualities like blue, soft and sweet, but such qualities belong to objects not to sensations. We have objects which are blue, soft or/and sweet, but the sensation of blue is not blue. The sensation of sweetness itself is not sweet. Blueness and sweetness belong to objects not to sensations.

The question may be asked: Why do we experience different qualities? Why is a sight so different from a sound? There is no satisfactory answer except that nerve fibres in our receptors are so constituted that they respond to such differences in external stimuli.

*Intensity.* All sensations are not equally intense or strong. Some colours are deep others are faint, some sounds are loud others are dim or some smells are striking others are weak. These are differences of *intensity.* A sensation may remain the same in quality and yet vary in strength or intensity. It is obvious that some stimuli are very strong as three spoonfuls of sugar in a cup of tea and some very week as half a spoonful of sugar in a cup. One cup will be sweeter than the other, and we will say that sensations of sweetness differ in intensity. We can compare intensity of sensations only of the same quality. We cannot compare the intensity of taste with the intensity of sound. Nor can these differennes of intensity be quantitatively measured.

Here it must be noted that there is a limit to which the intensity of a sensation can be lowered. If you add two or three particles of sugar to a glass of water you will not have any sensation of sweetness. Every stimulus must be of a certain strength or intensity before it can give rise to sensations. This lower limit is called the *threshold of consciousness.* Some lights are too faint to be seen, but as the intensity of light is increased there comes a point at which it is seen. This is the threshold of light. The point at which a stimulus just crosses the threshold should be fixed, constant and precise but it is not so because we are here dealing with organisms whose sensitivity varies from time to time. If we wish to find out such thresholds of different sense qualities we must repeat our observations and measurement and apply statistical techniques. But the result will be only statistical and not a concrete guide in practical life.

*Duration.* Sensations differ in duration or propensity. Sensations endure, they last for a shorter or longer time. They rise, poise and fall. This temporal character of sensations is found with greater distinctness and definiteness in some types of sensations than in others, specially in those of taste and smell.

*Extensity.* Extensity should be distinguished from extension which is an attribute of physical objects. The latter remains unchanged while the former keeps changing with varying distances of the object from the organism. Extensity or extensivenees is the voluminous or diffused character of sensations. Some sensations are more spread-out than others. William James says, "The quality of vluminousness exists in all sensations, just as intensity does. We call the reverberations of a thunderstorm more voluminous than the squeaking of a slate pencil; the entrance into a warm bath gives our skin a more massive feeling than the prick of a pin; a little neuralgic pain, fine as a cobweb, in the face, seems less extensive than the heavy soreness of a boil or the vast discomfort of a colic or a lumbago; and a solitary star looks smaller than a noonday sky."

To these four attributes of sensation some psychologists add a fifth, *place-differences and local signs.* An extensive sensation is a complex, within its unity it includes a number of sensations experienced together. Such "partial" sensations are distinguished from each other by assigning to them places. We speak of one as located here and another there, and can determine their distances from each other. This would be clear if we consider the apprehension of "apartnes" when we prick our skin with the two ends of a compass simultaneously. The sensation of two pricks is more than that of one and we can distinguish the two pricks as well as their "apartness." This apprehension is of place-differences or local signs. This attribute distinguishes a sensation of one part of a spread-out sense organ. The distance between the parts stimulated, for example, between the two pin pricks on the skin should be sufficient to give us two sensations. If it is very small, it is possible we may have only one sensation instead of two. The distinctness or apartness of two sensations is due to the fact that two distinct nerve fibres have been stimulated. Pain in the leg is different from the pain in the arm because of differences of local signs.

**Perceptual value of sensations**

The perceptual or presentative value of sensations is very great. They put us in direct communication with environment. The whole of our scientific knowledge is an elaborate reconstruction made out of sense experience. Sensations provide the raw material of such knowledge by presenting external objects to the individual. All that exists outside and independent of us manifests itself to us in sensations. A sensation always stands for some object.

When a sensation is very intense it compels attention to itself and the organism tries either to remove the object or to maintain it. Thus strong sensation with its capacity to draw attention leads to activities affecting the welfare of the oganism. It is the pain of the cut which tells us that some part of our body is being injured.

Again sensations help adjustment. Every change in the object when perceived has to be matched by adaptive change in the movement of the organism. In playing tennis every movement of the arm and the body is adapted in expectation of strokes from the other side. The sensations which have a high perceptual value are those of sight, hearing and touch and give us great discrimination in our environmental factors.

**Classification of sensations**

Sensations are classified on several bases. One is introspective analysis which shows that all sensations fall into groups on the basis of their resemblances. Colour sensations fall into one group as taste sensations fall into another. Since they come from different sense-organs we may classify them according to the sense organ through which they come. That is why we speak of eye sensations and ear sensations. But there are several sense organs which give rise to more than one kind of sensation. The skin gives heat, cold, touch and pain sensations and some of them are given by other sense organs too. Or we may classify sensations according to the nature of stimuli. Some stimuli come from without as light and sound are external, but other stimuli come from within as contraction of the muscles.

In this book we shall follow the traditional aproach by grouping sensations under sense organs.

**Vision**

The eye is a remarkable sense organ for its delicacy, sensitivity and usefulness. It is the most important source of our knowledge of the external world, it is most frequently used and relied upon for our accurate, detailed and complete information about things around us. It is the organ of vision or seeing, the vast reservoir of facts which we obtain by reading numerous books on a large variety of subjects is possible only through our eyes.

*The human eye*: In principle it is not unlike a photographic camera which has a lens in the front part and a sensitive curtain at the back. The eyeball corresponds to the box of the camera. its outer surface serves as the wooden cover and it is lined black with choroid coat which prevents any ray of light coming in. This dark chamber admits light through an opening in front which we call the ***pupil of the eye*** and which corresponds to the adjustable diaphragm of the camera. This pupil admits light to the eye; in dim light the pupil expands, thus increasing the amount of light passing through it, and in bright light contracts thus reducing the amount of light admitted. These adjustments permit a person to see in dim as well as bright light.

Light rays entering the eye through the pupil are focussed by the lens, which is just behind the pupil, upon the sensitive inner surface of the eye called the ***retina***. From the retina nervous impulses reach the brain over the optic nerve and are translated into visual perceptions. The retina corresponds to the photographic plate of the camera with the difference that the former recovers after an exposure so as to be ready for the next. If we examine the retina with a microscope we see that it is made up of two kinds of tiny cells, *rods* and *cones*. These cells differ in shape, size and function. The rods are longer and thiner than the cones. Cones are sensitive to all light and are essential to colour chromatic vision. Rods respond only to brightness and give us achromatic vision. In daylight or bright light we respond mainly to stimulation received by the cones; in darkness it is rod vision that is used.

In the centre of the retina there is a small depression where the light rays are focussed and which is called the *fovea centralis*. This is the part we use most in looking at objects, it is the point of clearest and sharpest vision, and is most delicately discriminative. It is closely packed with cones. As we move away from the fovea to the edges of the retina, the cones decrease and the rods increase. The best colour vision is at the fovea and the edges of retina where there are only rods can see only brightness and not colour. This can be easily demonstrated by looking through the edges to extreme sides.

The point where the optic nerve leaves the retina has neither rods nor cones; it is called the *blind spot*. There is no vision at the blind spot. From the retina the optic nerve takes the messages to the sensitive area of the occipital lobe of the brain.

To adjust the focus for objects at different distances the lens of the eye changes its shape. Such changes are called *accommodation*. A muscle known as the *ciliary muscle* so contracts and relaxes that the lens becomes flat and thin to focus on distant objects and becomes thick and curved to focus on near objects.

*The stimulus.* The stimulus of the eye is light. Light is a wave motion, its vibrations succeeding each other at the break-neck speed of 500 billions of vibrations per second, and travelling through space at the rate of 186,000 miles per second. The vibrations of these waves are focussed on the retina, the sensitive plate. There they are changed into nerve currents and these nerve currents are the basis of our visual sensations of brightness and colour. The nerve currents are communicated through the optic nerve to the brain centre where they are converted into visual sensations.

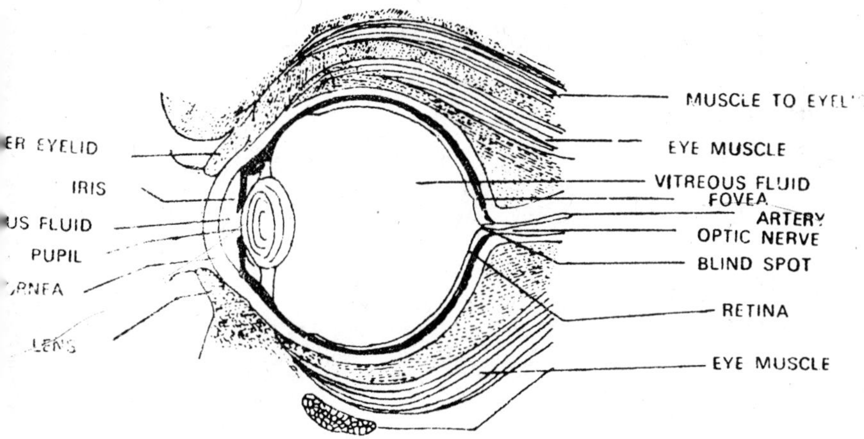


Fig. 7. The principal parts of the eye

## General characters of light sensations

Visual sensations show certain general characters which depend on the nature of variations in light waves. Scientists tell us that light waves are very short vibrations of ether. Ether is what fills all otherwise unfilled space. These light waves vary in three ways : in length, in amplitude and in form or complexity. Different characters of visual sensations depend on each of these variations in light waves. Colour or hue is related to wave-length of light, brightness to amplitude and saturation to form or complexity of the light waves.

Differences of wave-length provide us with different colours. The colours are the reds, greens, oranges, purples and other familiar ones. There is a fairly simple and consistent relation between wave-length and the hues, red, yellow, green and blue. These waves are extremely small. The shortest light wave that we can perceive is 390 millionths of a milimeter in length and the longest that we can perceive is about 700 millionths of a milimeter. The longest wave that we can perceive gives us red sensation and the shortest, violet, and in between are waves of every intermediate lengths, arranged in order from the longest to the shortest giving us other colours like orange, yellow, green, blue. When light from the sun is passed through a prism it gets broken into all the colours of the spectrum just as the rays of the sun shining through the rain break into a rainbow. Waves of light of shorter length then violet are not visible, and waves of greater length than red are perceived as heat, not light.

At one end of the spectrum we have red given to us by light waves of the length of 700 millionths of a milimeter and at the other end is violet given to us by waves of 390 millionths of a milimeter. As we pass from the red toward the violet colours become more and more yellow, and less and less red, passing from red-yellow series till pure yellow is reached at a wave length of 580 millionths of milimeter. Between 580 and 510 we have greenish yellows and yellowish greens till at 510 we have green. At 476 we have blue and between 510 and 476 we have similar shades of increasing blue and decreasing green. And at 390 or 400 we have violet. Most colours that we see are not pure, simple wave-lengths, but combinations of different lengths. The light reaching the eye from any point seldom consists of waves that are all of the same wave-lengths. Sunlight contains waves from all parts of the spectrum and appears as white. White is made up of the combination of all the different wave-lengths.

The *amplitude* of the light waves gives us brightness or intensity of visual sensations. It indicates the "energy" of the stimulus. We speak of the brightness of the object and brilliance of the sensation. If you look steadily at an electric lamp its brightness remains the same but its brilliance soon begins to decrease because the eyes are geting adapted to it. Variations in brightness may range from pure white at one end to pure black at the other end. It is possible to make any colour brighter or less bright by increasing or decreasing the intensity of light, that is, the amplitude of the vibrations. The colour tone may remain the same. The same red object is brighter in the noon and becomes less and less bright as dusk falls.

Thirdly visual sensations differ in the *degree of saturation*, or purity of colour. It depends on the form or complexity of the wave. We have seen how light is broken into many different wave lengths and that each wave-length gives us a specific colour. When there is a single wave-length we have pure colour, but usually a colour may be more or less whitish or on the other hand it may be pure red or green. In the latter case it is more saturated. Red is more saturated than pink. The more it approaches grey by mixing with other colours the less saturated it is.

Thus colours change due to changes in wave-length, in brightness and in purity or form.

Psychologically there are four primary colours—red, green yellow and blue. The popular notion is that green is a mixture of yellow and blue, but looking at it from the side of our own experience green is a pure colour. We see green as single colour. The layman and the artist speak of many colours and shades but they are all mixtures or blends of these colours in various degrees of saturation and brightness.

## Colour Mixture

We have seen that a ray of white light can be broken into its component colours when it is passed through a prism. It is possible to mix the different colours of the spectrum and get white light as a result. A sensation of white is the result of a combined action of all the wave-lengths. We may may have colour lights fixed on a wheel which rotating mixes them and gives white. Or we may have coloured discs fitted on a cardboard wheel which on rotating mixes them and gives white. Even if instead of all we were to combine only four colours, red, green, blue and yellow or even three, red, blue and green we would get a white light. When the wheel is rotated rapidly, the sensitive cells of the retina are stimulated in quick succession, first by one colour and then by another. Such experiments have given us three laws of colour mixing.

1. For every colour there is another colour which, when mixed with the first in right proportion, gives white or neutral gray. The wave lengths of both stimuli will be present in the mixed stimulus and the total energies of the two will be added. This is called *additive colour mixture*, and the two colours are called *complementaries*, for example., blue and yellow, red and bluish green. They will give us gray.

One thing should be clearly borne in mind. It is not painter's colours or pigments that are mixed, for them you would surely say that blue and yellow will give us green. We mix the lights by throwing them together. We may take two prisms and throw green light where the red is or blue light where the yellow is and the result will be either white or gray. Two colours are complementary when they mix to give white or gray.

2. Colour stimuli which are not complementary when mixed result in a colour of intermediate hue. Red and yellow give orange and blue and green give bluish green.

3. If, when mixed on the wheel, two separate colour combinations give the same colour sensation, these will in turn give the same colour sensation when all the four are mixed together. If a red and a green yield gray, and a certain yellow and blue give gray

then all the four mixed together will give gray. The mixture of mixtures should give the same result as the original mixture.

The laws of colour mixing apply only to lights and not to pigments.

**Colour-blindness**

A fairly small proportion of individuals, mostly males, are not able to distinguish between hues and are said to be colour-blind. About four per cent of the population, almost all males, never experience the colour qualities of red and green. They can see other colours. That is why they are called partially colour-blind. They see reds and greens as gray. Of course, since these persons have never seen these colours as an ordinary person does, they generally do not realize that they are colour-blind. Colour-blindness is not lack of ability to recognize a colour. Nor is it blindness. Most colour-blind people are not really blind to colour. They usually can see a great many colours but they confuse certain critical ones. They can distinguish between reds and greens but they do so by other means. Sometimes it is brightness which enables them to distinguish. Total colour-blindness is very uncommon. The individual who suffers from total colour-blindness sees objects as white, gray or black. Nor can he stand illumination even of ordinary strength. He can see things only in dim faint light.

In a way every one of us is colour blind, in certain parts of the retina. We see colours only in the central part of the retina. The outermost part of the retina corresponding to the margin of the field of vision is totally colour-blind. If we move out of the edges of the retina we see nothing but brightness or if looking in front of us, an object is introduced gradually on any of the sides, our first sensation is that of gray, black or white. Its colours will be seen only when it moves to the centre.

Again in faint light the whole of the retina with the exception of the yellow spot is totally colour-blind. When the light in a room becomes sufficiently dim, the entire coloured view passes into a gray one.

Colour-blindness is very uncommon in women, and is present only in three or four per cent of men. It is not a disease, cannot be cured, cannot be corrected by training and is not associated with any other defect of the eye or the brain. It is simply an inherited peculiarity of the colour sense. Careful study shows that the colours a red-green blind person sees are blue and yellow.

Between the outer edges of the retina and the yellow spot, there is an area which is partially colour-blind. It can see blue and yellow but not red and green. When the colours of the solar spectrum are seen sideways, the red and green appear gray and are not discernible.

Obviously colour-blind people are a great occupational hazard for railway drivers, pilots and all those who have to deal with traffic lights, red and green. Very rigid tests are therefore provided for their selection. Salesmen too who have to see coloured materials will have serious handicap if they are colour-blind.

### Adaptation and the sensation of blackness

On passing from a lighted room into a dark room, at first everything appears black. Gradually we begin to see for our retina is becoming dark adapted. Similarly in passing from a dark room into broad daylight, as in India we have to do often in summer, we get dazzled and are "blinded", but soon after we get used to it. Our eyes have now become light-adapted. Thus our eyes get adapted to the light to which they are exposed.

*Is there a sensation of blackness?* Physical science has taught us that black is the absence of light and this is very often taken to mean that black is the absence of all visual sensation. But it is not so. Black is as positive a visual experience as any other. There is no external stimulus which arouses it but on the contrary the very absence of light acts as a positive stimulus to give us a sensation of black. Sometimes this sensation arises from a contrast effect. Passing from a brightly lit room to another less lighted we experience this blackness. Thus it may be said to depend on the lack of adaptation of the retina to the stimulus.

### Constancy

We are able to identify visual objects correctly in spite of changes in illumination, white, gray or black whatever they are. This is called "brightness constancy" and is independent of the degree of illumination under which we see them. Thus objects which appear white in bright light look white even when light is dim, black objects look black in both bright daylight and in dim twilight. We are able to recognize our white shirt, black coat or red tie whatever the degree or intensity of light in the room, and we make no mistakes. It is because the brightness constancy of objects depends upon what percentage of the total light the object reflects. This percentage is called the *albedo.* When light falls on a surface or an object, some of the light is absorbed and some is reflected. A pure white object reflects all the light that falls on it but increasing shades of gray absorb more and more light, that is, the lighter the gray the greater the percentage of light reflected. This percentage of the total light that a surface reflects is called *albedo.* Whatever the intensity of illumination the albedo remains the same. That is why the brightness of objects remains constant because what we perceive is not illumination but the albedo.

### After-images

After-images are not really images but after-sensations. They occur in other senses also but more predominantly and definitely in vision. A sensation follows the presentation of a stimulus but sometimes the physiological processes involved in sensations continue even after the stimulus has been removed. The effects of the visual stimulus persist even after the removal of the stimulus and the longer the stimulation the more persistent are these after-effects. These after-sensations are called *after-images.* The cinema hall appears darker when we enter it on a bright summer noon than when we enter it on a cloudy day. If you are looking at some bright light, place one of your hands between the light and the eye, remove it for a moment, replace it again, you will continue to see the light even after the light has been screened by your hand. This is an after-image.

After-images are of two kinds, positive and negative. If you look at bright light and then quickly look at a dark surface the light will be seen for an instant after you look away. This is *positive after-image*, that is, the after-effects are of the same quality as the original sensation though fainter. It is because the physiological processes started by the stimulus persist for a time even after the removal of the stimulus. The colour mixing also depends on this factor. The colours are not actually mixed by the rotating wheel. Each colour disc leaves an after-image which mixes with the next and so on. The eye is stimulated by the second stimulus before the first one fades away, and the second blends with the first. Moving pictures work on this principle. One picture is seen and before it disappears another has come in. They follow in such quick succession that eyes get an impression of continuous motion in the picture. These pictures move at the rate of 16 per second. Small children move a burning stick round and round to create the impression of circular fire.

If you look at red paper for twenty seconds or so and then look at a white wall you will see a greenish spot corresponding to the red size of the red paper at which you have just looked. If instead of red paper you have blue paper you will see a yellow spot on the white wall. In such an experiment eyes should not be moved and the paper should be seen against a white wall and removed without moving the eyes. The new colour seen in the after-image is the complementary of the original colour. Such after-images are called *negative after-images*. Looking at a white paper the after-image will be black. Thus the negative after-image will be that which will produce gray when mixed with the original.

## Colour contrast

The complementary relationship of the opposing colour pairs brings out colour contrast. The negative after-image of red is green and it enhances the effect of red. If you place red paper alongside of green paper, the red will look redder as the green will look greener. Recently Indian women have been wearing red blouse with a green sari or red sari with a green blouse. Both intensify each other's effect. This is due to *contrast*. It shows that the quality of a colour depends on its background. If you take two pieces of the same gray paper and place one on a black sheet and the other on a white sheet the piece on a black sheet will look less gray, even brighter, than that on the white sheet. There is much truth in what ladies call "colour matching". Every colour affects and is affected by other colours, and there is one colour which intensifies its effect more than any other colour. There is much scientific basis of the advice given that a white bush shirt with a black pant or a coloured bush shirt with a white pant looks better. It is due to contrast.

**Theories of colour vision**

Thomas Young an English physicist put forward a theory of colour vision which was supported and elaborated by a German physiologist and psychologist H. Ludwig von Helmholtz and is now known as Young-Helmholtz theory. According to it only three kinds of receptors exist in the eye, one reacting to red, one to green and one to blue-violet. Stimulated in varying degrees these different receptors are capable of giving us all the colours. Corresponding to these three receptors there are three separate areas in the visual cortex and the mixing of colours may be done by the brain. White light, blending all colours, arouses all three receptors at once. There is no receptor for yellow as yellow results from the simultaneous stimulation of red and green. This theory is remarkable for its simplicity but does not explain all the facts. It does not recognise yellow as an independent colour but considers it as a blend of red and green wave-lengths. But when a person is colour-blind to both red and green he sees yellow. If this yellow depends on red and green the person should see only blue and not yellow. This means that there is an independent receptor for yellow.

This weakness of the Young-Helmholtz theory is overcome by the Ladd-Franklin theory which holds that red-green vision developed from the yellow. The vision of the primitive man was colourless, capable of distinguishing only white, black and gray, later white split into yellow and blue, and still later the yellow split into red and green. It explains red-green blindness by saying that the yellow-blue vision and the regions of the retina which react to them have not yet reached that stage of development where red and green can be seen. This theory does greater justice to facts of colour vision and recognises that there are separate zones in the retina for different colours.

Ewald Hering, a Prague professor, says that there are four primary colours red, green, blue and yellow, against three of Helmholtz. He found that certain pairs of colours mixed together give gray. This is true for red and green, blue and yellow, white and black. These he called "complementary colours". He also studied the phenomenon of after-images, that blue gives a yellow after-image and red gives green.

The retina is the most sensitive part of the eye and has only three receptors, one for red and green, one for blue and yellow, and one for black and white. Colour-blindness occurs when the red-green receptor is injured. Colour-blind people can see blue and yellow because that receptor of the retina has not been injured. Hering assumes two kinds of activity in the same neurone, but we know that each nerve fibre carries only one kind of impulse. Thus Hering creates a new difficulty which the previous two theories avoid. Secondly Hering seems to be assuming that black and white are also colours by giving them similar position in the retina.

Young-Helmholtz theory is more widely favoured because the physiological explanation it gives of colour vision explains more facts than the other two theories.

---

## QUESTIONS

1. What is meant by saying that sense-organs are the gateways of knowledge. Discuss the relation between sense-organs and stimuli and attempt to classify both.
2. What do you understand by sensation? Discuss the several attributes of sensations and illustrate your answer.
3. Give a list of the different senses and the sensations they give.

4. Describe the eye and indicate the functions of the important parts, particularly the retina, rods and cones, the optic nerve and fovea.
5. What kind of energy gives rise to light sensations? In what three ways light waves differ and what differences in sensations correspond to such variations?
6. What do you understand by colour-mixing? Describe the three laws of colour-mixing.
7. What is an after-image? Relate colour-mixing to the fact of negative after-images.
8. What is meant by colour-blindness? What are its different forms?
9. Explain:—colour contrast, colour constancy, adaptation and saturation of colours.
10. Examine critically the several theories of colour vision.

## CHAPTER VI

# SENSATIONS—(*Continued*)

### The ear

The ear is the organ of hearing and is almost as important as the eye. Through hearing we understand speech and speech is our most convenient and effective medium of acquiring and imparting knowledge, of communication on which our entire social living depends. Through hearing we receive a great many warnings and hints and thus adjust ourselves to the changing environment. Hearing foot-steps, horns, alarm clock or shouts we make changes in our behaviour. Through hearing we enjoy sweet music, laughter and good company. Sound sensations are capable of delicate discrimination and through them we can distinguish sounds following in quick succession and thus they give us a sensation of time.

It is common to speak of the outer ear, the middle ear and the inner ear. Hearing is accomplished by special receptors receiving sound waves and converting them into nervous energy. Sound waves enter the auditory canal and strike the ear drum called the *tympanum*. This causes the membrane of the tympanum to vibrate and three tiny bones called the *oscicles* carry the vibrations to the inner ear where the sensitive cells convert the sound waves into nervous energy which is transmitted to the brain. The external ear or lobe is larger in animals like cows, horses or buffaloes, it serves to catch and gather the sound waves and transmit them to the middle ear or the ear drum. The latter only carries through the hole the sound waves which set the inner auditory membrane into vibration and cause sound sensations. The auditory sensations are stimulated by vibrations of the air particles.

The middle ear has the *Eustachian tube* which opens into the *pharynx*. This tube serves to keep the air pressure in the middle ear the same as that outside. When one is suffering from severe cold the tube is closed by the infection causing unpleasant feeling.

The inner ear has two main parts. One is concerned with balancing the body, consists of semi-circular canals and has nothing to do with hearing. It will be dealt with in a later part of the chapter. The other is concerned with hearing and is called the *cochlea.* It is so called because it resembles a snail. It is large at one end and small at the other and makes nearly three complete turns. Each turn is filled with fluid and separated from others by membranes. The *cochlear canal* is the smallest of the three and is separated from the *vestibular canal* by *Reissner's membrane* and from the *tympanic canal* by the *basilar membrane.* The basilar membrane is the most important of these membranes, for it has the *organ of Corti* in which sound waves give rise to auditory impulses. These impulses travel along an auditory nerve which runs from the cochlear canal to the brain.

Most of the fibres from the right ear cross to the left temporal lobe and vice versa.

**Hearing and its stimulus**

While light travels through a vacuum, sound requires an elastic medium like air, water, bone or metal. This can be clearly proved by placing a bell under a jar from which air has been exhausted. As long as there is air in the jar, the bell can be heard, but when all air is withdrawn, the bell may work but there is no sound. The waves set up by a vibrating body are transmitted through air to the eardrum. There they produce certain changes which stimulate nerve fibres. From nerve fibres impulses are carried to the brain and we hear.

Sound is produced when an object is sent into vibration. A plate falls on the ground, a door bangs, a gate creaks, a horn blows and there is a single sharp sound. Rain on the tin roof, stone striking against a door, ironsmith striking a hammer or children shouting all these produce a series of sounds or they may be mixed up to produce a confused, discordant sound which we call *random noise.* These sounds may continue and persist

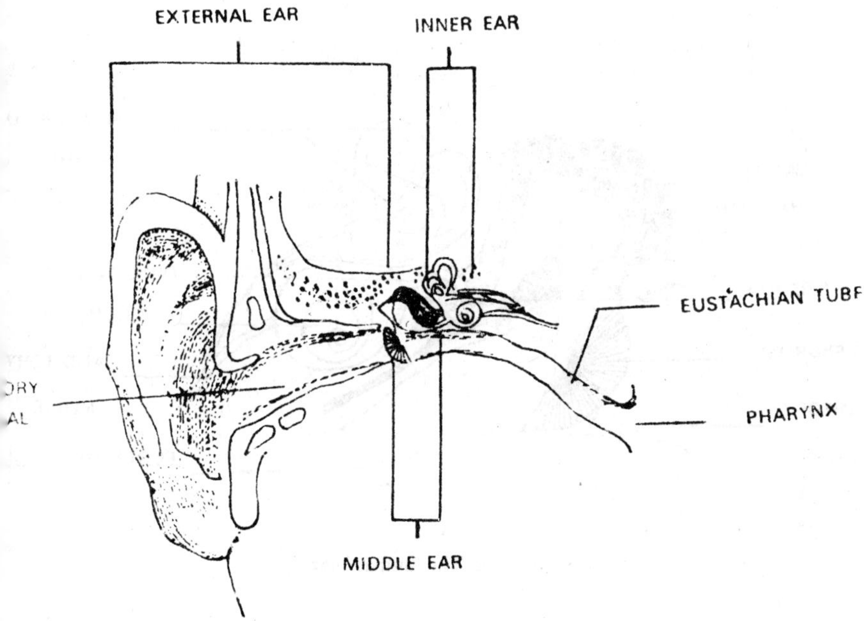


Fig. 8. The human ear

Fig. 9. The human ear

without any order in an utterly irregular manner. Noise is an irregular discordant jumble of sounds. But not all sounds are noisy. Sounds from musical instruments are simple and smooth, they do not jar on the ear, because they follow some order, are regular and successive and are sweet and enjoyable. We call such sounds *music.* But the distinction between noise and music is not absolute. Most of our sound experiences are partly music and partly noisy, it is the predominance of one over the other which makes us call it music or noise. Many people with a discriminating ear leave a music performance as it is full of noise, some folk music is just an attempt to bring in regularity in an otherwise hurlyburly of noise. Thus there is no clear-cut separation of noise and tones.

Tones have three characteristics or attributes which we should know in detail — *pitch, loudness* or *intensity,* and *timbre.* We usually divide tones into that of a harmonium, a violin or a pipe organ but that does not lead us far. A tone is described as of high pitch, medium pitch or low pitch ; a tenor voice is high pitched, a baritone voice of medium pitch and a bass voice of low pitch. The pitch of a tone depends on the vibration rate of frequency of the sound wave. Pitch rises or falls as frequency increases and decreases. With the help of cathode-ray osciloscope sound waves have been recorded and how often they go up and down in a measured time. This is their frequency and we state it in cycles per second. But it should be borne in mind that frequency is physical and pitch is psychological, and people judge pitch without knowing anything about frequency. A slow vibration frequency produces a low pitch and a rapid vibration frequency produces a high pitch. The lowest tone we can hear is about 15 to 20 vibrations per second and the upper limit for tones is 20,000 to 25,000 vibrations per second. But high tones often cause painful sensations in the eardrum. Older people are not able to hear high tones. Some persons have a musical ear and can catch sounds of lesser or greater number of vibrations.

The second characteristic of sound sensations is their loudness or *intensity.* It depends on amplitude or intensity of sound wa-

Sounds can be arranged in order of loudness, in a series of amplitude of the waves. In any stringed musical instrument a string has a fixed pitch which can be made softer by a light pluck or given a vigorous twang with greater amplitude. The pitch remains the same but its loudness or intensity has increased.

Sounds vary in *timbre*. It depends on the complexity of the sound waves, that is, on a mixture of waves of different vibrations. Most of our sensations are not simple as we consider them to be even if they rise from a single source. They are complex and can be discriminated by a musical ear. Differences of timbre would be clearly understood if we were to compare the same note sounded on a piano, a violin and a trumpet. Such differences are explained as arising from differences in the combination of several elementary tones.

Every sound has a fundamental tone which means that the vibrating body is vibrating along its whole length. It is the lowest tone which a given resounding body produces. But it also vibrates in parts giving off simultaneously various more rapid vibrations having frequency rates multiples of the rate given off by the whole string. They are *overtones* and give uniqueness and richness to the fundamental tone.

Another common phenomenon of hearing occurs when two tones sound together while differing only slightly in frequency. *Beats* sound like an alternate waxing and waning. The number of beats per second depends upon the difference in vibration rate of the two tones. Two tones of 256 and 257 vibrations produce one beat per second and two tones of 256 and 258 vibrations produce two beats per second, and so on. If this difference increases, beats are heard as rough or unpleasant in tone quality. Gradually the beats disappear and a new tone called the *difference tone* is heard. If we sound two tones of 556 and 856 vibrations together a third tone will be heard of 300 vibrations per second.

Suppose we sound two tones an octave apart and one is twice the vibration rate of the other. If one is 556 and the other is 278 the difference in vibration will be 278. Now when the difference tone is the same as one of the component tones, the difference tone will not be heard as a separate tone but will reinforce or strengthen the component tone. That is why two tones an octave apart blend together. They produce a tone higher in pitch than the component tone and the higher tone is called the *summation tone.* It should be noted that such differences cannot be experienced by a novice, only a practised ear can discern them.

When one sound drowns another we say that one *masks* another. In telephone and radio communication or in the choice of bells and alarms one has to see that sounds are heard in competition with other noises. The masking effect may be eliminated by raising the loudness of the masked tone.

**Sensations of balance**

We have already pointed out that a part of the inner ear consists of semicircular canals which have nothing to do with hearing and contain receptors which help keep body's balance or equilibrium, to maintain our upright posture, steady gait and direction of movement. It is spoken of as the "jar organ" giving us the "static sense". It tells whether we are falling or going up, spinning or standing still, going left or right, forward or backward.

Each semicircular canal is almost at right angles to others which means there is one canal corresponding to the three planes of space. These canals are filled with fluid and open into a common chamber filled with sensitive fibres to which the nerves are connected. It is assumed that a movement of the head will set up a movement of the fluid in the canals and that this movement will stimulate the fibres. They are strongly stimulated when we whirl round vigorously or turn somersaults and the resulting sensation is one of the giddiness or dizziness. Too much spinning or swinging persistently stimulates the inner ear and leads to a falling sensation. This dizziness is reduced by training in rotation. Unusual stimulation of these canals is conducive as it cures many people of motion-sickness. Those who get sick in a long bus journey or air travel or sea trip have their jar-organ to blame. Rigid tests of motion sickness are given to military personnel which has to be air-lifted. The tests include motion in long swings, rotating chairs, elevators and the like. Some people grow pale, perspire and fall ill. Some feel dizzy in the beginning but soon get over it. This means that their receptors have got adapted to the unusual movements.

The after-effects of persistent stimulation of this sense-organ are interesting. A person getting down from an aeroplane or a ship after a long journey feels that buildings around are going to topple and the ground is unsteady. This is enjoyed by children spinning round and round and then stopping, they feel dizzy and tend to fall. This is because violent turning has set the canals into activity and after stopping you must readjust yourself to the fact that they have become active. It is a common practice with naughty boys that they noiselessly step close to the back of another and give a slight slap on his ear to make him shake and jar. It is this organ which is stimulated.

**Sensations of smell**

Receptors for sensations of smell lie in the upper part of the nasal cavity. They consist of small sensitive areas in each nostril. In quiet breathing the greater part of the air is carried directly to the pharynx and very little reaches the sensitive areas. It is only in full breathing, particularly in sniffing that we are able to sense odours. In breathing out there are no odours. The organ of smell can be stimulated only by chemical substances in a gaseous form.

The sense of smell is the most primitive and oldest. Though it does not play a very important part in the life of man today it was probably used by primitive man in discovering and testing food and in protecting himself from harmful surroundings. Many animals use it for food-seeking and enemy-hunting, and they sniff at things before they eat them.

The sense of smell has a strong feeling tone. Every odour is either agreeable, disagreeable or a mixture of both. A very mild odour is pleasant but a very strong one of the same type may be disgusting. So fragrance has to be presented in a very mild form.

The sense of smell is easily fed and fatigued. A sweet smell fails to be sweet for long and a bad smell ceases being noxious after some time. Foul air of the slums is tolerated by their habitual dwellers, their sensibility has been blunted with use. Many people entering into a stuffy room wonder how people work there but a few minutes stay makes them insensible to the stuffy feeling. They get adapted and used to it.

The sense of smell is extremely delicate. This is particularly so with many animals, dog, for example. The dog can follow an individual odour with accuracy even though the material left on the ground is negligible. Dogs are being employed by the police for pursuing criminals. Even in man the delicacy of smell is very great ; camphor can be perceived even in the proportion of 1 part to 400,000.

*Primary odours.* Are there any primary odours out of which all other more complex odours can be made by simple mixing? Many attempts have been made to classify odours and no two attempts agree. Odours are generally classified by reference to the substances which give rise to them. Crocker put forward four primary odours — fragrant (musk), acid (vinegar), burnt (roast coffee ) and caprylic (sweaty), but Henning's classification of odours into six heads is more popular.

1. *Spicy* found in pepper, cloves and nutmegs.
2. *Fragrant* found in flowers like rose, violets.
3. *Fruity* found in apples, lemon etc.
4. *Foul* or putrid found in decaying things as bad fish.
5. *Resinous* as found in pine, turpentine.
6. *Burned* as found in tarred or burned things.

Most of the odours which we experience in our everyday life are mixtures of various odours in different intensities.

Smells not only mix with other smells but they also mix with other kinds of sensations like touch, taste and organic sensations. Pungent smell is not purely an odour but a peculiar kind of touch experience. Sneezing is not due to smell stimulation but to an irritation which is an organic sensation. Their mixture with taste sensations is a matter of common experience. What we call flavour is smell and taste mixed together. If one were to plug his nose while testing tea, onion or Coca Cola, the taste would be lost. When one suffers from a bad cold things seem tasteless because the sense of smell is not working

Unsuccessful attempts have been made to locate smells in different regions of the olfactory receptors..

**Sensations of taste**

The organ for sensations of taste is generally said to be the tongue but on closer analysis it is found that the tongue has also got all the skin sensations along with taste spots. These taste spots called *buds* are located in little pits opening upon the surface of the tongue. In the sides of these pits can be found little flash shaped chambers, each containing a number of taste cells. These cells have a large number of projections called *papilae* which when stimulated give us taste sensations. These projections are connected with brain and when stimulated send nerve currents along the axon to the cortex. Unlike the "spots" of the skin these papilae do not each give a separate sensation. Some of them give two, others give three of the tastes. However an attempt has been made to locate them in the tongue and it has been found that the sensation of bitter taste is aroused chiefly from the base of the tongue, the sweetness from its tip, the sour from the edges and the salty from both, edges and tip.

The appropriate stimulus of the taste sensations is of chemical nature. It must either be a liquid or a substance soluble in the mouth, for else it cannot get to the sensitive papilae of the taste cells. If the tongue is dried, and a solid lump of sugar is placed on it, it will not give us any taste of sweetness till some saliva gathers up and dissolves it What is the nature of this chemica stimulus is very difficult to say. A large variety of substances give us similar tastes, for example many acids and some non-acidic substances give sourness; sugar, sacharine, glycerine give us sweet and we have yet to discover what is common to substances arousing one type of taste.

In common language we speak of a large multiplicity of taste sensations ; everything seems to have a taste of its own, but this common language does not give us the truth. We have only four pure tastes —sour, bitter, salt and sweet. The rest are all blends of these and also of skin sensations which the mouth is capable of giving. A morsel of food is not only sweet but soft, gummy, hot etc. and all these fuse inextricably into a unity we call the taste of the food

In the first place sensations of taste are mixed up with sensation of touch. The tongue is fairly sensitive to stimuli arousing touch sensations and its tip can discriminate between touch sensations. Besides some tastes are uniformly connected with softness though when the taste is intense the sensation of smoothness becomes less prominent, almost obscured. In the case of acids we are aware of their "astringent character" and when the acidity is increased it is almost stinging. This has led some people to say that the sensations of taste are merely those of touch.

Secondly sensations of taste get mixed up with those of smell. This may be due to the proximity of sense-organs or the close association between their stimuli. As has already been pointed out flavour is mostly a combination of taste and smell. Food in the mouth constantly stimulates the smell organ both from without and from the back passage of the throat. It may easily be tested by closing the nose while eating something delicious. The flavour will not be what it used to be.

Sensations of taste can also be easily combined with organic sensations. Taste most often depends upon the stimulation of the alimentary canal. What we call relish is a mixture of organic sensations of hunger and taste.

Though tastes have no perceptual value, they afford us a great deal of enjoyment, and not only help us in discriminating and recognising chemical objects but warn us against foods harmful to the organism.

**Organic sensations**

Organic sensations have their source in such bodily processes as affect the nutritive or vegetative life of the organism; their stimuli are to be found in the varying conditions of the blood supply, the digestion and assimilation of food, the secretions, the supply of oxygen by breathing, and generally in such changes as make a difference to the efficiency of the bodily tissues in the performance of their vital functions.

Organic sensations are of three kinds, corresponding to the sources from which they come. Firstly there are sensations coming from the various parts of the alimentary canal. The extreme back of the mouth and top of the throat gives us thirst, the "dry throat". The tube running from mouth to stomach gives us nausea or the feeling of sickness, the stomach itself gives us hunger. The latter is aroused when the stomach, being ready for food, begins its churning movements.

Secondly there are sensations from the bones, tendons and muscles which are known as the *kinesthetic* sense, that is, the sense for movement. The movement of the joints or bone-sockets gives us the sensation of pressure. The contraction of muscles gives us pressure and pain. From the tendons we get a new sensation of strain, of effort when we are actively pushing or pulling.

Thirdly we have sensations of "bracing" and "stuffy" feelings from the lungs and the sensations of itching, tickling, "pins and needles" from the blood vessels.

Organic sensations in general are vague and diffused. It is not easy to localize them and they often so fuse into each other that it is not possible to distinguish one from the other. They are always accompanied by a high feeling tone, and it is their intense feeling tone which has prevented them from further differentiation. They have little or no perceptual value and the only knowledge they can give us is that of the internal organism. On the other hand they are very important as determining conditions of our affective and active life. Most of them are either always pleasant or always unpleasant. From the variety, complexity and persistence of our activities to eke out a living to satisfy our appetites like hunger we can infer about their important role in life.

**Skin or cutaneous sensations**

Sensations from the skin are known as cutaneous sensations. The skin is very often spoken of as the organ of touch but it contains a number of receptors for warmth, for cold, for pain as for pressure or touch. The *epidermic* or outer layer of the skin is thin and non-sensitive ; it is the *dermis* or the inner layer which contains the cutaneous receptors. If we explore the surface of the skin, point by point, with different kinds of stimuli, we find that it is not uniformly sensitive. It contains a mosaic of tiny sensorial areas, each yielding a certain special sort of sense-experience and no other. There are a multitude of minute spots, some of which give only a sensation of warmth, others of cold and still others of pain etc. Thus it is common to speak of *heat spots, touch spots* or *pain spots*. These spots are nerve-endings of small cones or corpuscles.

Though we speak of a large variety of skin sensations, roughness, smoothness, hardness, softness, moistness, dryness, warmth, heat, cold, aching, tickling, stinging, pricking and many others, it is customary to classify them under four heads. We have sensations of touch, warmth, cold and pain. The rest are more or less compounds of these four. Thus tickling is mostly touch or pressure, wetness is cold and touch, pricking is pain and touch, and so on.

Touch spots tell us of the weight, roughness and smoothness, hardness and softness of objects. The value of touch sensations also lies in the extent to which they help us to estimate the amount of pressure. Touch spots are not found everywhere on the skin. Some parts of the skin are more sensitive to touch stimuli. The tip of the finger is very rich in touch spots and everybody knows how much it can help in distinguishing objects in the dark.

Temperature sensations are not of heat and cold, but of warmth and coolness. Hot and cold are a bit painful. Beyond a certain limit the hotter or the colder the sensation the more painful it is. Too much heat and cold excite the pain spots as well as the warmth or cold spots. Thus we may say that a sensation of heat is a compound of sensations of warmth and pain, and the sensation of cold is a compound sensation of coolness and pain. Sensations of extreme heat and cold are difficult to distinguish from each other, for even very cold objects give us a burning sensation. According to Woodworth both types of sensations from extreme heat and cold are compounds of elementary sensations of warmth, cold and pain.

Skin sensations also show the phenomena of contrast and adaptation. It would be clear from a very interesting experiment in which three pots of water, one of very hot, the second of very cold and the third of fresh water are placed side by side. Now dip your right arm in hot water and the left arm in cold water. Let them remain there for a few minutes after which put both the arms in fresh water. To your surprise you will find the right arm feeling cold and the left arm feeling hot, because fresh water is colder than the pot in which you had put your right arm and hotter than the pot in which you had put your left arm. This is both an adaptation and contrast effect, receptors get adapted to one kind of stimulus show contrast effect when suddenly shifted to a different stimulus.

Cheeks are said to have the most sensitive temperature spots. It is the cheek to which a washerwoman holds the iron to judge its temperature.

Pain spots may be stimulated by almost any kind of stimulus, but it must be of an intenser type and tend to injure the skin. Pain sensations in a way give a warning that the organism is going to be injured. The fewest pain spots are found in the cheeks, the thighs and the ear lobes. A needle can be run through the cheek with comparatively less pain. Pain is given as a punishment to deter people from doing wrong but pain warns that something is wrong with the body and thus acts as its protector. It is a sort of danger signal.

### Weber-Fechner's law

We have seen that sensations differ in quantity or intensity though their quality remains the same. Now the question arises: Does the intensity of the sensation depend on the strength and intensity of the stimulus? How are differences in the intensity of sensations related to differences in the strength of the stimulus? It is possible to measure quantitatively the intensities of stimuli but it is not always possible to measure the intensities of sensations, and the question boils down to this : How much must two stimuli differ before we can notice the difference? In judging the cause-and-effect relation between the physical stimuli and resulting sensations our problem is to know how much a given stimulus must be increased or decreased to bring about a "just noticeable difference". The answer depends on several things. Very small differences may pass unnoticed. If you add a cupful of sugar to a bucket of water and then add another spoon you may not see any difference in the sweetness of water. But if you add two spoons of sugar to a glass of milk and then add another spoon to it the difference will be observed. If you add an inch to the height of a person you may not see the difference but if you add an inch to the length of his nose it will be more readily observed; the street light which passes unnoticed during day illumines the street at night ; if you add one ounce of weight to 100 ounces it will not be seen but if you add the same to 15 ounces it will be felt. The question was studied experimentally by E.H. Weber a professor in the university of Leipzig and was later further investigated by his colleague Professor G.T. Fechner, and they formulated what is known is Weber-Fechner's law : our perception of change is relative to the object changed, when stimuli increase in geometrical ratio, sensations follow in arithmetical ratio, and that equal differences in intensity of sensations do not correspond with equal differences in intensity of stimulus.

This means we must inquire what is the minimum we should add to the stimulus so that a difference in sensation should be perceptible. In other words what is the "differential threshold" of different sensations. Several experiments have been made and they show that it differs with different kinds of sensations. As a result of the study of general principle of relativity in the perception of differences, it has been found that for visual perception the fraction is 1/100, that is, to a light of 100 candle power at least a light of one candle power must be added before any increase in brightness can be perceived, to a light of 200 candle power a light of 2 candle power and to a light of 600 candle power a light of 6 candle power must be added to perceive an increase in brightness. For visual perception of lines it is 1/50, that is, to a line of 50 centimetres an addition of 1 centimetre in length will enable us to see the change, 4 centimetres to a length of 200 centimetres and so on. For taste the change must be 1/3 of the existing intensity of the stimulus. For weight and pressure it is 1/3. Any change below these thresholds of discrimination will not be observed.

There is a description of an experiment in some old books on psychology. A frog sat in water and the temperature of that water was gradually increased until it reached the boiling point. The frog was boiled alive and did not make any effort to escape. The increase in temperature was so small and gradual that the frog did not perceive the difference which was below the threshold.

Weber-Fechner law grew out of an attempt to see if the intensity of the stimulus could be related to the intensity of the sensation, and to measure and generalize about the relationship between stimulus changes and our perception of these changes. In those days such a field of study was called *psychophysics* as it attempted to relate the physical with the psychological. In finding out *just noticeable differences* between stimuli they discovered thresholds for each type of sensation. A given stimulus was made stronger or weaker by adding or subtracting very small amounts till the change was noticed This was the *method of just noticeable difference.* By another method a standard stimulus was compared with a number of stimuli to determine the smallest difference that can be perceived. This is the *method of constant stimuli*. In a third *method of average error* the just noticeable difference was considered as a measurement of the error of observation, of lack of sensitivity of the subject to any stimulus or its changes.

It is obvious that the basis of this law is physiological. The law holds good in the range of medium and high intensities but breaks down when we are dealing with stimuli and sensations of very low intensities. If a pinch of salt is added to a cup of water adding one-third may make a difference but if we were to use a bucketful of water the difference would not be noticeable.

---

## Questsons

1. Describe in outline how the ear works, and analyse the characteristics of sound sensations.
2. How would you distinguish between noise and music? Explain what you understand by overtones and beats.
3. The ear is an organ of balance, explain and discuss in detail.
4. Describe the different smell sensations. Why is it that a person with a bad breath never notices it himself?
5. Describe how sensations of smell and taste combine with other sensations.
6. Describe the organic sensations and name parts of the body which are most sensitive to each one of them.
7. Describe the skin sensations and mention parts of the body which are most sensitive to them.
8. Critically discuss the Weber-Fechner law giving illustrations.
9. Explain : — differential threshold, the perceptual value of organic sensations, psychophysics, kinesthetic sensations.

CHAPTER VII

# ATTENTION AND PERCEPTION

Ordinarily we speak of giving attention to objects, of concentrating attention on some object or shifting attention from one object to another. This may give the impression that attention is some faculty or power that we can use at will. But it is better to speak of attending, the act, process or function of attending rather than any power.

Psychology studies mental processes and activities but it is difficult to do this without attending to them. Attending to an object is to bring that object to consciousness. To perceive an object, to think about it, to solve some problem about it, to remember it and the like is not possible without attending to it. By attending to anything we bring it within the realm of consciousness. Attention is the heart of the conscious process and is basic to all mental activity and behaviour. Attention in a way precedes all mental activity.

**Nature of attention**

At any one moment we are aware of a large number of objects around us but we attend only to a few of them. Writing on my table I am conscious of things lying on the table, of the room in which I am sitting, of time and place, but I am attending only to the letter I am writing. The field of attention is narrower than the field of consciousness or awareness. It is concentrated awareness of a selected aspect of our environment. We are said to be attending to an object when our sense-activity is focussed on any particular stimulus. Such stimuli stand out more prominently from the rest of the environment and are more clearly perceived.

But we do not continue to attend to any single object for long. Any sound from outside will shift my attention from the letter I am writing to the sound I hear, and the next moment I feel a pin prick and attend to that. Listening to a lecture how difficult it is to concentrate attention on any one idea of the speaker. Attention shifts to companions, to the hall in which we are sitting, to the face and dress of the lecturer and so on. Attention is always fluctuating and shifting, our interest and needs are changing and they affect the process of attending, and then some outside objects by their force and intensity compel attention.

Attention is not just looking on. It is an active process, involving give-and-take with the environment. When we attend to anything we are inclined to do something about it be it simply to keep it before our mind or to remove it from consciousness.

Attention is a process of adjustment. By attending the individual adjusts himself to inner needs or to outer stimuli. We attend to sounds to find out what they mean and how they will affect us. We attend to traffic on the road for our safety and because the loud horns and bright lights compel us to do so.

**Importance of attention**

It is often of great importance to the individual whether he attends to an object carefully or not. Most of the accidents on the road, burglaries, even illness are due to our failure to attend carefully enough to small details. A slight lapse may mean a big injury or loss. Let us consider in detail some of advantages of attending.

In the first place by attending sensory discrimination is improved. At any one moment we are conscious of a large number of things but attention separates its object from the rest and enables us to observe it carefully. We are able to make fine distinctions in what we observe and to perceive things which otherwise would have passed unnoticed. I am vaguely aware of the clock on the wall but by attending to it I am able to know the exact time. Details come out by the act of attending, and impressions become clearer. If you are talking while eating you may not be perceiving what you are eating but if you are attending to dishes before you and discussing them with others at the table you will have clearer and more distinct impressions about what you eat.

Secondly attention directs our energies, we respond to some objects and ignore others. To be attentive is to concentrate one's efforts in a certain direction so that things and ideas we attend to are relevant to our needs and purposes. In the market you attend to only those shops where your needs can be met, the lawyer attends to only those ideas of the prosecutor which he can strongly contradict, a student attends only to those books which bear on his study.

Thirdly attention increases efficiency. It helps us to get ready to meet any situation. The runner jumps at the word "Go". The state of attention prepares us to respond and to respond immediately. A shooting pain compels attention and immediate response to remove its cause. Attention is a preparatory adjustment and inattentive people are seldom efficient and successful.

Fourthly attention helps us to remember experiences more accurately and fully. Those things to which we attended very carefully are recalled with vividness and in detail. That is why teachers ask students to be attentive and repeat lessons so that students may attend and be able to remember.

**Bodily adjustment in attention.**

We have pointed out that attention is an active process, it is selective in so far as we do not attend to anything and everything, it has a purpose and aim, it changes and fluctuates, and cannot be concentrated on any one object for long. We cannot attend to many objects at the same time, the range or span of attention is limited. And the objects attended are more clearly apprehended. In attending we make certain bodily movements by way of adjustment. If attention is a state of preparedness or readiness the body must also be suitably adjusted for action. In the first place all receptors are directed toward the object of attention, the stimulus. Our eyes and ears are directed to it and other sense-organs are also ready to receive any impression. Secondly the whole body posture is changed to enable the sense-organs to function best. We crane our head to catch every word spoken and see every object shown. Such bodily postures help to concentrate attention. Thirdly in any act of attention there is found some tension in muscles as if the body is poised for action. When sense-organs are in a state of readiness to receive impressions there is activity in their muscles and this leads to activity in the rest of the system, the entire body and the brain. Mind is active in any act of attending and so is the body, ready to respond by way of understanding and action if necessary.

**Laws of attention**

Why do we attend to some objects and ignore others. Psychologists have laid down certain laws or conditions which decide this. There are external conditions and internal conditions which determine what object will attract or compel attention. Some psychologists call them the *determinants of attention* and classify them as objective and subjective according as they are to be found in the external stimuli or in the individual himself. Let us study them in detail

*Objective determinants.* One of the important external or objective conditions or determinants of attention is *change.* Other things being equal, we are almost always more likely to notice a changing stimulus than an unchanging one. So long as the ticking of the clock goes on we do not notice it but as soon as it stops, it arrests attention. The change in the stimulus or its intensity should not be gradual, it must have a certain degree of suddenness. Such change may be in the qualitv, intensity or extensity of the stimulus.

Another factor of advantage in holding and securing attention is the *intensity* of a stimulus. A strong or intense stimulus will attract attention more readily than a weak one. A loud noise has the advantage over a low murmur, a street band compels attention while the hubbub does not. A bright colour or light will draw attention while a more subdued one would not.

Other things being equal the larger the *size* of a thing the more likely one notices it. A large building will be more readily attended to than a small one. The advertiser uses large types in his notices to attract attention. However a small picture in the middle of a printed page will draw attention.

*Repetition* is another such condition. Objects presented again and again are sure to secure attention. Advertisements in newspapers are printed and calls are made again and again to attract attention. Much of the power of propaganda lies in the potency of repetition.

*Novelty* and *contrast* also help in attracting attention. Objects different from the type we are accustomed to see are readily noticed. We do not pay any attention to household furniture because they are too familiar but a new arrangement is readily noticed. A lean thin fellow in the company of big stout men is attended to very soon. Clever speakers try to present things in a new and different way to draw the attention of the listeners e.g. "I have a very small objection" and the like.

Lastly the *importance of the problem* or the *meaningfulness* of objects is also as important. We pay attention to that which is of concern to us.

*Subjective determinants.* It is readily recognised that one person attends to, and another ignores, the same object or the same person at one time attends to it and at another time ignores it. So the personal or subjective factor is as important. The question is : Is there anything in the individual himself which determines what objects will be attended to and what will not be attended to? Such subjective determinant may be summed up in one word *interest*. We attend to objects which interest us and do not attend to those which do not interest us. Interest and attention go hand in hand. We are interested in that to which we attend, and we attend to that in which we are interested. Interest means making a difference. We are interested in objects because they make a difference to us, because they concern us. Interest is also defined as the "felt value of an end", the satisfaction that we get from the realization of goals.

An important source of interest is man's *native desires* and *needs.* A hungry person attends readily to food as a man in danger attends quickly and definitely to those features of his environment which promise escape and self-preservation. So many advertisements contain pictures of young ladies to appeal to the sex impulse of people. Today we are deeply desirous of gaining health, efficiency and smartness and advertisements of all those articles which promise these are of great interest to us. They appeal to our native urge and desire for esteem, recognition and praise.

Our interest may arise out of our *attitudes* too and they determine what we shall attend to. In a way we attend to what things confirm our attitude. One with a hopeful approach will attend to all things bright and cheerful, another with a hostile attitude attends to faults and shortcomings.

Attention is also determined by one's *education* and *training*. In a library a professor will attend to books on his subject, an artist will attend to books on art, a bookbinder to wellbound books. In a passing crowd a barber will attend to hair, a bootblack to shoes, a tailor to clothes. We attend to objects we have been trained to observe. A scientist sees things where a layman does not see anything.

The *mood* of the moment, the *purpose* in hand, our *goals* in life determine our interest and the objects to which we will attend. One in angry mood jumps at the slightest wrong and lashes out, he attends only to things which will feed his anger. Looking out for a lost child in a crowd we do not attend to other children. And a botanist attends to plants and leaves in a forest, a zoologist to insects and animals. A salesman attends to what people are considered capable of buying things, a beggar to people considered capable of giving alms.

Thus what a person is, his personality, attitudes, goals, desires, purposes, moods and the like, determine his interests and the objects he will select for attention.

## Kinds of attention

Attention is commonly distinguished into *voluntary*, *involuntary* and *habitual*. In voluntary type of attention we want to attend, we make an effort to do so, and we must attend. Even if our minds wander and there are obstacles to attending, we by our will-power concentrate our mind on a task and attend to what we have taken in hand. The lecture may be uninteresting and dull, but we have to attend as it bears on our course of study. More interesting things come to mind but we drive them away and attend to the lecture intentionally and deliberately. We have made up our mind against odds. This is voluntary attention.

But the blaring noise from a loudspeaker, the dazzling light from a very strong lamp or the very bright colours of dress compel attention. We are forced to attend to them. We have no alternative but to attend. Witnessing an absorbing motion picture, reading a very interesting novel or listening to sweet music we freely give ourselves away, and attend without realizing it. Such attention is *involuntary*. We pay attention inspite of ourselves. Involuntary attention is the most efficient type, and even though teachers have to force children's attention in the beginning their final aim is that children should attend of their own accord, that is, to convert voluntary attention into involuntary. It is, because, though through devices he may be able to draw children's attention he cannot sustain it or enable them to hold it for long. Voluntary attention is a good start but a bad ending because one's attention is seldom held for long unless it is sustained by his needs, desires, interests or goals. So all those whose aim is to secure other people's attention must present their material in such a manner that involuntary, effortless attention is developed.

Some people attend to certain kinds of stimuli because they have done so in the past, because they have developed habits of attending to them. A doctor attends to the telephone even if he is asleep as a mother attends to the cries of the baby sleeping near her. This is *habitual* attention. The boatman attends to boats on the horizon as a child attends to the shouts of a hawker. If attention is a state of readiness or is a mind-set some individuals are more or less permanently ready or set for a certain kind of stimuli. It is because our drives, needs, desires, attitudes or goals have a more or less continuous role in our lives.

### Control of attention

We have discussed factors which help to draw and hold attention, but some of them may be working to attract a person's attention away from the task in hand. This is *distraction.* Noise is a common distraction in study and we seek quiet for concentration. But too quiet a place may also work as a distraction. A person working in a town fondly hopes that sojourn in a quiet place in the countryside will help better concentration but when he goes there he is unable to concentrate because he is habituated to work and study in a noisy place. The novelty of the situation proves too much for him. Often, however, outside distraction is an excuse for inability to attend and one who is blaming external factors for his lack of concentration may be just deceiving himself. A student who does want to study is usually able to do so whatever the interference. Many people complain that there is so much noise in the library that they cannot study at all and yet if they have to read a captivating novel or a love letter they go to the same library.

Individuals differ in their ability to withstand distractions but here are suggestions which may help in doing so. One common way is to run away from distractions. Another is to make distraction a part of the whole activity and still another is to get accustomed to it. Going to the hills we find that the summer stream makes so much noise as to prevent rest or sleep but we soon get used to it. This is *negative adaptation.* Some people get negatively adapted to distracting stimuli sooner than others, partly because they are more alert and determined.

### Measurement of attention

Attempts have been made to measure the strength and vividness of attention. One such attempt deals with the *attention power of stimuli.* Some stimuli attract attention more readily than others and all those whose business it is to attract other people's attention are deeply interested in such attempts. It is important for an advertiser to know what sort of advertisements have the greatest appeal and how his advertisements compete with others. An eye-movement camera has been specially devised and it determines which of the two advertisements has the greater power of drawing and holding attention. A draft advertisement is compared with other advertisements and thus its attention-drawing power is tested before it is printed. Similarly attempts have been made to measure the *duration of attention*,-that is, how long a stumulus is capable of holding attention. Much depends on the make-up of the individual but the patterns of the stimulus may also determine it. A third field in which attempts have been made to measure attention is the range or *span of attention.* To how many objects can a person attend at any one time? The question may be analysed into two parts : how many things can we perceive at a glance, and how many activities can one carry on at the same time. The answer to the firct question depends on what we mean by a thing. We may attend to a word of four or ten letters because they are organized into meaningful groups just as we may attend to shoes, socks, tin of boot polish and brush at one glance because they form one whole. But if things are not so organized we can attend to only five things at a time. This number, however, may vary according to the context.

Stories are often told about Napolean or Ceaser dictating two letters at the same time or writing letters with both hands, but these are only stories. We can attend to only one thing at a time, to more things if they are organized into one thing, unless we are engaged in an automatic activity like cycling, spinning or running when we can also talk or think besides. In these cases the automatic activity does not require any attention. Normally we attend to only one thing at a time.

**Nature of perception**

Perception is the true beginning of knowledge. Sensations provide the raw material which perception elaborates into a definite knowledge of the external world, of the attributes and relations of objects around us. We sense the physical world; we perceive what it means. Sensation tells us that we see a black spot but it is through perception that we identify the spot as crow, black rag or kite of black paper. Sensation is the core of perception and perception interprets it by integrating it with other experiences. The two processes can be easily distinguished in everyday experience. We hear a faint noise and do not know what it is, the sound of an aeroplane in the distance, of an automobile or of a buzzing fly. It is just a sensation and becomes a perception when we are able to identify it. The act of perception is completed when the sense quality given by the stimulation of a sense-organ is interpreted to mean a definite object. Thus a perception is sensation plus meaning; sensation means a quality and perception means an object suggested by that quality. Sensation can give us form, shape, colour, taste, smell or sound but perception tells us what they mean and what objects they stand for. An element of thought, memory, learning, past experience and motivation enters into perception. A sensation thus is simpler than a perception, but both give knowledge and information about the external world.

### Processes involved in perception

Perception involves the presence of an object in environment and its knowledge. Our receptors are aroused and impulses are conveyed to the brain through in-going nerves. In the brain through the excitation of association areas past images left by previous experiences are recalled. The pink colour arouses the recall of shape, smell, softness and the like and the symbol rose comes to mind. This is the *symbolic process*. They may also arouse our likes and dislikes. We may be pleased or displeased with the object perceived. This is the *affective process* involving feelings and emotions. It may also give us *aesthetic* experience and we may consider the object ugly or beautiful. Lastly we perceive the object as a whole and do not see only parts or aspects as is done in sensations. There is an element of *organization* or *re-organization* in all perception.

**The Role of past experience in perception**

Perceptions become fuller, more accurate and more serviceable as a result of our increasing experience. We learn to supply more detail and to distinguish the nature of objects when only a slight clue is given. For example we may perceive the rose by smell alone or recognize a friend by his gait or voice alone. In all such cases limited sensory data provide sufficient clues for us to understand the whole object. This is what happens when a person becomes a rapid reader; a letter gives clue to the word and a word to the sentence.

Objects also become more meaningful through experience. The picture of the college which a student takes back home after the first visit is much meagre and vague than the picture he forms after attending the college for several weeks. You cannot appreciate the sorrow of another till you have had experience of sorrow yourself. One who has never done a good charitable act cannot perceive goodness in others. Experience sets limits to what we can perceive and understand; as our experience widens, objects become more meaningful.

Long experience also deadens our appreciation of things around us through familiarity so that we have to go out far to enjoy the beauties of nature. The farmer is indifferent to fresh air and green pastures while people from towns do not tire of enjoying the rural scene.

**External factors in perception**

Objects which are arranged in an orderly manner or which fall into natural groups are more readily perceived than confused collections of things. Noise may force our attention but tunes and melodies are better perceived. Odd jumbles of letters are not so readily perceived as meaningful grouping of letters into words. A group of words making sense is called a sentence and is more readily perceived than collection of a words which do not make sense. *Arrangement* and ***organization*** of objects helps perception.

There is a lot of experimental data about perception of dots in groups. If these groups have a meaningful structure and make a regular pattern their perception is more satisfactory. But if they are scattered about haphazardly it is difficult to perceive them readily. Even if there are gaps in any meaningful arrangement the gaps are passed over and the whole is perceived. Bulbs arranged to form WELCOME are read as a whole inspite of gaps in between them. The tendency to perceive gaps as filled in is called *closure*.

**Inner factors influencing perception**

Perception is selective and we do not perceive all that is presented to us. Let us examine the various factors that influence perception.

*Attention.* At any one moment a large number of stimuli are pressing upon our sense-organs but we perceive only a few of them—those to which we attend. We have already dealt with external and internal determinants of attention. They also indirectly influence perception as attention is the heart of all processes by which we acquire knowledge.

*Set.* We perceive what we expect to perceive. In our experience with our environment we become familiar with the world and learn what to expect from it. If changes occur in our familiar surroundings we often miss them because we did not expect them. The proof readers often fail to detect misspelt words because they expected correct spelling and were set for it. We all have built up expectancies in life and our mind is set to receive certain stimuli. When we change our house, job or city our sets are upset and for some time we are not able to adjust.

*Type of surrounding.* Happy beautiful surroundings are considered desirable and ugly drab surroundings are deemed undesirable for work and a great deal of time and money is spent in decorating the home and place of work. The idea is that people feel and work better if the general perceptual background is attractive and pleasant.

*Interests and values.* When a specific stimulus is of special importance to the individual he perceives it more easily and readily. A teacher is always perceiving goodness or badness of pupils' behaviour, a barber sees their hair-cut and a doctor their health. Our interests and values make us perceive certain objects to the exclusion of others.

*Mood.* The mood of the moment determines the nature of perception. In a happy mood everything appears sunny and rosy, even enemies are looked upon favourably and in a mood of depression even friends appear to be selfish and hostile.

*Social norms.* Social and cultural factors influence perception. Hindus perceive the cow differently from a Muslim. A bare-headed person in a church goes unnoticed but in a Gurdwara he would be considered a sacrilege.

*Social perception.* Things, situations and people are perceived according to the interests, attitudes and values of the group to which we belong. Group prejudices are very strong and colour our perceptions. Our perception of Englishmen before Independence was different from our perception of them today. Women perceive a social gathering differently from men. This is due to social training. A naked sadhu is an object of worship for some and of disgust for others. Thus our perception of the physical environment is affected by social influences and training. The background of attitudes and beliefs prevailing in society influences the selective character of perception.

Many psychologists distinguish between *structural* and *functional* determinants of perception. The former include the nature of the physical stimuli and the neural effects they arouse in receptors and the nervous system, and the latter are derived from needs, interests, attitudes, past experience and social training of the individual.

A large amount of experimental data is available on the effect of such factors in the selective character of perception. In one study semi-starved young men perceived only food objects and perceived them bigger than they were. In another experiment it was found that children from poorer homes over-estimated the size of coins than children from wealthy homes. Such studies show that needs and values affect perception.

### Organizing factors in preception

In addition to factors mentioned above there are several others in the environment and the individual himself which give meaning and organization to perception. These organizing factors are very important for they determine the nature and character of the world in which we live.

*Figure and ground in perception.* Objects are perceived against a background—moon against the sky, pictures against a wall, mountains against clouds or words against a page. The moon, pictures, mountains and words are seen as *figures* and the sky, wall, clouds or page is seen as *ground*. The figure seems to have some sort of shape, form, object or quality but the background is formless and vague. The ground seems to extend continuously behind the figure, and the figure seems to be in front of the ground. It has a colour and this colour is seen as a surface; it is dense and opaque. In contrast the ground is less definite, neither clear surface nor bounding edges. In any war when tanks are camouflaged confusion between figure and ground is deliberately caused, and the coverage of leaves and bushes mixes readily with the jungle. Many animals like parrot or squirrel are often difficult to distinguish from their background and are thus given protection by nature.

*Constancy of form, shape and colour.* The most convenient thing for an individual would be that things he perceives remain constant and fixed in relation to us, but as things actually are objects are constantly changing. Colour is changing with changes in light, size is constantly changing with change in angle and distance of the observer, but although physical impressions change from time to time objects retain their shape, size and colour. Seen from a hill-top cars appear tiny toys, so do men and animals. But this does not deceive us. White shirts are perceived as white even though they look gray in twilight. A rectangular table remains rectangular even though seen from a particular angle its shape is badly distorted. Seen from various distances, and angles, and under varying degrees of illumination men, animals and objects retain their shape, size and colour, that is, they remain constant.

The idea of constancy was not stressed when people believed that the knowledge we get in perception is an exact copy of the outside world or is a mirror of the world around us. But now when we recognise the elements of learning and experience in perception the idea of constancy has been recognized. We interpret changes and differences as due to changes and differences in angle and distance.

*Context and experience.* In a running train electric poles seem to be running backward while distant villages seem to be running with the train. Whirling round for a few seconds the world around seems to be going topsy-turvy. But we are not fooled. We know that our own movement is being transferred to the objects around. In a film show still shots are moved in so quick a succession that they seem to be continuous. We estimate the distance from the small size of distant objects. Such perceptual experiences are interpreted in their context in the light of our past experience.

The Gestalt school of psychologists emphasize that perception is the result not of separate, distinct impressions but of wholes. In recognizing a friend's face we do not react to his eyes and eyebrows, his nose and the shape of his head, mouth or cheeks, but we perceive his face as a whole. If the parts are seen at all they are seen in relationship to the face as a whole. These psychologists point out that perception is based on figure and ground. When attention is focussed on any object, it is seen as the figure and the rest is seen as the background.

## Errors in perception

"Seeing is believing" does not seem to be convincing when we consider that not only our sensory organs are imperfect but also our feelings, emotions and bias influence the interpretation of what we see. Perceptions involve an important element of meaning or interpretation which may go wrong. Desires, wishes and prejudices have a strong influence on our perceptions. No lover can judge his beloved fairly and reliably, mothers always think highly of their children and no staunch party man sees anything wrong with his party.

One important cause of errors in perception is emotional excitement. A frenzied mob does not see things correctly, an angry person does not perceive the right thing. It is difficult to find out the truth in an outburst of emotional rioting because everybody is violently excited about the incident.

*Suggestion* is another source of error in perception. Numerous experiments have shown that people have testified to an electric shock when asked to handle a wire and the button is pressed even though the main switch was off. Jugglers and magicians are able to get along by suggesting to the audience to see what they wish them to see.

*Illusions* are perceptions in which objects are mis-interpreted, that is, which fail to give the true character of the object presented. They are false interpretations. They are quite normal in so far as they are experienced by everybody. Every one is inclined to see a vertical line as longer than a horizontal line of the same length. It is a general error that coming out of a cool room into the hot sun we over-estimate the temperature outside. It is normal to mistake a string for a snake in the dark. Let us study some of the causes of illusions.

**Kinds of illusions**

Illusions are classified into three groups according to the nature of their cause, that is, (1) those that are due to the nature of the stimulus, (2) those that are due to subjective conditions, and (3) those that are due to the nature of the sensory organs.

1. Illusions due to the nature of the stimulus. Vision furnishes the best examples of illusions of this type. Several normal visual illusions are shown in figures X and XI. A very common example of illusions due to the nature of the object may be found in

motion pictures. We speak of "moving" pictures, but actually the movement is in our perception, not on the screen. A series of stationary pictures each slightly different from the preceding one, is flashed on the screen at the rapid rate of twenty-four pictures per second. We see these still picutres as moving; that is, we supply the movement as an illusion.

Within limits if two equal sqaures, one black and one white, are placed side by side against a gray ground, the white will appear usually larger than the black. To most people a red object will appear slightly larger, and nearer, than an equally bright blue object.

More examples are given in figures

2. Illusions are also caused by subjective factors. At any time our mind is so full of the thoughts of a particular object that any object even slightly resembling that object is mistaken for it. In a big crowd we have lost a child, any child resembling our child in gait, dress or hair is mistaken for that child. How often we shout to a friend in a large gathering only to find that by mistake we have addressed somebody else who resembled our friend in one respect or the other. We are so used to associating certain impression with specific objects that we are easily fooled when some other object gives us the same impression.

One of the oldest examples of this type of illusion is Aristotle's illusion. Cross two fingers, the fore-finger and the middle-finger and touch a pencil with the crossed part of both fingers, it seems you are touching two pencils. The touched sides of two fingers are normally not together in space and habitually never touch a common thing; the one which now touches them, therefore, seems in two places, that is, seems two things.

A similar thing happens when sitting in a railway train at the station platform we look out and find our train moving while it is the next train which is doing so. It is because we found objects outside our window moving backward when our train was in motion. Now that we see the adjoining train moving in the opposite direction, being habituated to see things move opposite only when our own

Fig. 10. The two lines of the same length although the vertical appears to be much longer than the horizontal

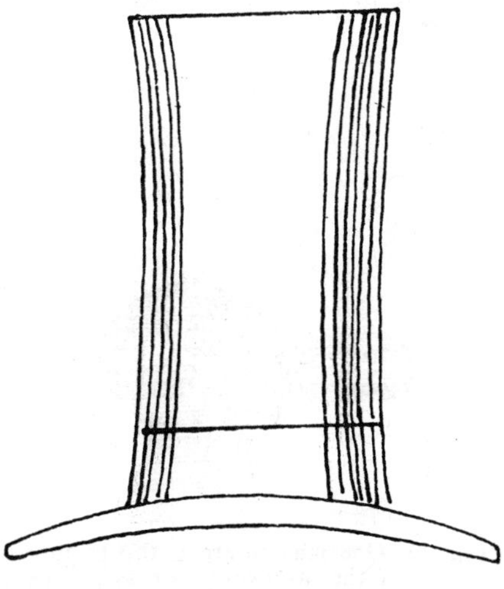

Fig. 11. The hat is just as high as the brim is wide It looks much higher

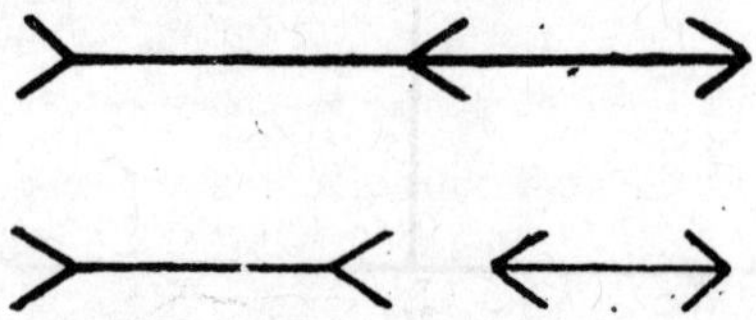

Fig. 12. The distance between the arrow points is the same in each case though it looks different

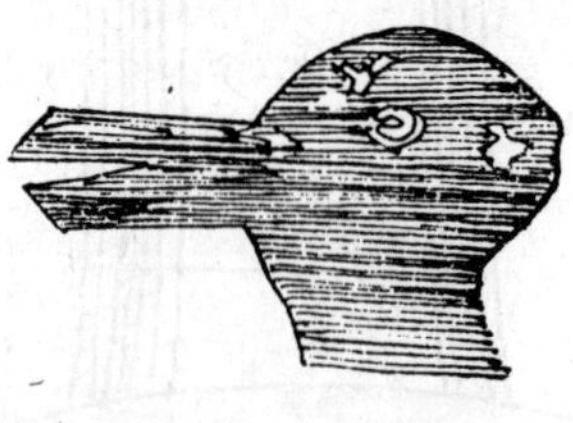

Fig. 13. One may interpret this picture either as a rabbit or as a duck

train was moving, we are led to perceive that this time also it is our train that is moving.

Again sometimes our mind is so full of certain thoughts and feelings, that is, we are so inclined to expect certain things to happen that any impression or suggestion may lead us to perceive that thing. In the dark the fearful mind perceives every bush to be a thief or a ghost. Mistaking the creaking of the house for the footsteps of a burglar shows the importance of anxiety and fear in causing illusions. Such illusions arise from mind-set and expectation.

3. Illusions may be due to sensory defects, or the nature of the sense-organ. A person suffering from jaundice sees everything yellow and a colour-blind person is unable to perceive objects of red and green colours, he sees them gray. When tongue is moved in the cavity of a tooth it looks disproportionately larger. It is another illusion due to the nature of the sense-organ.

## Questions

1. What is the value of attending to objects?
2. What are the determinants of attention? Why do we attend to some objects and not to others? Discuss in detail giving examples.
3. What do we mean by attending to an object? How does attention increase the efficiency of our activities?
4. Discuss the objective and subjective conditions of attention. Attention is described as selective, what determines its selective character?
5. Distinguish between voluntary and involuntary attention.
6. What are the possible methods of overcoming or reducing distraction? How many objects can we attend to any one time and for how long? Can we measure attention?

7. Discuss the nature of perception. How does sensation differ from perception?

8. What external and internal factors influence perception? Discuss social perception.

9. Discuss the organizing factors in perception by giving examples.

10. What is an illusion? How do illusions arise? Give examples and types of illusions.

## CHAPTER VIII

# LEARNING : LAWS AND METHODS

Learning is a universal experience, everybody learns at all stages of life and goes on learning from birth to death. Babies learn to feed themselves, to hold things, sit and stand; children learn to dress, button their coats and lace their shoes; boys learn arithmetic, hockey and manners; grown-ups learn their job, tact and adroit use of language. All that we do, think and feel from morning till night is the result of learning, and what makes a man, clerk, doctor, artist, engineer, salesman or hockey player is due to learning. It is learning which causes one man to be an honest citizen and another to be a burglar or pick-pocket. On Monday the child is told in the school that two and two make four and two and three make five. He is not sure, fumbles, hesitates, gets nervous and may or may not be able to repeat what the teacher has told him. But the next morning when the teacher asks him he answers with self-assurance readily and correctly. This is learning.

### The nature of learning

Learning is generally defined as more or less permanent changes in our behaviour as a result of experience. It is a process which, as a result of training and experience, leads to certain modifications in behaviour so that the individual makes new and changed responses to environment. When a person tries to learn riding a bicycle, his movements to begin with are awkward, he is not able to control the handle bar, he falls, if he attends to the road he cannot attend to his pedals or to his handle, all his attention and mind is concentrated on the cycle, and he totters from one side of the road to the other. But when he has learned cycling, he has perfect control over the cycle and his movements, he does not fall or attend to different parts of the cycle or his movements, his movements are correct and easy, there is no nervousness and strain, he rides smoothly on one side of the road, even takes one hand off, talks or sings while cycling. He has learned how to ride a cycle, and his performance is smooth and sure.

Now what changes occur when we learn? In the first place there is greater co-ordination and integration of movements. The beginner is not able to work his hands and legs together. If he tightens his grip on the handle his legs do not move or he is unable to keep balance on the seat. But on learning he is able to time and combine his movements carefully and accurately. Secondly he is able to organize his activity into wholes. In typing he is able to respond to words and even phrases and sentences into units and type them out. Thirdly he is able to eliminate unnecessary movements or activity. There is no fumbling and useless and unnecessary activity is avoided. This is *negative adaptation.* Many of the uncalled-for movements made by a novice are ignored by the expert. Fourthly the feeling of bewilderment and uncertainty gives place to one of confidence and assurance.

Learning may also be understood as a progressive adjustment to environment. The organism is placed in a new situation and in order to adjust himself to it he makes certain natural responses; some of these responses are based on past experience and some on reflex mechanism. He does not succeed and seeks new channels of behaviour to succeed. In doing so certain changes and modifications in his behaviour and experience take place. If these changes and modifications are effective they are repeated and become a part of his behaviour and experience. All this is learning, that is, acquiring changes and modifications in experience and behaviour to meet the demands of adjusting to new situations.

**Importance of learning**

Learning is the most important characteristic of man. Of all animals human beings have the longest period of immaturity, which means, that for a very long time they are helpless and dependent and are compelled to learn. A calf or a colt is able to look after itself at the age of a few months, but a human being may take twenty years to become independent of parental or adult help. There are many smaller animals whose young ones are able to perform adult functions within a few hours of birth. Their nervous systems are simple and their adjustment needs are few and simple. But man has a highly complicated nervous system which is capable of a very large variety of activities and movements and these are capable of manifold complicated differentiation, integration and development. Consider the very fine, complex and accurate movements we are able to perform in playing on a stringed instrument, in sketching a landscape, in writing or knitting. No other animal is able to do so. But it is also because man has to live in a very complex and complicated social environment and to meet the demands and challenges of that environment he must be equipped with a large variety of skills and insights, knowledge and understanding. No wonder then that nature has equipped him with a highly complicated nervous system and such a long period of immaturity during which to acquire the necessary learning. One can learn only from actual experience and one learns all sorts of facts and skills from his experience extended over a number of years. One learns as long as one lives, acquiring changes in behaviour and knowledge to meet the changing demands of this ever-changing universe and society.

**Learning and maturation.**

Our behaviour depends on both maturation and learning. Maturation is inner growth of the organism, organic processes increase the ability and efficiency of the individual, and this growth has a certain pattern. Parents say that a child should be able to walk or talk at a certain age or the baby should be able to hold its head, sit or stand after so many weeks or months. These changes are due to maturation and they are not influenced by outside conditions. Learning, on the other hand, is the result of environmental influences and experience as a result of which the individual is able to move and work more effectively. But learning depends on maturation. For every type of learning a certain stage of maturation is considered necessary. A six-month baby cannot walk nor a child of five learn writing free hand. They will learn when they grow mature enough to be capable of learning these activities. It is no use forcing children to learn things for which they are not sufficiently mature Thus learning and training depends on maturation but maturation does not depend on training. No amount of practice can teach a baby of six months to walk and run.

Modifications which come about in behaviour due to maturation are racial. They are inherent in a normal organism and will be found in every individual generally at a particular age. But learning is personal and each individual learns in his own way and manner. Again the individual does not have to make an effort to mature, maturation is inner growth. But to learn he may have to strive hard. Maturation is inborn and unlearned, learning is acquired. Lastly we mature upto a certain age but we go on learning all our lives. An old person has no more to mature but a lot to learn.

**Kinds of learning**

All learning involves activity but activity that leads to learning may be physical or mental. When we perceive, think, remember or solve a problem we are as active as when we learn riding a cycle or making high jump or planing a piece of wood. Learning that depends mostly on physical or motor activity and leads to acquisition of skill is called *motor learning*, and learning that depends almost wholly on sensations, perceptions, memory and thinking and leads to the acquisition of knowledge and understanding is called *ideational* or *verbal learning*. It is called verbal because ideas tend to be expressed in language and words. Learning to shave, skate, ride a cycle or climb a tree is motor learning; and learning to solve sums in arithmetic or that mangoes are sweet is ideational or verbal learning.

Some things we learn *deliberately* and *intentionally*. We discriminate and select what we want to learn and acquire and then make an effort to learn and acquire it. We select sensory stimuli and perceive them in the light of past experience. We assimilate new sensory experiences in the light of familiar experiences. Or in learning a new skill we combine already acquired movements into a new pattern, that is, organize them in a new way. In learning cycling no new movement is learned but a new organization of movements is acquired. Sometimes we learn although we did not make any clear-cut response to the situation or consciously attended to it. Such learning is *incidental.* School learning is intentional and deliberate but learning the names of shops on the way to school is incidental.

### Factors in effective learning

There are some important factors, conditions and influences, which make for effective learning and they are briefly described here.

The first important factor which even a layman will stress is *repetition* and *practice* of what we have to learn. We must repeat again and again the passage we have to remember, the movement we have to master or the skill we have to make perfect. Practice is the price we must pay for fuller and more effective and efficient learning. Many studies have shown that as practice increases errors are reduced till they disappear.

But mere repetition and drill is not enough. It must be strengthened by a *motive.* The learner must be deeply interested in what he is trying to learn otherwise practice becomes mechanical. Motives impart speed and efficiency to learning. Some of the important motives are hunger, thirst, sex, security, esteem and the like and if we appeal to them in learning, learning activity is more fruitful. In one study of maze-learning three groups of rats were used. One group of rats was hungry and was to obtain food at the end of the maze, the second group was also hungry but it was not to get any food after following the right path in the maze, and the third group was not hungry but even then on following the correct path in the maze it was to get food. Psychologists studied the effect of the motive of hunger on their learning the correct path in the maze. They found that the first group of rats which were hungry and got food on following the correct path in the maze learned to follow the correct path much more quickly and without making errors than the other two groups for whom the hunger motive did not exist. They thus concluded that motives, goals and purposes strengthen teaching and training and make learning more efficient and effective.

Psychologists have also studied the effect of prizes on learning. 16 children of the same age and intelligence were selected and were divided into three groups to learn to find out the correct path in a maze. The first group was not offered any reward at the end of the maze, the second group was offered reward in money and the third was offered only a psychological reward in praise and commendation. The group which was offered reward in money learned best, the group which was given only praise and compliments came next and the third group which was not rewarded at all was the slowest to learn thus showing that material rewards provide the strongest motive in learning activity. In another study it was shown that groups of children which are encouraged and stimulated by praise and words of cheer learn better than those who are rebuked and reprimanded.

Another factor in effective learning is *knowledge of results.* If in course of learning young people are told from time to time about the progress they are making and how satisfactory it is they do better. Knowledge of what they have achieved spurs them to strive harder.

*Intelligence* also affects learning, the more intelligent learn better and quicker. *Maturation* and *interest* are also important factors. An older, more mature person learns sooner and better and it is an obvious fact that those who want to learn and have a very strong interest do better.

*Methods of learning* also make a difference. For studying different subjects, for learning different types of skills or for assimilating different material of facts and thought we have to adopt different methods. Should we learn them at one sitting or space our learning? Should I commit the whole poem to memory all at once or should I do it in parts? Should there be periods of rest in between practice time? Psychologists say that effective learning requires that our methods should differ with differences in learning material.

## Laws of learning

From numerous studies and experiments on maze learning, on how children in a nursery school learn to lace their shoes or button their coat, on how young apprentices learn machine work or on how high school students learn a foreign language, there have emerged certain principles which govern all learning activity. Psychologists have formulated three laws : (1) *the law of exercise,* (2) *the law of effect,* and (3) *the law of readines* which we shall now discuss in detail.

*The law of exercise* is the law of use and disuse. In order to learn any activity it is usually best to repeat it again and again. We say "usually" and not "always" because sometimes a single strong emotional experience is enough to teach us, or one observation of activity performed by others makes us learn it. One instance of burning his finger is enough to teach the child to avoid fire and we learn to do simple skilful things by just looking at someone doing it, by imitation. But it is generally true that in learning any skill repetition and practice is necessary. The more frequently a performance is repeated the more prompt, easy and definite it becomes. The student re-reads a lesson a number of times to master it, he plays a musical tune a number of times before he is able to play it accurately and easily. Repetition and drill fix facts and activities to be learned. Skill in games, typing, craftwork and every human endeavour is acquired by constant exercise and frequent repetition. Practice is the price we must pay for being perfect. It is the most common law and is widely used in life and education.

It is also true that lack of practice weakens the quality of what we have learned. How often we apologize on the tennis court for our poor performance by saying that we are out of practice. An activity which is not used, exercised or repeated for a long time tends to be forgotten. We learn and retain by use and lose and forget by disuse. This is the *law of disuse.*

Thorndike arrived at this law through a number of experiments with animals on maze learning and puzzle-box. The puzzle-box was made of wires and its door could be opened by a button inside it. A hungry cat was placed inside with fried fish placed outside this box. The problem for the cat was to get out and eat fish. For a long time the cat jumped about inside, tried to cut wires with its teeth and made all sorts of movements to get out till it accidentally pressed the button, got out and ate the fish. Exercising and practising in this way a number of times the cat learned to open the door by pressing the button. The law of exercise is useful in acquiring habits. Repeating certain responses a more or less permanent connection is formed between the stimulus and the response so that the response follows whenever the sitmulus is presented. The connection has become habitual or the individual has formed a habit of responding in a definite way in a particular situation.

It has already been pointed out that sometimes we learn without drill practice or exercise as the child learns to dread fire by a single experience or we learn to work a radio by merely looking on once. But sometimes we do not learn even by exercise or practice. A student may go on repeating the multiplication table or geographical names without acquiring them mostly because he repeats them mechanically without interest. Too many students in schools are asked to write corrections in grammar and spelling 20 or 50 times, they do it and yet do not learn them at all. Teachers are justified in concluding that they did not put their heart in the task. Without interest and motive repetition and exercise does not lead us far. It is only when it is accompanied by interest, motivation, intelligence and understanding that practice becomes meaningful and effective.

*The law of effect* is the law of rewards and results, of satisfying experiences. Activities which are accompanied by a feeling of pleasure, which meet our needs, satisfy our motives, goals and purposes or in which we are interested are more readily and effectively learned than those which are unpleasant and annoying, whose meaning or purpose we do not understand or share, and whose value we do not recognize. This law stresses the role of feeling and motivation in effective learning and we have already discussed it in detail in the previous section. In all experiments of learning which have been described here the importance of rewards to which the activity leads has been indicated, motives, the prospect of reward and results and the desire to achieve certain goals help to keep the activity going and maintain the organism's effort. One set of activities contributes to the satisfaction of a need and another does not, and the former tends to be repeated and learned to the exclusion of the latter. When children succeed in solving a problem, performing a task or meeting a situation they are pleased about their achievement and this feeling of satisfaction spurs them on. Success leads to further success and failure is the fore-runner of further failure. The system of rewards and punishments in schools and colleges is based on this law. Patterns of behaviour which are rewarded are fixed and those which are punished or lead to unpleasant effects are discarded. The cat learned to press the button because it was adequately rewarded with fish, the activity had satisfying effects.

The law of effect is not able to account for incidental learning in which many useless and unnecessary things are acquired. Not all our learning is satisfying, useful or meaningful. Nor is it desirable that we should look for rewards and praise in everything that we do or learn. A number of things are learned because they are satisfying in themselves.

*The law of readiness* points out that we cannot learn anything unless we are prepared for it. Readiness or preparedness for a task is half the battle; if the pupil's mind is set on a task he will be inclined to work hard and learn it most quickly and effectively. Woodworth uses the word *mind-set* for this readiness. Much of the effort in teaching and learning is wasted because pupils' readiness is not taken into account. They go through their tasks indifferently and mechanically because they are being forced to. When students' mind is aroused, they are curious to know and learn, that is the best time to make them learn. Mental alertness is necessary for learning. Similarly when young people are taught skills before they are mature enough to acquire them they do not learn. In manual skills as in academic studies learning should be graded so that one thing leads to another and the learner is prepared for it.

**Methods of learning**

It has already been pointed out that for effective learning suitable method is no less important. Assuming that the individual has strong motives to learn and that other conditions are favourable the question is what is the best procedure for attaining proficiency. Two questions are raised : (1) should the learner go on repeating and practising without break till he has mastered the skill or information or should there be intervals of rest; (2) should the individual in order to commit a reading material to memory memorize the whole of it by repeating it over and over again or should he learn it by parts? The former is the problem of *massed* or *spaced method of learning*, and the latter is the problem of *whole* or *part method of learning*. These we now examine in detail.

*Massed or spaced learning*. Suppose you have to learn swimming, cycling, skating or typing, should you go on practising till you have learned the skill? Or should you take rest in between and practise for short periods? Continuous learning is called *massed learning* and learning with breaks or rest periods is called *spaced learning*. Several studies made with groups of children of the same age and intelligence show that those who distributed their learning surpassed in achievement those whose learning was more concentrated. Spaced periods of practice are more economical than unspaced periods. This means that if you have to learn an assignment it will be better to study it a short time on several days than to attempt to learn it at one sitting.

The reasons for this are not far to seek. In the first place the spaced learning is more advantageous because it rules out fatigue and interest is maintained. In massed learning continuous effort tires the individual, lowers his efficiency and reduces his interest. Therefore the individual has to make greater effort to learn and put in more practice. Secondly spaced learning helps to drop wrong associations and strengthen correct associations. The rest periods give time and opportunity to make such corrections as well as to strengthen correct associations. In continuous massed practice there is no such opportunity. Thirdly in spaced learning memory traces get opportunity to firm up during the rest periods. In continued massed practice there is no time and opportunity for consolidation, for allowing memory traces to settle down. Rest periods help such consolidation. Fourthly a mental process, once started, continues even though our attention is directed to other things. This is especially true if the final goal has not been attained. Once we accept a task, a state of mental tension persists until it is finished, whereas when a task is finished we tend to forget it. When periods of study are distributed mental tension persists between them; we learn not only during periods of study but also during the intervals. Moreover, the interval between study periods gives an opportunity for growth.

But we should note that such studies and experiments show that we should distribute and space our study and learning but they do not show that we should give up study or learning on the first sign of fatigue or we should never work when we are tired. In all learning there is a period for optimum efficiency, and there is as much danger in making learning periods too short as in making them too long. A person who gives up as soon as he feels tired does little to develop his stamina.

*Whole or part method.* Should a student read his lesson from beginning to end again and again till he has mastered it or should he break it into parts and learn the parts one by one thus learning the whole? The former is the whole method and the latter is the part method. In committing to memory a poem of 300 lines one may go on repeating the whole of it or spend some time on memorizing its several parts and then reciting the whole of it. Some people advocate the whole method others consider the part method more economical. A number of experimental studies have shown that when one has to memorize a long list of meaningless words the part method is more effective, when a short poem is to be memorized the whole method is more useful, and when a long poem like the Ramayana is to be learnt only part method is practicable. But one must organize the material to be learned into large units and study it as a whole. In this way one can reduce the material to a few meaningful units, each one of which is easily learned as its component parts would be if taken separately.

By learning things as wholes we understand the material better and see how the different parts stand together in a general pattern. But there is a disturbing factor that the learner may lose confidence in the face of a long assignment. However much depends on such factors as intelligence and experience, and individual differences are large.

## Plateaus

A common experience in learning is that after a period of satisfactory progress there comes an interval of little apparent improvement. Such periods when there is no progress or progress in learning is retarded are called *plateaus*. If we make a graph of the progress of learning such periods will have to be shown as level. Psychologists have tried to explain plateaus in many ways and suggest ways to get rid of them. When the plateau appears it causes further retardation because it tends to discourage the learner and he makes mechanical repetitions without making progress. Such plateaus are found much more in complex than in simple skills. In complex skills many minor skills have to be learned and while they are being learned the individual marks time and there is no progress. Experimental studies have shown that plateaus can be greatly reduced by a proper distribution of work and rest periods. Rest periods are useful in so far as they give time for assimilation of what has been learned, prevent fatigue and maintain interest.

## Theories of learning.

Psychologists have tried to explain how people learn and why they learn. They have carried on numerous experiments and studies on animals and children and come to certain definite conclusions with regard to different aspects of the learning process. They are not agreed about such explanations but such disagreement is natural in a developing science like psychology. To many it seems that they are dealing with different kinds of learning and in many books on psychology these explanations are treated as dealing with different kinds of learning. In a sense they are. But the term learning is so comprehensive and includes such a large variety of activities that such an approach is quite natural. We shall discuss them in some detail here as they are basic to our understanding of behaviour, both human and animal.

## Learning by conditioning or conditioned response

About 1904, a Russian physiologist named Ivan Pavlov began a series of conditioning experiments that were to have a tremendous influence on the psychology of learning. Although only a few psychologists have taken the extreme position that all learning is based on conditioning most agree that a great many of our responses are conditioned.

Learning by conditioning is learning to respond to a substitute stimulus, to a stimulus other than the original stimulus. A typical experiment of conditioning might be set up in this manner. We are familiar with the fact that when a dog is given a bit of food, saliva begins to flow freely. The flow of saliva is a reflex response, that is, it is a native, unlearned response of the salivary glands to a sensory stimulus. Now in the experiment a dog is tied to an apparatus that measures the amount of fluid his salivary glands produce and food is presented and saliva flows into a pot below dog's mouth. Now Pavlov presented a sound, say of a bell for example, at the same time food was presented to the dog. After twenty to forty simultaneous presentations of food and sound, it was found that saliva would flow at the sound alone. It means that the new stimulus sound has taken the place of the original stimulus food in producing the saliva. The response is now made to the substitute stimulus which is as effective as the original stimulus. The dog has learned a new response or has learned to respond to a new stimulus. This modification or re-organization of behaviour is learning by conditioning responses to a new stimulus.

A new terminology grew with the experiment. Food the original stimulus is called the *unconditioned* stimulus; the second substitute stimulus is called the *conditioned* stimulus, and the reflex is said to be *conditioned* to the new stimulus.

Conditioning is by no means confined to the laboratory. A small child reaches out to a table lamp and touches the hot bulb. It gives him violent burning pain and he withdraws his hand. Often one experience is enough to produce conditioning and later the mere sight of the lamp makes him withdraw his hand or avoid it altogether. Often one conditioning leads to another. If strong light is shown along with the sounding of the bell the dog may salivate when strong light is switched on. If people around shout when the child touches a burning object he will fear shouting too.

Many parents shout when a child approaches a dog, the child is frightened by the noise but the fear is conditioned to the dog. Later the mere barking sound may frighten the child even if no dog is to be seen.

All the laws of learning apply to conditioning. The connection between the substitute stimulus and the responses becomes firmer if the experience is repeated. Repetition is necessary to establish the conditioned reflex, the sound of the bell and the food should be more closely associated in experience. But as has been pointed out often just one very strong emotional experience is enough to fix the conditioning. The stimulus-response bond needs frequent *reinforcement*, that is, the bond will continue if the conditioned stimulus (bell) continues to be associated with food. But if the bond is not re-inforced it tends to weaken and may ultimately disappear. This is called *extinction*. Thus reinforcement is presenting the unconditioned stimulus (in this case food) which rouses the unconditioned response (in this case salivation) immediately following the conditioning stimulus (bell). When there is no re-inforcement, with repetition the stimulus-response connection will grow weaker and eventually disappear; this process is known as extinction. Extinction can be prevented by occasionally bringing back the original stimulus (food) when the conditioned stimulus (bell) is presented. It so happens that after extinction has taken place the extinguished response will sometimes return spontaneously after a rest period.

When we learn to respond to a new stimulus we also learn to respond to all stimuli resembling it. The dog learns to salivate in response to a bell but it will respond similarly even if the bell is slightly changed. or to a similar sound from some other source. The more similar a new stimulus is to the conditioned stimulus, the more likely it is to evoke the conditioned response. This is *stimulus generalization.* The child who has learned to be afraid of a dog also fears a cat, a rabbit or any fluffy toy. He has generalized the stimulus of his conditioned response. But he may also learn to discriminate between similar stimuli. When he discovers that a cat or a fluffy toy is not so aggressive as a dog, he may refuse to be afraid of them. This means that his response to these has weakened or become extinct. This is *discrimination.* Dying out of an un-reinforced response helps him to discriminate between similar but not identical stimuli.

A great deal of animal, and much human, learning is of the simple conditioned-reflex type. The burnt child dreads the fire; red chillies give him a burning sensation and he avoids even other red foods. Reflex behaviour is usually considered inflexible but these experiments show that even such behaviour can be modified through training. The stimulus-response connections, once formed, are direct and immediate. No amount of thinking or reasoning will have any effect on them. You cannot remove a child's fear of darkness or dogs by reasoning with him.

But the conditioned response is more flexible than the conditioned reflex. It is the method employed by those who train animals. Monkey trainers put the fore-foot of a monkey on a hot plate and raise a stick at the same time. The monkey learns to raise its fore-foot when the stick is raised in the air, after twenty to forty occasions of hot plate experience. Thus the trainer has taught the monkey to salute. In human beings the acquisition of fears, likes and dislikes, and many irrational attitudes are due to conditioning. In most cases such responses are forced upon the learner and he learns them involuntarily. A child who has been given a bitter medicine from a bottle may learn to dislike everything from a bottle; a nauseating experience from any food once makes people avoid it in future also; travelling in a bus the smell of petrol upsets many people, later even the sight of a bus or petrol pump does it. A child who had to be taken to a hospital for an injury and dressed by a white-coat doctor will shudder at every person with a white coat. Much of our knowledge is acquired through stimulus generalization as much of our irrational behaviour is due to it.

Much of what we have learned is due to what is called *secondary conditioning*, which occurs when a second stimulus is associated with the now effective stimulus and is able to substitute for it. A nod to a friend serves for the hand salute, even a smile may do, they all stand for the cordial greeting and serve as an effective substitute for response behaviour. The working of such signals or cues which have practically nothing in common with reaction-behaviour are examples of *secondary* or *higher order conditioning*.

Factors which influence conditioning learning are the strength or urgency of the need, expectation, repetition or exercise and proximity of time. The longest interval between the presentation of the natural and the conditioned stimulus should not exceed ten seconds.

The theory of conditioning does not explain all the facts of learning. It can deal only with simple responses. In learning cycling, for example, what responses are unconditioned and what are conditioned it may not be easy to say. This approach cannot explain complex types of learning. Secondly it takes a very mechanical view of learning, the two stimuli are associated by sheer repetition. It leaves out of account the mind-set of the learner, his interest and ability. But this theory is very helpful in analysing irrational fears and phobias and curing them. Its explanation of the process of habit-formation is also very satisfactory.

### Learning by trial and error

Alexander Bain, Lloyd Morgan and Thorndike argue that learning takes place through trial and error. We seem to learn by random and blind efforts; we try one solution, we try another till by sheer accident or by exhausting possibilities we hit upon the correct solution. When faced with a problem situation the individual however strongly motivated, is often compelled to resort to tentative and experimental attempts to find an adequate answer. All are agreed that this is the most primitive and least efficient technique of learning to respond to a difficult situation. When a rat is placed in a maze with correct pathways arbitrarily chosen, the animal has little choice but to engage in a trial-and-error behaviour until it reaches the goal. Even a grown-up person when trying to tackle a mechanism which he does not understand such as the radio, a typewriter or a sewing machine starts fumbling with it till he accidentally hits upon the right solution or does not hit upon it. Trial-and-error behaviour is most often aroused when a logical solution is not to be had. Parents do not understand why the baby is crying, they hug, pat, laugh, give milk or pay attention to him till they find out what it is that the baby wants.

When any attempt succeeds the individual is likely to repeat it, it is re-inforced and gradually errors are reduced and eliminated. Trial-and-error involves much waste of effort and time, but gradually both time and effort are reduced and the number of errors is diminished. Thorndike conducted numerous experiments with maze and puzzle-box learning in which rats and cats were used to find out the correct way of reaching the solution, and these experiments enabled him to lay down the following steps in any process of trial-and-error learning:

1. Presentation of a new situation which is seen as a problem.
3. Natural responses to seek adjustment to the new situation.
3. Hitting upon success by chance after trying a number of unsuccessful ways.
4. Gradual reduction in time and errors in reaching the correct pathway, and their ultimate elimination.
5. Repetition of successful attempts.
6. Fixation of the correct attempt or solution.

Thorndike thinks that all the laws of learning are used in this method or type of learning, and there is no doubt that through numerous trials the animal learns much and gradually improves his effort. We all learn a new skill like cycling, swimming or riding through this method but it involves considerable waste of time and effort. Again learning is often based on single strong emotional experience. We like and dislike at first sight, our loves and hates are often based on single experience, and these cannot be explained on the basis of trial and error. Another drawback of this method or type of learning is that it gives no place to the role of intelligence and understanding in learning. Stressing blind, if not bewildered effort, it does not recognize the role of perception and insight in learning. Lastly in this theory the entire learning is sought to be explained by practice and exercise in utter disregard to the individual's interest, attitude or purposes. Such learning is to be found more among animals and children.

**Learning by insight**

But man also learns by understanding, by perception of the situation. Learning proceeds by the more efficient process of trying those methods which are seen to have a relation to the solution. Such learning, we say, proceeds by insight. Insight may be defined as the awareness of the consequences of performing an act. Wertheimer, Kohler, Koffka and several other psychologists carried out a number of studies to show that even higher animals learn by insight. Kohler's experiment during the first World War when he was interned by the Spanish government in one of the Canary Islands are now a commonplace. He spent his time there in conducting learning experiments with chimpanzees. The animal found bananas near him but beyond his reach. It wanted to reach the fruit, grasped a stick lying near by and tried to reach the fruit. It found that the stick was too small to reach it. Outside its cage a longer stick was lying but this too was beyond his grasp. It looked at it for a while, then pulled the longer stick with the help of the shorter stick he had in his hand. Having grasped the longer stick it reached the fruit. The final attainment of the goal must therefore be attributed to his understanding and perception that there was a longer stick which could do what the shorter stick failed to achieve.

Insight occurs when the individual sees in a flash the solution to his problem or difficulty. It is not blind and stupid learning by trial-and-error, it is intelligent learning by insight and perception. People try to size up the situation, reason things out and arrive at a conclusion. It is learning by thinking. Linfley and Dunker carried out studies with human beings and found that learning by insight may be gradual based on the analysis of the problem and exploring the possible solutions one by one in the light of goals and purposes. Many psychologists hold that this learning by insight is just trial-and-error behaviour through the use of the thought process, the person turns over in his mind and thought the several alternative solutions instead of going through the actual physical motions of solving a problem. To find out the shortest route to the college you do not have to try all the possible routes physically but you go over them without being aware of the act and hit upon the correct solution. Because the success is sudden many call insight learning an "Aha" experience. However it seems reasonable to suppose that man's most novel solutions, most creative ideas, and most new inventions owe their origin and development to insight. Perhaps trial-and-error could lead to the same results but would have been less efficient costing more time and effort.

With experience man is able to solve problems better and sooner. His knowledge and information serve as a strong base for this process. We may say he has learned to learn as a result of his knowledge and past experience. He now exercises discrimination in solving problems and learning becomes a matter of insight rather than of trial-and-error.

**Learning by imitation**

In acquiring complex skills of everyday life like typing, cycling, playing on the violin one may learn by observing and watching others doing it, by following demonstrations given by the expert, by imitating his movements. By copying the behaviour of others he avoids the waste of time and effort of the trial-and-error method and the strain of thinking in insight learning. In imitating the presented sample through demonstration or moving picture the individual saves a great deal of time which otherwise would be spent in blind fumbling involved in trial-and-error and acquires a number of insights at the very beginning of his performance. He thus benefits by the experience of others. A boy sees how a skilled player of tennis holds the racket and moves about the court, a girl sees how her mother spins, sews and goes about the household chores, a student attacks problems as his teacher does, children learn to speak as their parents do, and scores of other things we are learning by and through imitation.

Psychologists like Millar and Dollard have tried to show that the tendency to imitate is itself a learned response and if re-inforced, the individual will be more likely to continue to imitate.

Too many people believe that imitation is a lower type of learning, something slavish and unworthy, and is characteristic of the raw and immature. Still others hold that imitation can never lead to novel responses and is fatal to creativity, originality and initiative. But many educationists believe that only the imitative individual is capable of learning and the more imitative he is the more educable he is. And no imitation is an exact reproduction. It does include some variations which indicate individuality and may lead to novel responses.

**Animal and human learning**

Man is more intelligent than animals, his nervous system is more complex and complicated than that of animals and he is called upon to meet more difficult challenges and to solve more complicated problems as he has to live in a more complex social environment. Therefore there are bound to be differences in the learning of man and animal. Animals cannot and do not learn complex types of behaviour.

Animal learning is largely confined to learning of movements and physical adjustments, but human learning is marked by mental activities, by processes of perception, imagination, memory, thinking and reasoning. An animal only runs, jumps and bites or indulges in other bodily acts.

Human learning also makes use of signs and language. Man counts and gives names to objects, movements and situations which an animal is unable to do. With the help of language man is able to conserve his past experience and present thinking, and is able to bear his past learning on present and future problems. He can anticipate events and difficulties in a way which is beyond the mental reach of animals.

Thus man learns sooner and better. Animal learning is mostly by trial-and-error or by conditioning, but human learning is mostly by insight, understanding, imitation and observation. By virtue of the wide range of his mental powers man is able to foresee his needs, problems and difficulties, he is able to imagine future situations, to formulate future goals and purposes. And then he strives to work for them, getting training, observing what others do, studying and obtaining understanding of his environment. His learning therefore is multiple, wide, deep and comprehensive. He is more sensitive to his environment and seeing finer shades of differences makes equally finer adjustments to them. He deduces general principles from his past experience and to turn over several alternative solutions in thought before taking physical action.

**The nature of habits**

One immediate result of the process of learning is the ease and promptness with which learned actions are performed. Actions which at first appearance require effortful attention come to be performed without that effort and attention if they are repeatedly performed under similar circumstances. Such habitual actions become automatic and mechanical. They have a quickness and accuracy which the first performance of an action lacks. Thus habitual actions are the final stage of the learning process. It is that mode of behaviour which through repetition has become so perfected that it neither requires nor undergoes any further adaptation. Thus habits may be said to have three characteristics : (1) they are acquired through repetition, (2) they are semi-mechanical and automatic, that is, they do not require any effort and attention once they are acquired, and (3) they can be performed only under similar circumstances. An Indian, in the habit of eating with his hand, on going to England starts learning to eat with fork and knife. At first he blunders and often pokes the fork into his nose, but gradually he begins to eat with the ease and grace of an Englishman. It is because the use of knife and fork has become habitual. Previously he could not talk while eating because he could not attend to two things at a time but now eating having become habitual, it is done automatically in a stereotyped way, and he can talk or think while eating.

Habits are not confined to bodily actions alone. We may have habits of thought also. The suspicious person is one who is in the habit of suspecting everybody. Some people have a habit of replying to letters the day they are receivedor of making puns.They are all habits of thought.

One practical result of forming habits is that the performance of habitual actions costs no effort. One who is in the habit of studying regularly at a fixed hour does so without having to make up his mind about it but another who has formed no such habit finds it extremely difficult when near the examination he has no choice. Another advantage is that more than one thing can be done at a time. When spinning becomes habitual women can talk, sing or think while they spin. But habits have drawbacks too. They do not permit adjustments to novel situations and keep a man in the rut. They are a conservative factor in human behaviour and retard the quick flow of energy into new channels, to seek new means for our goals. They are a good servant but a bad master.

### How habits are formed

It would be useful to inquire what principles should be followed in the cultivation of desirable habits. Habits have an expulsive force, good habits kill bad habits and to get rid of the latter we must form counter good habits. The principles are the same.

1. The cultivation of good habits should begin early in childhood when the child has not yet formed any habits and is receptive to all influences. Childhood is the formative period of life and the advice to begin early is the advice to begin on a clean slate.

2. Habits are formed by frequent repetition and it takes time. We cannot form habits in a day or even in a week. It is an uninterrupted continuation of performance under similar circumstances which tends to strengthen particular modes of behaviour.

3. The new habit should be launched with a strong emotional stimulus. A dramatic public announcement, a public vow that we will not smoke or drink provides a strong motive force to shed the old habit and form a new one. Hindus make a ceremony of everything that a child is called upon to do and a good reason is that such ceremonies provide an emotional stimulus to new habits.

4. Once the habit has started there should be no exception or break, no return to the unwanted habit, and the action should be performed persistently. Never say "I will let you off this time but you should never do it again." By letting him off this time you are making him do it again. You are not merely neglecting a particular habit that you wished to encourage but actually encouraging a counter habit you wanted to discourage or suppress.

5. Good habits should be strengthened by voluntary practice. One makes up his mind to salute people first, to call on his neighbours frequently without caring whether his neighbours return the call, to avoid speaking ill of others and the like is on the road to gain not only good will of others but also valuable social habits.

6. Good habits should always be rewarded. Children should be praised for good habits and punished with disapproval for their bad habits. Adults should have some satisfaction in building good habits. Such rewards re-inforce the performance of the habitual action.

As has already been stressed in breaking bad habits the best plan is to cultivate the opposite good habit. These very principles will operate in the breaking of bad habits.

**Transfer of training**

Do abilities acquired in one situation help in another? Does training in one kind of performance lead to improvement in some other kind of performance? Many controverseys have been waged over the influence of learning one thing upon the learning of another. It was held for a long time that the study of classical languages like Latin and Sanskrit, of mathematics and science trains intellect and memory so that we are able to memorize words, dates and names in history and geography better. Others believe that the study of science trains the powers of observation so that one can be an accurate observer in social and personal relations as well. Training is transferred from one skill or mental power to another. This is known as the doctrine of *Formal Discipline* or *Transfer of Training*. Older psychology analysed mind into separate faculties and each faculty had its own peculiar sphere. Memory, imagination, reasoning or observation are strengthened through prolonged exercise and can subsequently be used with equal advantage in any situation. Certain subjects like classical language, mathematics and logic were considered to have higher training value and students doing well in these subjects were supposed to do well in other spheres of life also.

Obviously this problem is of great importance to education. Only such subjects should be included in the curriculum which have disciplinary value and they should be taught in such a way that this value is secured in the maximum. Fifty years back young men were given intensive training in classical languages and mathematics in public schools of England so that they do well in public life as administrators, doctors and educationists. Their success was attributed to such training. But the critics argued that it was not due to the training they received but due to the careful selection made for admission to public schools. Such students were usually bright and came from better homes.

Faculty psychology on which this doctrine of formal discipline is based is entirely rejected these days. If thinking, judging, remembering, reasoning, observing and other mental activities are due to independent faculties of mind, how can there be any transfer? And yet many philosophers and educationists believe that some kinds of training help to build up such general power.

Fifty years ago William James made an experiment with learning. He committed some lines of Hugo's *Satyr* to memory and then portions of Milton's *Paradise Lost*. Later he went back to Hugo's *Satyr* to see if he could memorize more rapidly than the first time because of his practice on *Paradise Lost*. He found he could not and concluded that there is no such transfer of training.

But all learning involves transfer. Our present learning is largely influenced by our past learning. One who has repaired watches can repair fountain pens and clocks more easily. Learning at home transfers to the school setting. What we learn in the school transfers to the college and it is hoped that learning in the college transfers to later life. It is stumulus generalization that makes such transfer possible. We have a vast netweork of educational institutions and huge sums of money are being spent on them. It would be all wasted if there was no transfer of learning. Common sense rightly assumes that what young people learn in schools and colleges will be applied in later life to some advantage. Engineering colleges admit students who have studied mathematics and physics in school, medical colleges want them to have completed a course in biology and chemistry; business and industrial concerns employ those who studied book-keeping and commercial subjects in the college. They all assume that such studies and learning will be transferred to new learning and profession in life. When previous learning is favourable to present learning the transfer is said to be *positive*, and when it is unfavourable, thwarts, interferes and obstructs present learning it is said to be *negative*. *Negative transfer of training* is also called *habit interference*. Transfer of learning takes place in all types of learning, motor, ideational and verbal. Many skills learned with the right hand can also be learned with the left hand and with greater ease and speed, and it is a common experience that after passing M.A. in one subject it is easier to pass the examination in another subject of similar nature.

The factors which facilitate transfer of training are *similarity of content, similarity of method or technique, similarity of principle* or a combination of all three. Psychologically speaking we may say that transfer from training takes place when there is similarity of stimuli and similarity of response. One who is proficient in one language is generally proficient in another. One who can drive a truck may not fiind it difficult to drive a bus even though of a different make or model. Mechanical engineers are able to handle machines which they see for the first time because of their rich background. When components in the two situations are identical or similar transfer is easy for stimulus is generalized, and when material is organized in a meaningful manner transfer is possible through understanding of the general principles. There it is not power, ability or talent that is transferred from one area or situation to another area or situation but specific knowledge or skill that is used in the new situation or area. We expect a knowledge of history and political science will make for better administration as a study of civics will make for a better civic sense.

Recently a large number of experimental studies have been made of the phenomenon of transfer of training in several subjects of study and in several areas of learning skills. It has been found that such transfer is more likely to be specific than general, that subjects taught in school differ in their transfer value—mathematics has more transfer value than history or literature and no subject is specifically a mind trainer, that transfer depends very largely on intelligence and educational attainments of a student, and that varied and numerous practical applications of what is learned to daily needs and realities of life make for greater transfer. It is possible to teach school subjects in such a manner that their transfer value is enhanced. A comparative study of the methods of teaching languages has revealed that some methods are more suitable for transfer. This means that students can be taught for transfer. Besides certain attitudes of mind like neatness, openmindedness, good work habits, desire to relate and apply knowledge to life, and the like are helpful to ready and close transfer of all that is learned.

## QUESTIONS

1. What is the nature of learning. Explain and illustrate the several laws of learning.

2. Describe the different types of learning. What factors are effective in learning?

3. Distinguish between maturation and learning. Does learning depend on maturation? What is the law of readiness?

4. Discuss the value of massed and spaced learning, and learning by part and whole method.

5. Write short notes on (1) plateau, (2) negative adaptation, (3) motivation in learning (4) Formal discipline.

6. What do you understand by learning by conditioning? Explain the phenomena of re-inforcement and extinction by giving examples.

7. Explain learning by trial-and-error and learning by insight. Give examples from actual life.

8. Explain briefly different kinds of learning, and bring out the importance of learning by imitation.

9. What is the nature of habits? How are habits formed? How would you proceed to break a bad habit?

10. Define learning, and distinguish between animal and human learning. Is it correct to say that animals learn by trial and-error and men learn by insight?

11. What do you understand by transfer of training? What factors determine it and to what extent transfer does take place?

CHAPTER IX

# REMEMBERING AND FORGETTING

In everyday speech we speak of having a good memory, of having a poor memory, of having a better memory for faces than names, of having memory that is failing, and so on. Such usage suggests that memory is an object or power which we may possess or lose. Yet it is true that there is no such thing as memory, and the word is used to denote a large variety of activities which may be distinguished from each other. It is better to confine our study to activities which are denoted by remembering.

The word "to remember" is used in two broad senses. We speak of, on the one hand, of remembering names, dates or events, and on the other, of remembering how to ride a cycle, play tennis or drive a car after several years. Obviously these two usages are quite different, the first refers to revival or reinstatement of words and ideas and the second to certain responses or behaviour of muscular type. Both refer to what took place in the past and which may be revived or made active again in the present.

Stout confines remembering to ideal revival, so far as ideal revival is merely reproductive, in which the objects of past experiences are re-instated as far as possible in the order and manner of their original occurrence. Some writers like Beatric Edgell use the word memory as equivalent to retentiveness, such retentiveness being subservient to reproduction or recall. To many people memory means memorizing or learning by rote. This activity depends entirely on repetition and is very mechanical leaving little room for choice of responses. But though it is rigid and mechanical, it is a type of learning all the same.

For convenience modern psychology analyses memory or remembering into four aspects or processes *fixation, retention, reproduction* and *recognition*. Fixation is just having impressions and fixing them in mind through effortful attention. Retention is conserving or maintaining that experience for future use. Reproduction or recall is the re-instatement of that experience, it is the ideal revival of what happened in the past. Recognition is identifying the recalled ideas as known before in previous experience. Every one of these aspects or factors is equally necessary and important. Remembering does not merely consist in reproducing or recalling past facts, ideas or words as most students think. It involves all the above four processes. We shall now discuss them in detail.

## Fixation

Fixation means that impressions must be registered so to say before they can be remembered. It is just the existence of experience, we must have experience before we can try to reproduce or recall it. To register it properly we must pay attention to it. Students may fail to fixate or register because they are not sufficiently attentive to what they listen or read. Active interest and attention are essential, and when students just hold the book without earnestly grasping what they are merely scanning or listen to the radio while they supposedly read, they cannot retain or recall much. Obviously factors which detract or interfere with attention interfere with our remembering. People involved in riots are not able to recall much and their testimony may not be reliable because in the throes of emotional excitement they failed to attend to essentials or they were so overwhelmed with a large variety of experiences that they could not fixate them, so many stimuli all struggling to gain attention and jostling each other out. When stimuli fail to register, attention is poor and remembering meagre. Attention of young children is always flitting, they cannot concentrate their attention on any one object for long and hence their memory is not satisfactory. People who are mentally disturbed and incapable of concentrating attention have a wandering mind and a very unreliable memory. Thus whatever factors disturb attention and its concentration lead to weak and vague attention and memory

**Retention**

The problem of retention is one of the most interesting for students. How much of what they learn is retained? Why do they forget? What factors make for better and more useful retention? Why do they find it difficult to remember even very common things? These questions are natural and basic and an attempt will be made to answer them in the pages that follow.

Retention and forgetting are but two sides of the same process. We learn a large number of things but some we retain and others we forget. In certain mental diseases like aphasia and in extreme fatigue retention is very low because in the former brain tissues are injured and in the latter they do not seem to work. The ability to retain is by and large a physiological affair, a matter of associations or connections in the brain and the nervous system. That is why many emphasize that retentiveness is inherited and we can do little to improve it though we can improve it by improving fixation. Retention is influenced to some extent by intelligence, motivation and interests.

There are several different methods of measuring retentiveness. We shall describe here three of them : *recall, recognition* and *savings*.

The *method of recall* measures retention by showing how well the past knowledge and experiences persist over a period of time. It is more suited to the study of retention of verbal material like a poem or a part of the textbook. The essay examination is a good example of the recall method of measuring retention as the student has to reproduce without any cues subject-matter that has been learned before. Obviously this method measures a very small amount of what is retained.

A second *method of recognition* is a slight improvement on the method of recall because one may not be able to reproduce what he has learned but may be able to recognize it as having been learned before. It is frequently used when in objective tests students are asked to identify true-false statements or to choose the correct statement from among a number of statements. As it is very often employed in class-room teaching and testing this method may be found useful in measuring retention. But there is a good deal of chance in it and that fact makes it less trustworthy. A number of definitions of psychology both correct and incorrect are given and the student is asked to underline the correct. It would be a reliable test of his retention but it is possible that without actual recognition he by chance underlines the correct definition.

A third method of measuring retention is that of *savings* or *relearning* and it is frequently used in experimental studies of remembering. Here the subject is asked to learn again material which he had learned before. Retention is measured by the reduction in time employed in re-learning that material, the saving effected in time or the number of trials. Suppose a student took 30 repetitions to memorize a poem and then after a fortnight were again asked to learn it If he can do it in only 15 repetitions there is a saving of 50%. This method is much more reliable and is capable of measuring small differences. Besides it would also show up negative savings, if for example he took 40 repetitions against the 30 original. The comparison of original performance with the re-learning performance will show how perfect retention has been. There is a danger that on re-learning the student may try to learn too well or too much as some over-cautious students are likely to do. So there must be one criterion for both original learning and re-learning.

Ebbinghaus carried out a number of studies on retention. He memorized a list of nonsense syllables and then allowed a period of rest varying from a half hour to a month. In this way he was able to measure the savings for different intervals of time between learning and re-learning. The savings were greater for short intervals. The decline, however, for the first day was much greater than the day after original learning and thereafter was less abrupt. In another study he found that the meaningful material is more likely to be retained.

Bartlett made a study of the qualitative changes in retention and found that details are lost in a verbal narrative and the story is retained only in outline losing much of its wealth of detail.

**Factors influencing retention**

We have already hinted briefly as to what factors influence retention. It is a commonplace that some people are strong in retention and others are weak, and it is a pertinent question to ask what factors influence retention. As has already been pointed out retention is a physiological affair and depends on heredity. The power to retain is innate and inborn depending on the memory traces left in the brain by past experiences. These traces may be weak or strong determining the quality of retention. A person in good health has better retention than one in poor health. Old and ill persons have poor retention in comparison with young and healthy ones. Besides health age also bears on retention. Young children cannot be expected to retain complex and difficult subjects as old people cannot learn and retain new material. We have already seen how learning depends on maturity and the law of readiness operates. Intelligence too is an important factor in retention. One who is intelligent enough to understand things can retain them better than one who is dull. An intelligent person memorizes after understanding but one less intelligent commits to memory blindly and mechanically by rote and retains less. An earnest and abiding interest in the subject together with a suitable mind-set makes for better retention. Over-learning helps retention and a student about to make his first speech, and meaningful material is easier to retain than meaningless matter. Sleep immediately after learning strengthens connections and the material is retained longer, as things memorized immediately after getting up are remembered longer and better. Speed of learning also affects retention, the quicker the learning the better the retention. These conclusions have been reached after numerous experiments made by psychologists.

**Recall**

We all know from our everyday lives what it is to recall successfully. We repeat what we ate yesterday for dinner, we recite a poem we learned several weeks back, we see a person we met last year and dish out his name from our mind, we re-live the experiences of early childhood. In all such cases we are trying to reproduce, here and now, the important features of some past experience or event. We reinstate, from the retained effects of past experience, a copy of the experience.

But this duplicative nature of recall is not as smooth and exact as it is assumed to be. Any illustration of recall will show that it is selective and constructive. Not all that was experienced is reported, only some details are selected for reproduction. And in reproducing past events people do add, change and exaggerate details so that the reproduced version is never an exact replica of what happened in the past. When a person is recalling, he is essentially engaged in selectively constructing the salient characteristics of the original event. Even in such a simple act as that of recalling a person's name we do engage in selective constructing. Sometimes we recall it promptly and easily but sometimes it is "nearly" "on the tip of our tongue" but does not come out. We think of his nationality, province or caste or where we met him last or how his name begins and the like. We may have to recall his mannerisms, profession or the circumstances in which we met him last. Throughout this activity we are selecting and constructing and we are aware of it.

Not all experiences are retained and there are some experiences which can be recalled with great difficulty and perhaps not at all. We all are assimilative and what we experience is somehow assimilated and affects our subsequent experience and behaviour. Just how this assimilation takes place we are not yet able to say but this is an obvious fact that our likes and dislikes, our attitudes, our understanding, our thinking and problem-solving all are affected by what has happened to us in the past, and we know and are aware of the road we have travelled in the past. Recalling is one of the ways in which we are affected by our past. There is nothing like recall in the inorganic world.

Recalls are made in the process of making adjustments. Sometimes the information needed to make an adjustment has not been adequately acquired or assimilated and we cannot make a proper recall even though we need to do so badly.

**Factors influencing recall**

In the first place the desire to avoid the disagreeable influences recall. This is commonly recognized and no lover will ever say that he forgot to keep an appointment. We all recognize that it is the unpleasant engagements that we fail to remember. In a general way we forget experiences which cause pain, blunders which injure our self-esteem. In this way we get rid of the tension. For the same reason we forget acts contrary to our moral code. Forgetting in such cases is a protective device which we use as a last resort. We repress unpleasant experiences and they cannot be recalled in normal circumstances.

Secondly our emotional states or moods influence our recall. Only those events and experiences are recalled which are in harmony with the present mood. In moments of anxiety we recall all those events and experiences when we were beset with dangers and dwell on our misfortune. When we feel tender toward our dear ones we recall happy memories and when we are angry we recall those occasions when they did something wrong. When friends quarrel they recall only those events when they differed. Our recollections therefore depend on our moods.

Thirdly the need of the moment influences our recall, to pull into consciousness as it were the memories we need. On examination days we recall information dealing with that subject alone in which we are taking the examination and not of any other subject. Only facts related to the task in hand are attracted as if by a magnet.

But very often we need information and facts and are unable to recall them. We are sure we know them but are unable to reproduce them. Speakers forget their speeches, we forget the name we need most to recall. Sometimes even very familiar names and events are missed and the relevant things are not recalled however urgently they may have been needed. It shows that there are several other factors influencing recall besides the need of the moment. The need of the moment is very important but it is not the only important factor. Distractions, emotional states, weak associations between the present problems and the relevant facts may interfere with recall. It would be very cumbersome to expect normal people to employ technical aids in recalling difficult phenomena but a few suggestions are made here for everyday lapses of recall.

1. For effective recall the person should cultivate an attitude of confidence. Anxiety often blocks recall. A young speaker anxious to make a good speech forgets his important points. If he were to undertake speech-making with confidence and control his nervousness and anxiety he would be able to recall successfully. The same is true of students taking the examination. Some of them become so nervous due to anxiety that they fail to recall details which they had learned only the previous day so effectively. A person who is assailed by fears of failure will not be able to recall effectively.

2. If you find you are unable to make the desired recall, it may be dropped for the time being. You will find that it comes back to mind after some time. When a mathematical problem eludes solution it may with advantage be given up for some time. May be that you were following the wrong track, and when you return to it with a fresh mind and a new approach you are able to tackle it. Often students who follow this advice are delighted that the correct recall flashes across their minds without much effort, by itself as it were.

3. Failure to recall is often the result of poor initial learning. If at the time of learning we paid concentrated attention to it, if for example, on being introduced to a person we took him full, observing his dress and deportment, and made a careful note as to things for which we might need his help and support in future, we will be able to recall successfully.

4. The fact to be recalled should be associated with as many things as possible. Numerous associations will help recall. Many times students know the answer but they are unable to recall it as they had never associated their learning with the problem in hand. That is why many good teachers teach a topic from many points of

view and review it from different angles and cite numerous examples of its application. Such an approach helps to form many associations and make ready recall effective. Rote memory is mechanical depending entirely on repetition and has no reference to meaning or value of the topic and fails miserably. It is the least permanent form of retention.

### Common sources of error in recall

It would be worthwhile to know what factors make our recall erroneous. As has already been pointed out we forget unpleasant experiences, ignore objections to our views and shut our eyes to things and events which injure our self-esteem or prestige. And we remember pleasant experiences, arguments which strengthen our position or things which flatter us or boost our esteem. This is a major source of error in our recall. To be judicious in our recall we should remember all relevant data favourable as well as unfavourable. Wise public men, scientists and philosophers take pains to note down points for and against their proposals or investigations so that they may not miss the unpleasant and unfavourable aspects of the issue.

Secondly many people in reproducing past experiences or arguments over-simplify them. They thus lose richness of detail and often recall skeletal outlines. Of course by simplifying they use less effort but then details of events fade out.

Thirdly in recall there is a tendency to supply details so as to make the reproduced account interesting, reasonable and intelligible. There is a common desire to make it look an interesting story and in doing so the true order is often changed. The person deceives himself that he is recalling true facts.

Over and above these sources of error there are certain general factors which falsify the recall. Excitement, emotional repression, fatigue make the recall defective. There are certain mental disorders in which memory suffers and recall is vitiated. Injuries in the head may wipe out memory of events. Some factors spoiling recall are to be found in organic defects. Old age may involve degenration of brain and lead to forgetfulness. Or the degeneration may be due to disease, paresis and high blood-pressure are known to affect memory.

**Recognition**

To *recall* is to think of an object experienced in the past but to *recognize* is to identify a present object and to place it in one's system of memories. It is knowing the object again and the person is aware that he is knowing it again. We show a person a photograph. Does he recognize as a photograph of a woman rather than of a man? Does he recognize it as a woman he has met before? Does he recognize her as some one he has met only last week or as one who works with him in the office? Does he recognize her as Mrs. X? There are three essential features in an act of recognition. First, the object is present here and now. Secondly, the person supplies some characteristics of that object, for example, the photograph is that of a lady colleague working with him. Thirdly, this characteristic is made possible by the past experience he has had of that object. In looking out of the window I see a moving object. I recognize it as a car, the car looks familiar, I recognize it as the car of a friend. We recognize an object present before us, supply an essential characteristic and relate the object to our previous experience.

The basis of recognition is the feeling of familiarity. In recall an experience, event or object has to be reinstated or reproduced but in recognition only identification and familiarity is all that is essential. But recognition is more than familiarity. The act of recognition is not complete till the object recognized is placed in our past experience. Recognition is easier than recall; we may recognize a person without being able to recall his name. Recognition may later lead to recall.

Students engaged in learning and teachers engaged in teaching should know what they are learning and teaching for recall and what they are learning and teaching just for recognition. Unfortunately teachers and students are racing to master everything in the course but there are many things which they need only recognize. Several grammatical usages, arithmetical formulas and the like have to be over-learned so that they can be reproduced at a pinch but there is a host of facts which they need only to recognize.

Recall is a more severe test of retention than recognition. In recall one has to reproduce details but in recognition one only says that he has seen the object before and where and under what circumstances he has seen it. But in both some characteristics have to be supplied. Can you recall what happened in the main street yesterday? This question is as much a clue as the photograph of woman whom we wish you to recognize. Thus in both retained effects of past experience are used to supplement the present activity.

**Association of ideas**

For a long time psychologists explained learning and recall as a process of association. The laws of association stressed the general principle that ideas recall other ideas along with which they were previously experienced. Peacocks shriek when clouds thunder, children are afraid when they spill milk, dogs run away when you raise your arm to strike. It is because these experiences are associated with others whom they recall, and arouse original responses.

Such an association of ideas is governed by certain factors like recency, frequency and intensity of experiences or mood or attitude of the person. If you ask a person the first word that comes to his mind when he hears the word *day* he will most probably respond with *night*. This association is determined by frequency but if day has been hot, he may respond with *hot*, in which case the association will be based on *recency* or *intensity* of the connection. Again in a happy mood he may recall sunny thought and in a depressing mood he may think of sad and gloomy things. What he will recall depends on these factors.

There are two ways in which different things may be associated so that recalling one leads to the recall of the other. In the first place, things may in some way resemble each other. One story may remind me of another with the same plot; a dog may remind me of another dog, wolf or fox. This is *association by similarity*. But the story may make me recall the person who told it last time, the dog may make me recollect the child who was bitten last week by another dog. This is *association by contiguity*. Facts experienced and thought together are so associated that the thought of one recalls the other. Some psychologists put forward another law of *association by contrast* according to which a thing recalls its opposite as summer may remind us of winter. Contiguity may be in space or time. Associative thinking opens up a vast vista of past experiences and thoughts.

## Memory Span

One of the simplest methods of finding out the efficiency of immediate memory, that is, fixation or registration is to test the *memory span*. It is the simplest type of recall test with verbal material. The subject may be presented with a series of digits gradually increasing in length. Each list is presented only once. The first series may have only four digits, the next five, the next six and so on. The subject's memory span is the longest group of digits he can recall in correct order, regardless of the length of the series of digits shown or read out to him. He may recall the entire series till he gets to six or seven, but when he is given a dozen he may recall only eight. Then his memory span is eight. This span may vary from one presentation to another and then an average is taken. The presentation may be visual or auditory. Memory span differs with age and with the type of material presented.

## Perseveration

Sometimes snatches of what we learned before, a poem or a song burst into our consciousness, all of a sudden, without any effort on our part and without any apparent stimulation. Such an unintentional recall is called *perseveration*. The part of previous learning persists unless we are busily engaged in any serious task and push it out of consciousness. These responses are stronger when a person is tired or ill. Often they come up at odd hours just before sleep and if they happen to be associated in the past with something nasty they may disturb sleep. Individuals differ widely in their tendency to perseverate and the best way of overcoming it is to get busy in an absorbing task like reading an interesting novel or listening to sweet music.

**Retroactive inhibition**

A lot of research has been devoted to finding out how activities intervening between learning and recall interfere with the latter. This interference or confusion between two learning activities is called *retroactive interference* or *inhibition.* It is the harmful effect of learning or activity on the retention of previous learning. Such inhibition is a special case of negative transfer of learning. It is the most important factor in forgetting. Our activity after we learn something somehow works backward to inhibit or interfere with memories of what we have learned. That is why being aware after learning causes more forgetting than does being asleep. In sleep there is no interference and in waking state something is always going on.

A sample of an experiment on retroactive inhibition may be given here.

| | Time 1 | Time 2 | Time 3 |
|---|---|---|---|
| Subject 1 | Learn A | Activity X | Remember A |
| Subject 2 | Learn A | Activity Y | Remember A |

Subjects 1 and 2 may be two persons but usually they are two groups of people of the same age, sex, educational standard and the same ability to learn. They learn the same thing in the same time and follow exactly the same procedure. They learn the same lesson indicated by A, and are called upon to recall it after a specific lapse of time. But the two groups differ in the intervening activity between Time 1 and Time 3. For group Subject 1 this activity at Time 2 is X and for group Subject 2 this activity at Time 2 is Y, and Activities X and Y are different. Thus the two groups differ only in the intervening activity and any difference in their remembering must be due to this difference because they are similar in all other respects. Group 1 engages in activity X which is very much similar to what he learns but activity Y for group 2 is light and entertaining like reading a joke book or learning nonsense syllable. In one study the subjects were university students and they were asked to learn a list of adjectives ; their activity X was memorizing another list of adjectives more or less similar and the activity Y was reading jokes. The result was that those who read jokes could recall 45 per cent. of what they had learned and those who were engaged in learning a similar list of adjectives could remember only 12 per cent. of what they had learned. The similarity between what they had learned and the intervening or interpolating activity interfered or impaired their recall. These findings have been supported by other investigations, and three conclusions have emerged from this research :

1. The amount of interference increases with increase in similarity between the learning activity and the intervening or interpolating activity.
2. The amount of interference also depends on the intensity of the intervening or interpolating activity. If we are more active in the interval, the more likely we are to forget.
3. The greater the degree of original learning, that is, the better we learn the original lesson the less likely it is for the intervening activity to impair our recall.

Retroactive inhibition affects not only how much we are able to recall but also the quality of what, we recall. The contents of recall are distorted.

## Forgetting

Forgetting is a universal experience. We do not remember all that we experience. Perhaps it is necessary too. To remember well we must forget. Forgetfulness is very essential. We must forget all irrelevant details so that we may be able to remember the relevant well. In economical learning we must select. Every moment of our waking life is full of teeming details of experience and it would be a catastrophe to try to remember each one of them So we must select a few and forget the rest.

Forgetting is the failure of recall of past experiences. All experiences leave traces or after-effects in the brain and forgetting is the failure of retention of past experiences in the form of memory traces. With the passage of time memory traces grow weaker till they ultimately disappear. This is a widely held view that as time passes, the impressions of what we learn just get weaker and finally fade away. Psychologists accept that there is much truth in the commonsense view but they hold that it is not just time that makes us forget our past but what happens during that time, between learning and recall, which is responsible for forgetting or failure to recall. This has been demonstrated by experiments or retroactive inhibition described in detail in the last section.

Another experiment which supports this view is carried out on retention after sleeping and waking. The ability to remember after a period of sleep was compared with ability to remember after an equal period of waking. Two subjects were compared on retention of nonsense syllables after varying periods of sleep and of wakeful activity. The retention after sleep was much better and it showed very clearly that the intervening activity causes forgetting much more than sleep.

In the last section it was pointed out that retroactive inhibition is a special case of negative transfer of learning. Later activity or learning has a harmful effect on the retention of learning that has already taken place. What facts explain retroactive interference also explain negative transfer.

Other psychologists stress that forgetting is not a negative or passive activity. It is a positive response or activity and the individual is responsible for it. It is not merely lapse of time that leads to forgetfulness but the person himself actively tries to forget past experiences. We have already seen how Freud stressed that we forget because we want to forget. Experiences which are unpleasant and injure our self-esteem are deliberately and intentionally forgotten and repressed, that is, banished from the conscious life of the individual. Thus forgetting is both a passive and active mental process. We may forget with lapse of time or we may forget because we want to.

**Causes of forgetting**

By now readers must have grasped the several causes which lead to forgetting but for convenience of understanding they are reviewed in this section again. Defects in retention and recall have already been indicated and there are defects of learning.

When material is unmeaningful, when experiences are unpleasant or uninteresting, when they serve no purpose and the person does not accept or appreciate their relevance, it is difficult to recall them and we tend to forget them.

Often the forgotten material was not well learned or was under-learned. To be able to reproduce satisfactorily we should always over-learn. To avoid forgetting we should over-learn material by 50%.

Recall depends on repetition and if for a long time experiences do not recur or are not refreshed, if what is learned is not repeated, it tends to be forgotten. Again material which is learned by cramming and blind repetition without much understanding or appreciation of the material is soon forgotten.

Another cause of forgetting is retroactive inhibition which has already been discussed. Numerous experiments by a number of independent investigators have demonstrated the truth that such interference by interpolating activity causes forgetting.

We have already referred to mental shock, brain injury, mental ailments as causing loss or fading of memory.

Finally trying to recall or reproduce in an emotional situation often fails. Failures of recall in the anxiety and fear ridden situation of an examination hall are well known to students.

## Theories of forgetting

Psychologists are not agreed about the explanation of forgetfulness, and several theories have been put forward about their possible causes. We shall examine only a few of the common and important ones.

Perhaps the most universally held view is that forgetting is due to *disuse*. When a person learns anything and does not use it for a long time what was learned tends to be forgotten. Not refreshing it, not repeating or using it, we tend to forget a lot of facts of history, geography or science which we so assiduously learned in our school days. Lapse of time is really lack of use, and old people often excuse thmselves that with lapse of time their memories are not as active and strong as they used to be. But do they forget their date of birth, their date of retirement? How often do they recall very minor details of their childhood which they never refreshed in previous years? How often they wonder why very unimportant facts about their childhood experiences crop up in memory without any rhyme, reason or effort? They are amused by such tricks of recollection and share their amusement with others. All this shows that it is not merely lapse of time or lack of repetition or use which is responsible for forgetting. This theory is therefore partial and one-sided.

Another theory is that of *interference*. The phenomenon of retroactive inhibition or interference has already been explained and illustrated. During the period of retention, and between the time of learning and reproducing a number of activities take place which may interfere with or weaken the memory of what was learned. There has been some after-learning which obstructs original learning from getting into our consciousness again. Those psychologists who have made use of experiments of retroactive inhibition argue that this explanation is satisfactory and valid. But it does not explain all kinds of forgetting. We forget many things because we are not interested in them, they are of no use to us, and we drop them in a way. The selective character of memory makes for economy in learning and forgetting is very useful.

Psychologists of the psychoanalytical school have formulated the theory of *repression*. Repression is a protective mental mechanism to which an individual resorts to escape unpleasant, unsatisfactory and humiliating experiences. The function of repression is to reject and keep out of consciousness memory of unbearable experiences. Repression blocks them from conscious states and gets rid of the problem for ever. Such experiences have been recalled by techniques of hypnosis and psychoanalysis and their recollections were very vivid showing that they were strong enough to persist in memory but were deliberately forgotten. Such forcible forgetting is very taxing for the individual. But repression does not explain all our forgetting and Freud was conscious of this fact. Students study and learn but they are not able to recall in the examination what they studied and learned so carefully. They cannot be said to have repressed their learning. This theory too is not adequate in explaining all the facts of forgetting.

**Can we improve memory?**

Memory is the storehouse for knowledge for every man and woman and its improvement and training is of vital interest and importance for all of us. Students in particular are anxious to know if memory can be trained or improved so that they collect as much knowledge as they can and deliver it in the examination. We have already indicated that retention is mostly a physiological affair depending on heredity and there is little scope for its improvement or training except by way of improving the individual's health and removing fatigue so that he learns with freshness and efficiency. Effective recall and recognition depend mostly on fixation and registration and most methods which are put forward for the improvement of memory are designed to improve fixation. From times immemorial philosophers and wise men have been laying stress on the fact that attention is the heart of the learning process and of memory. Habits of active concentrated attention and development of keen interests help memory as nothing else does. Memory depends on associations between stimuli an responses and if such associations are made stronger and larger they will certainly help memory.

We have already dealt with steps which may usefully be taken to to help recall and recognition. Woodworth points out two things which should be done to facilitate recall and recognition. (1) "Give the stimulus a good chance. Look squarely at the person whose name you wish to recall, avoiding doubt as to your ability to recall it, for doubt is distraction," (2) "drop the matter for a while and come back to it afresh."

Teachers and others have made up mnemonic lines by which dates and names in history and geography can be more easily memorized. It is partly because this material is organized into a rhythmical order that we are able to commit it to memory more easily and partly because students take to it with interest for its novelty. A meaningful organization of the material and some rhythm do help our memory.

William James held that memory cannot be improved but Stout is of opinion that practice in any sphere improves memory in that sphere. By long practice actors are able to learn their parts more rapidly and easily. The same is true of clergymen who learn their sermons by heart. These effects of practice however seem to be strictly confined to that sphere alone.

Sometimes multiple approach in learning is advised for better memory. Hear the name, read the written name, speak the name and write the name a number of times to remember it well and recall and recognition will be facilitated.

The advice to organize material into logical wholes is also very useful but such organization is based on associations, relations or meanings whose importance has already been stressed.

## Questions

1. What is memory ? Discuss the several processes involved in it.
2. What are the principal forms of memory ? Analyse them in detail indicating factors important for each of them.
3. What do you understand by retentiveness ? Can we improve it ? Describe the several methods of measuring it. What factors influence retention ?
4. Discuss the nature of recall. What factors influence recall ? What are the common sources of error in recall ?
5. Distinguish between recall and recognition. What factors influence recognition.
6. What is retroactive inhibition ? Describe an expriment on retroactive interference and show how it is a case of negative transfer. Can it explain forgetting ?

7. Write short notes on :–perseveration, Memory span, Contiguity, and Repression.
8. What do you understand by association of ideas and show how it helps remembering. What are the laws of association ? Illustrate them.
9. Why do we forget ? Discuss the principal theories put forward to explain forgetting. What are the main causes of forgetting ?
10. "To remember well you must forget". Bring out the truth of this statement. What are the causes of forgetting ? What steps should be taken to avoid forgetting ?
11. Can memory be improved ? What steps a student should take to remember better ?

CHAPTER X

# IMAGINATION AND DREAMS

## The general nature of imagination

When we are hungry we think of food, when lonely we think of friends. In such instances we become conscious of what would satisfy us, though the desired object is not present before us. We picture it in our mind. These are instances of imagination. I think of remodelling my house, and create in my mind pictures of what my house should look like. These pictures are new, they refer neither to what is present nor to what is past. They are only expected to be present in the future. But imagination does not involve a reference to time. It is mental activity about things, persons and situations even when they are not present to sense. There are animals which when dissatisfied are in a state of restlessness and tension, they do not know what will satisfy them unless and until the thing is present before them. Such a thing often happens to man also. He may feel restless and not know what he wants. Then suddenly he meets a friend and his tension is over. He was in need of company and the presence of the friend helped him to define his need. But often man is able to imagine what will satisfy him even though the object is not present before him. Imagination is the process of forming images or mental pictures. In perception the perceived object is before us here and now, it belongs to the system of present reality. In memory the object is something I perceived or experienced in the past, it belongs to what happened some time back, in imagination I call up a mental picture or copy of an object which may happen, is about to come up, may be isolated from all existing systems of things or may belong to a new system or an old system in a new way. I am expecting the arrival of a friend and may picture how he will look, I may imagine him to be wearing ordinary clothes or dressed as a joker with a beard on or as he is usually dressed but carrying a big trunk.

Imagination is picturing objects in their absence. Woodworth calls it "mental manipulation". It is recalling mental pictures of objects previously observed and then re-arranging them into new patterns or relations.

## Images

What we recall when we think of an object without its being present to the senses is an *image*. Sometimes instead of the whole object, only one of its qualities is present and a more or less vivid picture of the whole object is recalled. This picture of the object when the object is not present is an image, a memory image or a mental image. It is possible for every sensory experience to have its counterpart in an image. We may have images of lights, colours, sounds, smells, tastes etc. After taking a cup of tea I may have an image of its colour, temperature, taste or smell.

Just as we cannot have a pure sensation but only a perception, that is sensation plus meaning, so we cannot have pure images without any meaning. We have *ideas*. Images are to ideas what sensations are to perceptions.

We have three kinds of mental images. One is the *after-image*, which we have already studied and wherein we see, hear or feel an object for a brief instant after it is removed. And there are positive and negative after-images. In the positive we see an object as it was just before disappearing. After a light is put out, for example, we have a fleeting image of the bulb. Negative after-images are an opposite or "complementary" sensation of colour or brightness. If we gaze for half a minute at a spot of bluish green and then look right or left we see a red image of the same size and shape. The negative after-mage of bright light is black image of the bulb. After-images result from a lag in our sensory receptors.

Memory images, less vivid and accurate than after-images, are duplicates of original sensations and perceptions which may occur when we recall past experiences.

Eidetic images are amazingly vivid, almost photographic, reproductions of objects recently seen. They are common among children but rare among adults.

Most of the early research was carried on only in memory images.

## Sensations and images

Images being incomplete copies of sensations are naturally inferior to the latter, "both in the enjoyment they afford and in the use that can be made of them". Let us consider how inferior they are.

1. Images are more fragmentary than sensations. The latter have a background which the former lack. When I see a flag flying on the top of a building, this sight sensation may be accompanied by sensations of warmth, sound, organic sensation. But when I recall a mental picture of the flag the image is cut off from the context in which the original sensation occurred.

2. Secondly there is a difference in intensity. The image called up of a fine picture or music does not possess the vividness of the sensation of watching that picture or hearing that music. The percept has an aggressive character and strikes the mind as it were. Images are not so aggressive. In a very conspicuous manner the whistle of an engine or the flashing light of a car set up motor and organic sensations which are sure to be absent from their images. The image of a piercing sound or a dazzling light could never be so disturbing.

3. Percepts are more distinct than images and images are more sketchy and fainter than sensations. It is partly due to "oblivi-scence", that is, leaving out certain details in the image, and partly due to "reduplication", that is, every image is based on a number of sense impressions and only those details in which they agree are recalled.

4. Images are unsteady and fleeting as compared with sensa-tions. So long as the stimulus is present before the senses the sensation stays, but in the case of an image the stimulus is absent and it is very difficult to keep the image in the focus of attention. The image is much more fluctuating.

5. In receiving actual sensations we are more or less passive and just receive impressions from outside, but in calling images mind is more active. Sensations are objective in that they are determined by an external stimulus but images are subjective being determined by internal factors.

6. Images are inferior to actual sensations in their practical usefulness. In perception the object is actually present and we can continue to observe it and gain more knowledge. But images cannot give or add to our information. We cannot observe facts in the image of a thing that we did not observe in the sensation.

7. Lastly sensations and perceptions are related to motor activity whereas images are not so related. If we see a mad dog running toward us we perform certain movements to get out of its reach but the images of hundreds of mad dogs will not force us to budge an inch, except in abnormal condition. Often the perception is preliminary to some sort of action while an image is seldom so.

### Relative independence of percept and image

However the image is not entirely determined by perception. While we see the sky to be blue we may easily imagine it to be red, and our imagining it to be red does not in any way come into conflict with the percept. Nor do they combine as most sensations do. It is impossible to see the sky both red and blue or a combination of two colours. It is because an image and a sensation are independent processes and two different nervous tracts are excited in the occurrence of percepts and images.

### Confusion between imagination and perception

Children and adults are often unable to distinguish between perception and imagination. The images of children are much more vivid than those of adults and they often confuse between what they see and what they merely imagine. Returning from school a child makes up a number of stories of what he did on the way, parents think he is telling lies but he is just not able to distinguish between fancy and fact, images and percepts. In everyday situations mothers are not always able to tell whether they hear or only imagine that they hear a baby crying. Jugglers and magicians raise our expectations in such a manner that they make us see things as magical what is merely a sleight of hand.

A number of experiments show that the distinction between imagination and perception is puzzling. In one experiment subjects placed before a screen in a darkened room were told to judge whether or not dimly coloured lights appeared on the screen. Though sometimes no stimulus was shown, the subjects thought they saw it. Thus images were wrongly assumed to be sensations. Occasionally the reverse occurred: subjects thought a patch of light merely their own image.

Edmund Jacobson, a physiological psychologist, made an experiment in which electrodes placed near the eyeball showed the eye muscles active during visual imagery. Tongue and lip muscles contracted slightly when subjects imagined talking to a friend or thought about abstract ideas like "eternity". So he concludes that imagery cannot occur without muscular activity.

There are some persons who report that they experience colours when they hear sounds, that is, they perceive a definite colour patterns when they hear a particular sound. This is known as *coloured hearing*. *Synesthesia* is the general term for such relations between sense qualities. One man reported seeing a different colour for each orchestral instrument Cases of coloured odours and coloured tastes have also been reported. Such associations when stimulation of one sense-organ evokes a different sensory image are called synesthesia.

Francis Galton found that some persons visualize numbers in spatial patterns. C.C. Pratt found a subject who thought of a point directly before his eyes when number 1 came to mind. Five is higher and a little to the left. Twelve is farther away and still higher and so on. With colours Galton's subjects noted many curious associations. One man saw his numerals in this way: 1 was black; 2 yellow; 3 pale-brick-red; 4 brown and so on. It is believed that synesthesia and *number-forms* result from early forgotten associations that continue till they become habitual reactions.

### Eidetic imagery

As already explained eidetic imagery is vivid, clear imagery and an eidetic person is one who after looking at a picture for half a minute or so has a clearer, more intense and detailed memory image than an ordinary persons. Often an eidetic image includes details which the person failed to note in his original observation. Certain details may be larger in the image or even may appear to move. Eidetic imagery is common among children. Studies of young people from six to fourteen show it in about two-thirds of the cases.

G. W. Allport carried out a test of eidetic imagery on 30 English children. He showed them a picture for 35 seconds. It was a German street scene, with men, dogs and a wagon and over the door of a building the word *Gartenwirthschaft*. Projecting their image of the picture on a screen and describing it, the youngsters noted many small details when questioned about them. Some could read off the long German word, though they did not understand the language. A few even could spell it backward. Allport considers eidetic image as a variety of memory images.

### Experience and imagination

Imagination is based on experience and however bizzarre imaginary objects may be, the elements of which they are composed are all drawn from previous experience. A person born blind has no experience of light or colour and cannot imagine them. In a sense therefore imagination may be defined as the re-calling and re-arranging or re-combining of experience. Such a definition will help to distinguish memory from imagination and indicate the essential role of experience in imagination. Recall is based on past experience, it is a reproduction of what happened before; imagination too is based on previous experience but it combines past experiences into a new pattern and does not claim any accuracy in recalling the past.

### Reproductive and creative imagination

Reproductive imagining as the name implies just reproduces in thought previous experiences. By re-instating the past the organization and structure of the past is preserved. We may recall what we did in the last summer vacation and make it out into an interesting narrative as often students are called upon to do. But when they are asked to describe an imaginary flight in an aeroplane or what they would do if they became the prime minister, they draw their material from past experience but weave it into new patterns altogether as is done in a story, fairy tale or novel. This is creative or constructive imagination. Many theories of scientists are efforts of creative and constructive imagination and try to explain things in a new way by using terms and concepts which have been used in the past. Art, music, literature, philosophy and science are full of examples of creative imagination.

### Functions of imagination

When a schoolboy tries to think out what he would say if the teacher rebukes him for negligence, when a salesman thinks of alternative schemes for promoting sales or a general decides about different types of strategy in meeting the challenge of the enemy they are using imagination to guide their action and adjust their behaviour to meet new challenges and difficulties. But when we after a hearty dinner indulge in happy dreams of what we may do in the next vacation, when a student builds castles in the air about his ambitions in life after passing the examination or a young girl makes up glorious picture of her future doings as the bride of a handsome, rich and strong young man, they are using imagination for enjoyment and as a guide to action. But life is hard and we are all beset with uncertainty, failure and sorrow. In such a context we all dwell on our troubles and misfortunes and call up possible sources of further trouble and sorrow. Such imagination is an outgrowth of anxiety, worry and fears. We shall discuss them in detail.

### Imagination and adjustment

We have alrady learned that imagination functions as guide to action and makes for better and more effective and efficient adjustment to the needs and problems of life and environment. Too many people give themselves away in moments of stress, bemoan their bad luck and accept what fate has decreed for them. But some do not accept defeat. They explore possibilities of meeting the challenge circumstances have posed before them. They may consult other members of the family or their friends, they turn over the alternative methods of solving the problem, borrow help if necessary or take such measures as will help them to get over their difficulties in course of time. They are using their imagination to best advantage. One student goes on with his studies from one class to another but another visualizes what he would like to become in life, considers the alternative course of studies available to him, what subjects he should take up as a suitable preparation for different courses, how able he is to do well in some of them, assesses the possible expenditure of time and money required for different courses, the prospect different careers hold out and the like. He is using imagination to chalk out his course of action and the pattern of adjustment to life situations. Before committing himself to any definite course of action he considers possible alternatives and objections.

All rational and intelligent guidance of behaviour requires the use of imagination in the above manner. When people meet in committees to decide if English should be abolished from the curriculum, if food stuffs should be rationed, if railway passengers should be provided with cold water in summer, if family planning should be enforced in the country, if education should be made compulsory for all children upto the age of ten or fifteen, the most useful members are those who see in advance what difficulties are likely to arise in any programme of action and how they should plan to meet them. They suggest advantages and disadvantages of every course proposed, they examine different proposals critically and they suggest steps and cautions. All this is imagination.

That is why employers insist that people at the top positions should be men with imagination, who in moments of crises quickly imagine new situations which may arise and take prompt decisions. One of the important qualities of a great leader is to see beforehand the needs and wishes of the people of their party or group. Many people boast that they do not think or imagine but they act and bungle through. But do they realize that this is what animals do? All great courses of action are planned with imagination bearing in mind all alternative programmes, policies, strategies and steps. Of course if one just stays at the stage of imagination without doing anything, allows problems and difficulties to torment him, exaggerates them out of all proportion, loses confidence in following up action, imagination instead of being a spur and guide to action, may serve only to make people timid and useless. But that is the abuse of imagination.

**Imagination as a source of enjoyment**

Imagination is the spice of life. Without imagination life would be a dull and drab affair without hope, dreams and ambitions. Whenever man is surrounded by troubles, sorrows and difficulties he sees a ray of hope in them and builds up relieving dreams of possible success and happiness. We ignore reality and look beyond it weaving incompatible desires free from annoyance into a cheerful world of comfort and prosperity. Man has a strong tendency to shake off apathy and indifference and move into a new environment, imaginary if it cannot be real, where his hopes and desires will be fulfilled. This is made possible by imagination. It is true that most of us are disappointed when our dreams and hopes are not fulfilled but in the first place those hopes and dreams made us happy while they lasted and secondly we are for ever building new dreams and hopes. Life is hope, and imagination adds strength to our hopes. There are people who accomplish what they hope and there are people whom success is denied but who enjoy make-believe success in their dreams.

There are four ways in which imagination gives us joy, in play, daydreams, dreams and aesthetic experience. Much of the pleasure people get in play depends on the degree with which they are able to invest play with their fantasy. The little child playing with a stick which he believes to be a horse, the little girl playing with a doll which she believes to be her friend or child, children playing policeman, a cook or a postman live in a world of fantasy from which they draw happiness. Even in the games of adults this make-believe attitude is very prominent. They enjoy their games only so far as they take them seriously. They attach too much importance to winning and losing which an objective assessment of the situation does not justify. Play is spontaneous activity and does not turn entirely on imagination, but it is imagination which makes it all the more enjoyable.

Daydreams satisfy our desires which are difficult to satisfy in the real world, and night dreams too are an escape from the drudgery and worries of life. We shall deal with them in detail in the sections that follow.

The enjoyment that comes from the appreciation and creation of a work of art depends on imagination. Such enjoyment lies in the fact that we appreciate many things which though of no practical use appeal to us as beautiful. We enjoy physical activity, colours, tones, cool fresh air, companionship, peace and love. Imagination by investing experiences with new meanings and by enabling us to enter into the sorrows and joys of others adds greatly to the depth and range of all enjoyment. People without any imagination are not able to appreciate and enjoy artistic creations and the beautiful things of life because they are not able to get deep into the values and meanings of things. And the creative artist through his imagination rises above individual thoughts and feelings and gauging what is felt and thought at the universal level through their imagination are able to create what appeals to all mankind. Works of art express the longings of man and both its creation and enjoyment requires imagination of a high order.

**Imagination and Worry**

We have already described worry as an outgrowth of imagination. When we fail, when some dear one is seriously ill or we are late for the train we worry because we are not able to do anything about it. Such worrying is a normal process. But some people worry to pass time as a sort of fighting against boredom and monotony, as an "indoor sport" as Woodworth puts it. A mother has sent out her child to play; her love for him and her fear for his safety even though she does not doubt it may cause her to imagine him in all sorts of accidents and troubles. Such mild worries seem pleasant just as mild fears are a source of pleasure to the young and old. Unless they are too disagreeable such experiences involving mild fear and anxiety raise the level of consciousness and give pleasure. The mother would rather be worried than bored. Her worries give her mild excitement in an otherwise monotonous day, and the relief she feels when her child returns makes up for the unpleasant experience of worry she had earlier.

But excessive worry is serious. It may be the result of timidity, lack of self-confidence and/or mental conflict. Children and adults who have led a protected life and for whom decisions have been made by others may feel very much worried because they are called upon to stand on their own and take vital decisions. Similarly people who are always afraid of making mistakes are very much worried about the outcome of their efforts. Some attach excessive importance to what others will say about them and worry a lot. Mental conflict leads to worry. When we are not able to decide between two equally pleasant courses of action, when we are torn between our loyalty to parents and our future career, when temptations go against social codes, or when we are trying to reconcile two diametrically opposed courses of action, we are victims of intense conflict and excessive worry.

Many people indulge in too much worry about their health and are always seeking information about health, medicines and diet. This is *hypochondria* and like the mother's worry is an escape from some sort of boredom and monotony which is disagreeable. Such worry gives the individual pleasure, otherwise it would not be indulged in. He exaggerates his ailments to escape action and responsibility and yet he would not admit it. Such worry is congenial and if the person is more imaginative becomes very much heightened.

Of course everybody recognizes that worry is useless and does not lead us anywhere particularly when things about which we worry are beyond our control. The advice to face problems realistically and stand up to obstacles manfully is frequently ignored. Strong imagination supports worry.

### Hallucinations

Hallucination is false perception. When a person hears voices which others do not hear or sees things which others do not see, he is supposed to be suffering from hallucinations. Hallucinations are different from illusions. In illusions the object is there but it is wrongly perceived, in hallucinations the object is perceived when it is not there. Waking up at night you may think some door creaked and a burglar came in. If it was some rat making that sound it was an illusion but if there was nothing to cause that sound it was a hallucination. *Hallucinations* are images mistaken for perceptions and are a disorder of the imagination. They show that the individual's hold on reality is weakening by his absorption in his own fears and anxieties, desires and whims. He sees visions, smells odours or hears voices in line with his desires and fears. Woodworth defines hallucination as false sensations, "a memory image taken for a sensation."

Some drugs cause hallucinations, they make our images so vivid that we mistake them for perceptions. A drunkard is apt to see snakes or other frightening objects, and drugs like opium, hashish have a similar influence. Hallucinations are also caused by very intense emotions. A person dying of thirst in a desert sees mirage of water, and one who has lost a dear relative recently may see his presence. Hallucinations are highly individual and can be understood only in terms of the inner mental states of the individual concerned. Illusions on the other hand depend more on the external world and can be understood only in reference to outside objects. Illusions are normal while hallucinations are pathological. Unless caused by a drug or by some acute crisis hallucinations are symptoms of a diseased mind. If they persist, they call for treatment by a psychiatrist. Some of the common causes of hallucinations are repressed memories of painful experiences, feelings of extreme unworthiness, frustrated desires and the like.

### Daydreams

Daydreaming is an easy way of satisfying desires left unfulfilled in real life. It is building castles in the air like the well-known milkmaid, an unpopular girl, who dreams, as she carries milk, of the eggs which she will buy after selling milk, of the chickens she will raise, of the new dress she will wear, of how pretty she will look, of how young men will seek her hand in marriage and how she will scorn them. Unfortunately she acted out her scorn and shaking her head spilt the milk and killed her dreams. Day-dreaming is fanciful imagining of situations, adventures and events in which the dreamer is usually prominent and important. The disappointment we feel if the day-dream is interrupted is evidence that we actually enjoy daydreaming.

Mandel Sherman divides daydreams into the casual and the systematic. Most of us have casual daydreams about our momentary aspirations or conflicts. Systematic daydreams occur again and again, they are due to permanent motives. E. Bleuler calls daydreaming "autistic thinking" which shows it is self-centred, illogical and unrealistic. Most common is the "conquering hero" type in which a person imagines himself doing grand things of strength and bravery.

According to G.H. Green daydreams are of four kinds, the "display" daydream in which the dreamer wins applause for doing something big, the "saving" daydream in which he rescues another bravely, the grandeur daydream in which he does something grand, and the "homage" daydream in which he helps some needy person. Abnormal psychologists add two more types, the "death" daydream in which somebody's death is imagined for hostility or jealousy, and the "martyr" daydream in which he imagines himself dead and people mourning him.

The pleasure we get from reading a novel or watching a film show depends on the help they give us in daydreaming. We identify ourselves with the hero and carry on. Sometimes we indulge in daydreaming because we having nothing to do and lazily allow our mind to run as it may ; sometimes to compensate for a defect or handicap or for a life of monotony, sometimes to offset the effects of discouragement and sometimes to pass time in a pleasant way we have recourse to daydreams. In all such cases daydreams are an agreeable substitute for effort and vigorous activity.

Daydreams of persecution and suffering though unpleasant provide us opportunities to feel important and to raise ourselves in our own esteem. Such dreams are also excuses for lack of effort.

Daydreams are a perfectly normal activity and a number of scientists, inventors, explorers and social reformers were day-dreamers, it is an innocent and happy pastime, but these people followed up their daydreams with positive effort and action. But they become abnormal and dangerous when an individual indulges in them too much and thus withdraws from reality and everyday trials and tribulations of life. Children who spend too much time in daydreaming are unable to distinguish between fact and fancy, and adolescents given to daydreaming may develop disorders of imagination. Certain types of daydreaming may influence one toward crime.

**Dreams**

Dreaming is usually described as mental activity during sleep, it is an activity in which imagination plays the role of perception. The activity is bizarre and disconnected. Many assume that most sleep is dreamless, it may be that man is not able to recall all his dreams. If on waking up he fails to recall his dream it is believed that he did not dream at all. Dreams may be continuation of our waking activity. Often very strange and queer things happen in dreams and equally queer explanations have been offered of absurd dreams. The old view that they are messages from spirits and the like is no longer held.

Most dreams consist of visual imagery. Some are auditory. Practically all are one or the other or a combination of the two. J. Jastrow showed that dreams depend on past sensory experience. Testing blind persons, he found that none blinded before the age of 5 had visual imagery. Of those becoming blind after the age of 7, all had visual dream-images.

What causes dreams? How can they be interpreted? *Sigmund Freud's theory* is best known. According to him sleep is a mans of escaping the boredom of waking life to the more exciting and satisfying world of dreams. In support of this theory he argues that people in quiet uninteresting communities sleep more and appear less alert, that people engaged in interesting work sleep less than those not so happily placed, and that in dreams we derive a sort of satisfaction for many unfulfilled desires. If this theory is true it would mean that we dream all the time we are asleep. But this cannot be tested and it is not possible to find out what proportion of sleep is passed in dreaming.

Since dreams do not appear to be satisfying our desires, Freud and his followers insist that these desires are disguised and can be known only when they are interpreted. And interpretation of dreams can be understood only in terms of the psychology of psychoanalysis according to which there are three levels of mind, the unconscious, the foreconscious and the conscious. The unconscious is the source of all psychic energy, our instincts and repressed painful desires and experiences are rooted in it. The foreconscious consists of all processes of mental life which can be brought back to consciousness through conscious memory, and consciousness consists of that part of mental life of which we are aware at any one time. Desires or memories that are painful are driven into the unconscious. Our ideals are regarded as maintaining a close censorship over what is admitted into the unconscious. But in spite of the control of the censor some contents do slip into consciousness in a disguised form so that their genuine nature may not be known.

Dreams are a good opportunity for such repressed desires to enter consciousness though even in dreams they come in a disguised form. That is how Freud describes them as wish-fulfilments, they are symbolical fulfilments of sexual wishes. By "wish" Freud means all kinds of motives though there seems to be no justification for such a usage.

Another theory suggests that dreams are caused physiologically, like sleeping in odd positions or from sensory factors like smells or sounds which disturb sleep. Knight Dunlap suggests that dreams of nakedness arise from chilliness. L.H.W. Horton thinks that dreams are misinterpretations of sensory impression; a student with toothache dreams of boxing with a friend and getting a blow on the jaw.

Holingworth describes an experiment in which a subject was stimulated in several ways while he was asleep. When tickled on the nose and lips with a feather, he dreamed that his skin was being torn from his face. It is common to dream of a watchman's beat or a soldier's footsteps when a timepiece is ticking on the head side of the bed.

Another theory connects dreams with real experiences and indicates that dreams of people of different occupations differ and are connected with their daily environment.

Alfred Adler interprets dreams as turning over unsolved problems or anticipating new ones. The problems are presented symbolically. An imminent decision may be represented by an impending school examination or a strong opponent by an elder brother.

Psychoanalysts claim that certain images or pictures in dreams are symbols of the same thing for all dreamers. For example, they claim that a snake has usually a sexual significance; the failure to catch a train frequently means missing something of great importance; having to take an examination means facing a great ordeal which the dreamer fears he may not be able to face successfully. It is this similarity of meanings represented by dream pictures that is known as ***Dream symbolism*** and has given rise to dream books seeking to interpret dreams for us.

Dreams are interpreted by psychoanalysts by the method of free-association. The dreamer is asked to think of certain dream images and to tell the analyst whatever comes into his mind when he thinks of that image. After a number of sittings it is presumed that the dreamer has provided enough material which may reveal the mind of the dreamer and help to interpret his dream.

Freud and his followers have added much to our knowledge of dreams. They have stressed that dreams have a purpose and a meaning and have helped to make dreams intelligible. But they have attached exaggerated importance to sex in causing dreams. Sex wishes are not the only wishes. In war it is fear that is more dominant than sex. Freud's theory of dream motivation is too narrow. In his later life Freud seemed to have recognized this. We have already discussed some of the theories offered by other psychologists. We may not accept any one of them as the whole truth but all of them have contributed to make our understanding of dreams fuller and clearer.

Attempts have also been made to classify dreams. Some dreams warn us about coming events, others simply foretell future happenings, still others are caused by bodily conditions. Then there are night-mares. But such a classification is not scientific or exhaustive and superstitious people derive all sorts of meanings from their dreams. Woodworth's suggestion deserves careful consideration. He says that the object of interpreting dreams is not to understand that particular dream but to discover something about the personality of the dreamer. If we learn something worthwhile about him it is better than trying to find out what a particular dream means.

## QUESTIONS

1. What do you understand by imagination? Distinguish between a sensation and an image.
2. Explain how perception and imagination are confused ?
3. Explain :—Eidetic imagery, Synesthesia, Coloured hearing, After-image. Give examples.
4. Discuss in detail the function of imagination as means to adjustment, as source of enjoyment and as source of worry.
5. Discuss how imagination is necessary for a position of responsibility in administration ?
6. What are the kinds of imagination ? Is experience necessary for imagination ?

7. Discuss how imagination is necessary for the enjoyment of art, literature and play ?
8. What is worry ? What is the role of imagination in worry ?
9. Is daydreaming normal ? Discuss the advantages and disadvantages of daydreaming.
10. How are dreams caused ? Discuss Freud's theory of dreams bringing out its merits and defects.
11. Discuss the nature of dreams. How are they related to the life of the dreamer ? What factors determine their nature ? How would you interpret dreams ?

CHAPTER XI

# FEELING AND EMOTION

## The nature of feelings

Our feelings are the most common and simplest experiences. This is shown by the large frequency with which we use the word "feel". But the word is used in many senses and our first problem is to know in what sense it is used in psychology. In the first place it is used for *touch sensation* as when we say that the surface feels rough or smooth, it may be used for *sensation of temperature* as we say we feel cold or warm, for *organic sensations* as I feel thirsty or hungry, for *emotions* as I feel angry or sorry, for any *mental state* as I feel doubtful or certain and for *feeling pleased* or *displeased.* It is in this last sense that we use feeling in psychology to denote a primary, simple state of consciousness or an aspect of behaviour. Sensations of touch or organic sensations give us apprehension and apprehension is not feeling, they give us a sense quality. Emotions too are highly complex and should not be mixed with feeling though feeling is an aspect of every emotion. Feeling or affection as we call it in psychology consists in being pleased or displeased with something, in liking or disliking it. It is the simple emotional aspect of our daily activities.

No scientist has yet discovered just what goes on in the mind when we have a feeling reaction such as the above, but no one can be ignorant of the importance of feelings in our life. Feelings tell us how we are situated in regard to anything. "I feel good about the weather, some friend, some achievement, some purchase and so on". The feeling reaction tells us that all is well and that we are pleased about the thing or situation, we like it or find it agreeable. "I feel bad about things" means that I dislike them, am dissatisfied about them and they are disagreeable. When things begin to matter to us, we have feelings about them. Much of our thinking is also in the service of our feelings. Man is for ever wanting and desiring things, and doing something about his wants and desires. He is also for ever feeling and doing something about his feelings.

Few things can be counted upon as always giving rise to a particular feeling. Sweets, tennis, fine clothes, jokes we may say are always pleasant but are there not times when we get "fed up" with them? Often the feeling of "fed up" passes into a definite turning away, a positive dislike. No doubt they are more or less permanent and uniform sources of pleasure, but they may be pleasant at one moment and otherwise at another. That is why feeling is often called *subjective*. Pleasing things do not always please and displeasing things do not always displease. The feeling-tone often depends on the mood of the moment. A dish may be greatly enjoyed because you are in a mood to eat and extremely stale if you have had an annoyance just before. Secondly the pleasantness and unpleasantness of an oject depends on how often a thing is repeated in experience. Even the best song repeated a number of times becomes dull and hackneyed. On the contrary objects lose their unpleasantnes also because of constant repetition. Quinine loses its bitterness if you have to take it for a week.

The feeling-tone is estimated by two methods. In *order-of merit* method people and objects are ranged in a series of increasing pleasantness or unpleasantness, but the feeling-tone does not vary with the intensity of the stimulus alone. It also depends on frequency as has been shown in the section above. In the method of *paired comparsions* a judgment of preference or liking is obtained on the basis of comparison. As an example of the first method it has been found by experiment that 9 per cent. sugar and 2 per cent. common salt give the more pleasant taste than other intensities.

### Sensation and feeling

Let us compare sensation and affection or feeling. In the first place feeling or affection is blunted by repetition. Objects lose their pleasantness or unpleasantness if they are presented again and again. But more often sensations are repeated the more organic and familiar they become till they enter into our mental life as its part and parcel. Affection grows weaker and weaker till it disappears altogether. Our books, room, home, college are no longer pleasant or unpleasant, we have lost that feeling through constant use, but our knowledge about them has grown more definite.

Secondly sensations are objective and feelings are subjective. Sensations to some extent are determined by the objects but feelings are personal, they belong to ourselves and they have no objective reference. We speak of objects being bright, red, sweet or hard, but we speak of ourselves being pleased or displeaesd.

Thirdly sensations can be easily attended to, selected and observed, and become clearer when so brought into attentive consciousness but feelings if attended to become vague till they elude attention.

Fourthly sensations are "localized", it is some object that is presented and a particular sense-organ that is stimulated. But feeling is diffused over the whole organism. It is the entire person that is pleased or displeased. But it is one sense-organ that gives us a sense quality.

Fifthly, distinct feelings cannot exist side by side in the same pulse of conscious living, feelings get fused, and we cannot be both pleased and displeased at the same time. But two or more sensations may exist together at the same time, numerous stimuli may be present and a number of sense-organs may be stimulated at the same time or even the same object may give more than one sensation. But we cannot be both pleased and displeased in the same breath. Whenever there is a conflict between the two they blend and which ever is more intense overpowers the other. They are incompatible.

**Mixed feelings**

Common sense generally accepts the view that pleasure and pain may be present together, for in common talk we do speak of joyful sorrow or painful delight. The child may be seen to be weeping and laughing at the same time. Now in such states we do not have a mixture of pain and pleasure but only an alternation. Joy and sorrow succeeed each other in quick succession that we cannot distinguish between succession and co-existence. Pleasure and pain follow each other so rapidly that we think they are present together.

Again it is asked if at any time we are neither pleased nor displeased. Most of us are inclined to agree that there are moments when we feel indifferent, neither pleased nor displeased. At such moments the feeling tone is so low that we are not even aware of it. Feeling is always present though it is noticed only when it is more pronounced. Feelings do not obtrude unless they are very strong, if they were to do that they would hinder both knowledge and action. Secondly all activity even of the most passive sort involves attention and we do not attend unless we are interested, unless they affect us pleasantly or unpleasantly, until they make a difference to our feeling. Feeling is always present in our behaviour and experience.

## Development of feeling

Are there any likes or dislikes which are common to all men? Are there any objects or situations which everybody likes or dislikes? What feelings are inherited and inborn and what are the result of experience and training? Sweet taste, bright colours or harmonious tones seem to be liked by everybody as bitter taste, dull colours or discordant noise are disliked by everybody. We may say they are inborn and inherited. Again children and primitive people like loud bright colours like red and orange whereas adults usually prefer mild green, light blue or grey. The former are warm and the latter are soothing. Pain is usually disliked though in a relative way light pain may be pleasant. We like familiar scenes and young people always love what they know already, but we are often bored by many familiar things which surround us.

Then there are certain things which are widely disliked and we all feel annoyed with them like spitting in public, nagging, coughing loudly in one's face, bullying and similar vulgarities.

We also learn to take pleasure in some things and activities and to resent and dislike other things. Here the law of effect operates in learning. Whatever gives satisfactory results comes to please and whatever gives unsatisfactory results is disliked. One may like to flatter people because it pays dividends. Some feelings are social, our prejudices against certain races and in favour of others are social likes and dislikes. What foods, manner of eating and cooking and standards of conduct at dinner are approved and liked by Hindus may not be liked by other communities. So many of our likes and dislikes are acquired through social experiences.

**General nature of emotions**

Feelings of pleasantness and unpleasantness are associated with emotions of fear, anger, sorrow, joy, wonder. Like feelings emotions too are general reactions to our environment but they are more complex and specific and involve feelings. In fact the feeling-tone in emotions is very significant and it is possible to classify emotions as pleasant or unpleasant. Emotions are also more forceful than feelings, and stronger bodily changes are involved in them Let us analyse their character more fully, by enumerating their common features.

In the first place emotions have a wide range, they are found in all levels of behaviour. From the lowest animal to man it is the the same anger or fear that is foun A dog is angry when the bone is taken away as a man is angry when he is obstructed or misunderstood. Secondly emotions are capable of being excited by a wide variety of stimuli. They have no specific stimulus which alone can arouse them. Any kind of obstruction may cause anger as any kind of danger may arouse fear, but they are typical and there is a typical mode of behaviour which they arouse.

Thirdly emotions have a disturbing, even a paralysing effect on our behaviour. We know too well how anger gets the better of us and incapacitates us for effective action. Similar effect is felt in thinking also. A person in the throes of any emotion nnot think clearly or coolly. We speak of being "over whelmed", "engulfed" or "swept" by emotions. The difference between disliking and hating a person brings out the difference between feeling and emotion clearly.

Fourthly emotions excite vascular muscular apparatus which is connected with involuntary movements. That is why under the sway of emotions we act in a way which we ourselves in our quieter moments will find difficult to justify. How often in anger we utter words which we are later on ashamed of. We never meant them and still we uttered them.

Fifthly there are two sources of emotions. They may be aroused by definite perceptions or ideas, as when a good news excites joy or they may be internally aroused by organic changes such as those which result from the use of intoxicating drugs. It is too common a fact that a man's a temper changes with changes in his health.

Sixthly the occurrence of an emotion tends to leave behind it an emotional disposition or mood which makes the subject more sensible to certain emotions. A mood is a heightened tendency to feel a particular emotion. A man in angry mood frets at every object. It is because his emotional disposition tends to fasten on any object that presents itself.

Lastly all emotional experiences involve organic sensations. The excitement which accompanies anger, fear or joy is familiar to all of us. Some psychologists have emphasized this characteristic so much as to make it the basis of a theory of emotions. These we shall discuss in detail later.

An emotion is therefore a conscious experience arising in a specific kind of situation accompanied by disturbing bodily and mental changes of both internal and external variety.

**Bodily expression of emotions**

Emotional behaviour is largely an attempt by the organism to mobilize its resources to meet a situation. Bodily changes are an important part of all emotional behaviour. We may study such changes.

People ordinarily interpret emotions by *facial expression.* We often speak of people "looking" angry, afraid or happy and recognize these emotions in a person's face. Yet experiments show that we are often mistaken.

Several investigations with the help of photographs depicting emotions show that while certain major emotions may be correctly identified they also reveal an astounding disagreement in many cases. H. S. Langfield asked subjects to identify emotions portrayed in 105 photographs posed by an actor. The best subjects judged 58 per cent correctly, the worst 17 per cent. Correctness means agreement with the actor's intended emotion Langfield found that his subjects not only judged emotions wrongly, they were uncertain of their judgments, and were easily led astray by suggestion.

E.G. Boring and Titchner also showed that subjects are suggestible when judging facial expression. They prepared different expressions of the mouth, eyes, nose and brow that could be combined in various ways into different profiles. Practically all of the composite faces, when shown to subjects, were judged to portray actual emotional states, even when the parts, arbitrarily assembled, were inconsistent.

Knight Dunlap tried to study whether eyes or mouth express more emotion. He cut portrait photographs in half, crosswise, then combined the parts so that the eyes of a face expressing pain, for example, were put with the mouth of the same face showing pleasure. The general notion is that "eyes are the mirrors of the soul" but subjects were influenced more by the mouth than by the eyes.

A woman psychologist A. Feleky asked a hundred persons to identify emotions in 86 pictures, posed by an actress. Judgments varied. The highest agreement was 52 per cent. One picture was identified in 39 different ways. C. Landis photographed faces in real emotional situations. He shot off guns unexpectedly, gave electric shocks, showed bawdy pictures and the like and the pictures he took showed no characteristic facial expression for pain, surprise

or disgust. The only response common to many persons was a smile. The same subject showed similar expressions in various situations, and Landis concluded that no specific facial reaction characterizes a given emotional state. So we may conclude that facial expression, while it yields some knowledge of emotional conditions, is by no means a certain guide to the kind or degree of emotion being experienced.

Every one recognizes the role of *voice* in showing the presence or absence of emotions. We frequently judge about the emotional states of others by how they speak, the loudness of their voice and the like. In anger the pitch and intensity of voice rises and the pauses between phrases are shorter. By an investigation M. Sherman showed that in new born babies cries of pain, hunger, fear and anger cannot be distinguished. Fairbanks and Pronovost show that the emotions of contempt, anger, fear, grief, as presented by actors are more correctly identified from the voice in 66 to 88 per cent. trials. While vocal expression is more reliable than facial expression in revealing emotional expression the difficulties of relying solely on it are quite formidable.

Emotions make a difference to *bodily posture*. How the individual stands, sits or moves may often reveal his emotional state. Strong emotional experiences paralyse a person and he is unable to decide what he should do. In panic he runs, in anger he is in an attacking posture, in love he rushes to meet his dear ones. Emotions affect his entire body.

**Internal bodily or visceral changes in emotions**

Certain internal visceral changes also accompany emotional experiences. The first type of changes are of *respiration*. When we have emotions our breathing changes. Fiction writers often refer to people "gasping with amazement", "sighing with relief" or "catching breath in fear". Psychologists, however, try to measure the ratio between time taken for inspiration and for expiration with the help of a pneumograph. Usually it consists of an air-filled rubber tube strapped about the chest, with an outlet at one end connected to a recording needle. The needle, moving up and down as the subject breathes, records on smoked paper a wavy line showing inspiration and expiration. One psychologist found the ratio to be very low in laughter and very high in wonder or surprise, inspiration taking two or three times as long as expiration. With fear the ratio rose to 3 or 4 times.

*Changes in blood-pressure* are the best indicator of emotions. It is found that fear and surprise raise blood pressure by about 20 beats a minute. Hunger, fatigue and pain combined also raise blood pressure. W.M. Marston studied blood pressure of ten men and ten women in varying situations, and found that conversation with a new acquaintance of the opposite sex shot blood pressure up twice as much as did reading a story or a newspaper. Testifying before a jury shot up blood pressure ; the blood pressure changes were greater when the individual was telling lies before a jury than when he was telling the truth.

*Changes in digestive processes* are also produced by emotions. Meals eaten in a happy state of mind, laughing and joking, are digested sooner than meals taken in a mood of anger, fear or hatred. Many psychologists have reported that a family quarrel after dinner has made people develop digestive troubles and consequently sleepless night.

One of the most interesting of the many physiological changes which accompany emotional activity is the *psychogalvanic reflex*. It means change in the resistance of the skin to an electric current. By placing properly constructed electrodes on the surface of the body we can demonstrate that resistance of the skin to an electric current decreases during an emotion. With the help of a delicate galvanometer this change in electrical resistance is recorded and one may determine when an emotion is present and approximately how intense it is. It is not possible to discover what emotion is present but in spite of this limitation many interesting investigations have been made possible by this technique. C.G. Jung used the skin response to reveal personality complexes. He read off, one at a time, a list of words asking the subject to respond to each by giving the first word that came to mind. A galvanometer was applied to the subject's hand during the word association test. When a word aroused emotion, the instrument registered a higher current. Analysing the responses Jung could detect emotional tensions like love, guilt, inferiority feelings or thoughts of suicide.

Emotions bring about many changes in the working of the *glands*. They affect adrenal, tear, saliva and sweat glands which become very active. In moments of extreme tenderness people have tears in their eyes or perspire in anger ; in terror their mouth becomes dry. When the adrenal becomes very active it secretes more adrenin and sugar into the blood and the organism feels very strong. Many abnormal performances have been recorded of people overpowered by violent fear or anger.

*Hypothalamus* is regarded as the seat of emotions, their origin and control. If it is removed the person has no emotions. When the hypothalamus is excited messages are sent to the cerebral cortex and the entire autonomic nervous system becomes active. The hypothalamus is located in the mid-brain, but the activity of the cerebral cortex is involved in so far as any situation has to be perceived before an emotion is aroused ; often the association areas are aroused before an emotion is experienced.

**Lie-detector**

With an instrument recording blood pressure, pulse rate and breathing changes, Keeper and Larson tried to detect guilt in many legal cases. The subject is asked a number of questions, some unconnected with crime and some closely bearing on it, and his reactions are recorded. Almost always a guilty person shows greater upset than an innocent person at crucial questions. The subject is told that this instrument will find out the truth and this itself makes many confess. But there is always a possibility that an innocent person may get upset and may respond like a guilty person and be charged with the offence. However the lie-detector has given 80 per cent. accuracy in its findings, though its evidence is not admitted in a law court.

## James-Lange theory of emotions

William James, a leading American psychologist and Carl Lange a leading physiologist and psychologist of Copenhagen, put forward independently and at the same time, the theory that an emotion is the awarness of the bodily changes we have described above. It is difficult, they argued, to imagine a person angry without experiencing bodily changes. Could there be an emotion of fear, grief or tenderness without bodily changes? Assuming that it is not so they concluded that the awareness of the changes was the emotion. In the words of William James :—

"If we fancy some strong emotion and then try to abstract from our consciousness of it all the feelings of its bodily symptoms, we find we have nothing left behind, no "mind stuff" out of which the emotion can be constituted, and that a cold and neutral state of intellectual perception is all that remains . . . . what kind of an emotion of fear would be left if the feeling neither of quickened heart beats, nor of shallow breathing, neither of trembling lips nor of weakened limbs, neither of goose-flesh nor of visceral stirrings, were present it is quite impossible for me to think. Can one fancy the state of rage and picture no ebulition in the chest, no flushing in the face, no dilation of the nostrils, no clenching of the teeth, no impulse to vigorous action, but in their stead limp muscles, calm breathing, and a placid face? The present writer, for one, certainly cannot . . . . . Our natural way of thinking about these coarser emotions is that the mental perception of some fact excites the mental affection called the emotion, and that this latter state of mind gives rise to the bodily expression. My theory is that the *bodily changes follow directly the perception of the exciting fact, and that our feeling of the same changes is called the emotion.* Commonsense says that, we lose our fortune, are frightened and run; we are insulted by a rival, are angry and strike . . . . This order of sequence is incorrect, that the one mental state is not immediately induced by the other, that the bodily manifestations must first be interposed between, and that the more rational statement is that we feel sorry because we cry, angry because we strike, afraid because we tremble, and not that we cry, strike or tremble because we are sorry, angry or fearful, as the case may be."

His main argument may be analysed into two parts : (1) Emotion is nothing but the awareness of organic sensations, (2) Bodily expressions and organic disturbances which are said to be effects are really causes of emotions.

His argument in support of the first proposition is that if we take away bodily changes there is no emotion left. No doubt such a step will weaken emotions. We can destroy emotion by withdrawing attention from them but can we destroy bodily changes by withdrawing attention from them ? Even if it were so it would only prove that the two go together not that the two are identical. For the second it is enough to argue that organic changes may be artificially aroused without feeling any emotion as actors do. Sometimes an emotion disappears while bodily disturbances persist. Walking on the road I see a fierce dog and am awfully frightened. The organic changes and bodily disturbances expressive of the emotion of fear are aroused. But soon after I find that the dog is chained and can do no harm. I feel joy but the bodily changes of the emotion of fear still persist. If the emotion and the bodily expression are causally related or identical how is it that the latter persists even when the former has disappeared.

There is a considerable truth in the theory that bodily changes are an important part of our emotional behaviour and experience. If we behave in a kindly manner we do feel kindliness, trying to be a little critical how often do we fly into rage, irritation leading to more irritation, and whistling in dark does boost our courage. So bodily changes are important in emotional experiences but several lines of argument can show that there is more to emotion than merely our awareness of bodily changes. Many actors feel no emotion at all when they portray emotions on the stage. And what is more differences in organic changes do not seem to be sufficient to account for differences in emotional experiences. Fear and anger, for example, are radically different and yet the bodily changes accompanying them are very similar. It is very difficult to explain the large variety of higher and lower emotions from the simple bodily movements or organic changes.

By cutting the spinal cord of a dog physiologists have demonstrated that an animal may continue to show emotional responses even though it is deprived of sensations from the organs of the body. The experiment seems to prove that the awareness of organic changes is not essential for an emotional response. However it may be contended that all bodily changes have not been eliminated.

Finally adrenalin injected into the blood stream will induce the various organic changes characteristic of emotional excitement without any emotional experience on the part of the individual. He feels tense and agitated but the emotion is not experienced. Again there are bodily changes which it is difficult to classify emotionally, laughter may be due to joy or sorrow.

With all the arguments against James-Lange theory of emotions it cannot be denied that it has served to highlight an important truth, that the bodily changes and organic excitement is an essential part of emotional experiences, but it mistook a part of the truth for the whole truth. Emotions are more than these changes, they involve an impulse to act and the anticipation of a value which may be gained or lost.

**Hypothalamic theory of emotions**

Cannon and Bard traced the origin of emotions to the hypothalamus which is located in the mid-brain. Their theory is that both emotional experiences and emotional behaviour and bodily changes arise independently through excitations in the hypothalamus. Perception of any situation sends messages to the brain but before they enter the cerebral cortex they pass through the hypothalamus. The excitation of the hypothalamus leads to impulses one of which goes to the brain and the other to visceral organs and muscles. Impulses going to the brain produce emotions and impulses to visceral organs and muscles produce organic and bodily changes.

Cannon also held that strong emotions prepare the organism for an emergency. It is a sort of defensive preparation for a dangerous situation. Such a view held good in olden days but modern civilized living has no place for violent emotions and strenuous physical effort. We are often angry but we are not compelled to fight nor obliged to run when in panic.

Experimental investigations demonstrate that there is much truth in the hypothalamus theory. The important fact is that there can be no emotion unless there is a perception of the situation and this can be done only by the cerebral cortex.

### Development of emotions

The emotional behaviour of a newborn infant is simple. The baby is calm, contented or active, and when distressed it is tense, red-skinned, flourishing arms and legs, crying or twitching facial muscles. This is a mass excitement in which distinct emotions are not present and there are no specific responses to stimuli. Observation of infants shows that occasionally they are intensely aroused or stirred, their entire being flares up and they express their feelings openly and loudly. It is difficult to say what their specific emotions are and distinct and separate patterns of emotional expression such as fear, anger or joy are not yet formed. With maturation this condition changes rapidly and soon it is possible to distinguish between emotional responses expressing fear or anger. A number of studies have been made of emotional responses of infants but the most prominent is that of J. B. Watson who points out that there are three innate emotions, anger, fear and love, and they are aroused by restraint, lack of support and striking of the skin respectively.

Now it is generally recognized that early emotional experiences are very significant and largely influence the pattern of adult personality. The psychoanalysts believe that early emotional shocks handicap an individual for the rest of his life. Infancy and early childhood is the most formative period of life and emotional experiences have an enduring effect for the simple reason that they are the first to occur.

It is difficult to say what changes come about in the emotional experiences of an individual with age but broadly with maturation and growth two types of changes occur in emotional experiences, changes in conditions which excite or arouse the child's emotions and changes in emotional responses or the manner in which he expresses his emotions. With growth in abilities, interests and understanding the individual is able to respond to a wider range of objects and situations and see finer shades of differences and his emotional reactions not only become more varied but also more numerous. Needs grow in number and complexity and so do emotional responses. Secondly changes take place in the expression of emotions. In infancy the entire body shakes with emotions, legs and arms are flourished, the body becomes red and the entire organism is affected. But in course of time these expressions are limited. Children do not cry but place their hands on their eyes or make grimaces or say surly things. As they grow up socio-cultural influences restrict their emotional expressions. Society and culture look down upon unreserved expression of emotions and they have to abide by social standards of emotional expression. Highly cultured people do not betray their emotions and the concealment of emotions is considered a sign of both culture and maturity. Self-control is enjoined and expected.

**Significance of emotions**

Emotions are described as the prime movers of behaviour, these stirred-up states are storehouses of energy which may work for both intense vigour and efficiency and strong disruption of mental life. Very often the story of a successful man is the story of effective and satisfactory emotional adjustments as that of an unsuccessful man is of gross mismanagement. Some very highly intelligent people fail because of their raw and disorganized emotions and some people of mediocre brains are able to get along because they are able to manage their emotions effectively and harmoniously.

Emotions are funds of energy and prepare the organism for some emergency. The several organic and bodily changes have a purpose that they make the organism ready to meet the challenge of new situations. In the grip of strong emotions people have performed Herculean tasks which under normal conditions they could not handle. But modern civilized living does not need such energy-releasing aspects of emotions, and too much emotion and violent expression and behaviour may land us in trouble. Emotional gestures in anger, fear or love make for better adjustment in social situations. Angry sniffs help to intimidate, smiles help to ingratiate and the like.

Emotional excitement stimulates both bodily and mental activity. The individual begins to think more rapidly and of other ways of meeting the situation. But though emotions stimulate the quantity of thinking they do not improve the quality of thinking. Emotions do not make thinking more trustworthy nor do they help better understanding which is the result of intelligent and logical approach to a situation. Emotions have a great value in liberating us from inhibitions. A slow and quiet person when roused to anger may act very energetically and quickly. That is why modern education insists on developing and expressing emotions rather than checking and controlling them.

But emotions may be a great obstacle and handicap to adjustment. In the grip of emotions many adults behave like children, they break down and childish ways reappear. Emotions smother intelligence and confuse our understanding, they weaken our skill and obstruct close co-ordination between different parts and functions of the body. Sometimes intense organic changes instead of giving energy paralyse the organism for any activity. Many people become powerless to act in the grip of fear and anger. Many emotional responses last much longer and continue to thwart us for the rest of our lives. Many grown-up people are not able to get over their dread of the headmaster acquired in schooldays. Our phobias and fears, loves and hates continue in life and hamper adjustments. Emotional tension may impair the efficiency of an individual in his studies or occupation. Much of un-social or immoral behaviour is due to violent emotions. Anger, hatred, sex passion and the like are responsible for much crime in society. Although man is described as a rational being most of his behaviour is due to strong feelings and emotions which are able to suppress reason and understanding.

Emotions are a great asset but may be used to advantage or disadvantage according as the individual is able to manage them effectively.

### Some major emotions

We may briefly discuss some of our major emotions like fear, anger, wonder or joy.

*Fear.* J.B. Watson studied a large number of infants and found that originally they are afraid of only two things, loud sounds and lack of support. All other fears are learned and acquired in the course of experience. An infant's pillow falls and he is frightened. If he is in a dark room the fear will be transferred to darkness, if he is alone fear will be transferred to loneliness. Loud sounds made when there is a cat or dog nearby makes the child fear cats or dogs. Most of our fears are acquired in this way, and from cats and dogs children begin to fear all furry animals like rats, rabbits. People are afraid of high places, snakes, lightening, of ridicule, disgrace and insults, of financial loss and failure. All these fears they have learned in the social and cultural environment in which they live.

Fear responses are marked by withdrawal and shrinking. Children may take to flight and adults may withdraw in fear. Children run and hide themselves when they see a bear, a policeman or a dog. A grown-up person may avoid attending a function or a party if he or she fears that people will not accept him or her or will laugh or poke fun at him or her. Fear of failure in examination or profession may make a person turn away from it.

*Anger* is caused by any type of obstruction, restraint or injury, and the person moves to strike or injure the source of that obstruction. Children get angry when parents interfere with their activity or force them to do things which they do not like. For many of them anger pays and by becoming angry they are able to make their parents agree to their demands. Grown-up young people get angry when they are teased, ridiculed, punished or unfavourably compared, and instead of hitting back they may criticize parents and teachers, disobey them or develop a hostile attitude to all authority. They may nurse a grudge and take revenge in other ways. Some students neglect work because of resentment against teachers or the institution. Some become sulky, quarrelsome and negative. Grown-up people may express their anger with their family because they cannot do it in the office. Such displaced anger is common in the lives of all of us.

*Wonder* is excited by anything new, strange or unusual and the individual is impelled to know more about it, to explore and discover its nature. Children break things to find out what is inside, older children ask questions to discover and explore things. Older people have goals and purposes which lead them to acquire more knowledge and when their interest and curiosity about nature weakens they are unduly curious about the personal affairs of others.

*Joy* is an undifferentiated emotion and we all seek pleasure, excitement and happiness without having any precise idea of what we want. Children seek pleasure in activity itself and indulge in all kinds of play just for the fun of being active. In older people laughter may be excited by a large variety of situations from the bizarre to funny. We try to prolong our delightful moments. Some pleasure may result from vigorous activity and some pleasure accompanies a state of relaxation and rest. Mountain-climbing gives us pleasure and so does just reclining and dozing off after lunch.

**Mood**

Mood is a long drawn out emotion. It is a temporary emotional set. We experience some strong emotion and its after-effects endure even after the emotion has passed. Mood is always of the recent emotional experience or organic states. We speak of angry, despondent or confident mood. A series of successful experiences give us a mood of confidence while a series of defeats make us despondent. In a joyful mood we are inclined to be generous and forgiving. Some moods are due to organic states, anxiety and depression may result from digestive disorders.

Some psychologists hold that moods change in cycles, but if these changes in mood are too rapid it is a case for the physician and the psychiatrist. Modern life moves fast and there is hectic and busy activity throughout the day. Such a pattern of life breeds nervous ailments in which moods alternate quickly.

Moods affect our behaviour, efficiency and endurance. They make us extremely sensitive to certain stimuli and the pattern of work also changes with a change in mood.

**Sentiments**

Sentiments too are powerful sources of energy. They are organizations of interests around a common centre. They are much more complex than attitudes and they have an emotional core. Shand describes them as emotional dispositions. A person who has a strong sentiment for his family is engaged for most part of his life in promoting the welfare and happiness of members of his family. He enjoys their company most, he spends much of his time with them and his efforts and goals are centred round them. A man in love is engrossed fully with his companions, all his interests and wishes, hopes and ambitions, his activities and efforts revolve round her happiness and welfare. She is the centre of his life and striving. For him every event is related to his central need which is the important sentiment in his life. As sentiments are based on emotions and needs they energize behaviour in a powerful manner. They also distinguish one individual from another and are important constituents of total personality. They sustain man's life and activity through emotions and goals which form their core. Anger is short-lived but the sentiment of hatred endures in life and colours the personality of the individual. Sentiments are more enduring than emotions, more complex and more stable. It is because they include the individual's values which are so intimate and close to him and which pervade his life and behaviour.

**Complexes**

Complexes are groups of related interests and activities centred around an emotional core. A complex may be beneficial or harmful to the total personality. A research scholar may have his knowledge and interests organized around his subject so much so that he may be said to be in love with his research. Wherever he is and whatever he does he is obsessed with his study and research. All his other interests are influenced by his dominant activity and concentrates his effort and attention in a direction which promotes this study. This is a beneficial complex. But he may be dominated by inferiority complex and may be thinking all the time that he is not acceptable to others. Whatever he does betrays his inferiority and he is obsessed by the feeling that he is inferior to others. His life becomes miserable and he is not able to do full justice to his ability. In fact the term complex was first used in this harmful sense, for those organized groups of ideas which are injurious to the individual. Our behaviour and thinking must be understood in terms of our complexes also. Emotions also colour our complexes.

## Questions

1. Distinguish between feeling and emotion. Can we feel pleased and displeased at the same time? Are there mixed feelings?
2. Distinguish between sensation and affection or feeling? How do you estimate the feeling-tone?
3. Discuss the general nature of emotion. What are its chief characteristics? Describe some of the important bodily and organic changes accompanying emotions.
4. Discuss some of the problems of bodily expression of emotions, and enumerate some of the important organic changes in emotional experience.

   Explain :—Lie-detector, psychogalvanic reflex, mood, sentiment, complex.

6. Discuss critically the James-Lange theory of emotions.
7. What is the emergency theory of emotions? Discuss the hypothalamus theory of emotions.

8. What is the significance of emotions in life and adjustment? Illustrate your answer with examples from life.

9. What are the major emotions, in what situations do they arise and what are their bodily expressions? Discuss the development of emotions.

10. People say we run because we are afraid but the correct thing to say is that we fear because we run. Discuss critically the underlying theory.

# CHAPTER XII

# THINKING AND REASONING

Man is commonly described as a rational being and his rationality consists of his ability to think and reason. His superiority over other animals in learning and adjustment lies in his capacity to make adjustments to his environment and solve his problems on the strength of thinking. The great civilization he has built up in the course of history is the product of thinking in clear and bold ways. Thinking and reasoning is a very complex human activity of wide range and value and affects all types of human endeavour. What is the nature of thinking? How does it differ from remembering and imagining? How are thought and language related? What is reasoning? How can thought and reasoning be stimulated? What is the nature of creative thinking? These are some of the problems which will be dealt with in this chapter.

## The nature of thinking

Every living being is for ever seeking to satisfy its wants—wants for air, food, shelter and the like. Human beings in addition, want knowledge, education, new experiences, clothes of a certain cut, wealth, security. Some wants are easily satisfied and some can be satisfied after a long and hard struggle. It is these wants, possible but difficult, which pose a challenge to the individual and oblige him to think and reason. People think and reason to overcome a difficulty, to meet the challenge of a new situation and to solve a difficult problem, for difficulties, new situations and problems interfere with and obstruct the satisfaction wants. We think and reason to facilitate adjustments to a new situation, to remove an obstacle in the satisfaction of wants and goals.

In a broad sense thinking includes all processes of gaining information and knowledge, that is, perception, memory, imagination and conception. But in a narrower sense it means either imagination or reasoning. Imagination may be described as *mental manipulation* while reasoning is *mental exploration.* In imagination facts previously observed are recalled and these images are combined and manipulated into new patterns. In reasoning we mentally explore new relations actually existing between these facts. Both are independent of the present and seek to meet a possible situation in the future. In actual experience it may be difficult to separate the two but when we think without images or mental pictures and in terms of words alone, the activity is described as pure thinking. But both lead to the solution of problems we anticipate. In imagination there may be a number of possible solutions, but in reasoning there is just one solution that is to be found and which is considered quite adequate.

Thinking is a type of behaviour which is aroused by a stimulus present or absent and satisfying an immediate or remote practical need. Thinking takes place to adjust the individual to the needs of a new situation. It is often described as adjustment to a hypothetical situation. In a difficult situation an animal tries one way or another to solve it but man sits down and thinks. He goes over in thought the various possibilities of action, tries them out in imagination and selects one for action. Thinking is a delayed response in which an absent or future situation is responded to.

In all forms of thinking the items within the stream of consciousness are connected by some sort of associations but man does not go by those associations alone. He selects items and re-organizes them to suit his problem. Whatever ideas bear on the issue in hand are selected and association is controlled. The problem is analysed and the items are grouped into new wholes.

Thus thinking is a mental activity which arises to solve a problem in which perception, memory and imagination, and ideas, symbols, images and signs are used, there is some mental trial-and-error, and sometimes some parts of the body like the tongue, fingers, throat and the like also become active.

## Problem-solving

Human problems are complex and need continued thinking based on interest, ability and experience. He is able to recall and recreate the past, extend his thought and knowledge beyond the limits of space and time, and plan and foretell what is going to happen. With the help of language he is able to foresee problems long before they confront him, to weigh alternate solutions and their consequences; to inherit the accumulated wisdom of the past and apply it to fresh problems and situations. Language is the vehicle of thinking and through it thought is communicated, defined, made more determinate and clear, and held together in a system. With the help of language thought is communicated through speech or writing, it may be repeated to oneself, and what we call judgment or the relation of concepts is the use of sentences. Through the use of sentence language we are able to turn over in our minds various alternate solutions of our problems, to weigh their advantages and disadvantages, to assess their consequences and to select those that look favourable.

Human problems are difficult and of large variety, some arising from individual needs others arising from social, economic, political and academic needs. National problems and scientific difficulties are no less important, and the first need at all levels is that such problems should be clearly defined and their scope fully understood. We may raise difficulties and ask questions but we must know what our urgent problem is and should express it in accurate terms.

The second step is to collect data, information and knowledge about how other people have solved their problems in the same sphere. Our own experience as well as the experience of others must be pooled to find out what relevant material is available.

The third step is to frame a hypothesis or a provisional solution. After considering the various alternate solutions one may be accepted as more plausible for further investigation and verification.

The fourth step is the testing of that hypothesis, judging and evaluating it, to see if it can explain all the facts and meet the needs of the situation, what consequences follow from this hypothesis and how do they agree with facts already known.

Finally if the hypothesis is found valid, it is accepted as a true explanation or solution of the problem. This is the final verification of the provisional solution and it becomes a general law. Usually in everyday life thinking or problem-solving does not follow these detailed steps. Human ingenuity may skip some steps but in general this is the main procedure.

Problem-solving may be done by the individual or co-operatively by groups. But groups should be controlled and small.

**Thought and Language**

Some psychologists hold that there is no difference between thought and language and the two are identical. Talking and thinking are the same, thinking is self-talking, it is sub-vocal speech. J. B. Watson, the behaviourist, says that in thinking the individual is talking to himself. Children talk to themselves loudly when they are trying to solve a problem. Adults do not do this because of social restraint but they too start whispering to themselves. On this Watson argues that thinking is self-talking.

But other psychologists argue that deaf people who cannot use language are able to think. They cannot speak and if thinking is self-talking they should not be able to think. But they give evidence of thinking. Patients suffering from aphasia lose the power of speech and their vocal organs do not function. If thinking is self-talking there should be no thinking in them but they give evidence of thought. Woodworth holds that though the connection between thought and language is very intimate the two are different. We often think of things but are not able to express our thoughts which shows that thinking goes on independently of language. Some psychologists hold that it is possible to think without images also. This too supports the view that language and thought are not one.

Some psychologists point out that in thinking muscles of lips, tongue, fingers also become active. Thinking therefore cannot be identified with inner speech.

## Conception

An important element in the process of thinking is formation of concepts. We not only retain mental pictures of objects and experiences but on their basis form general ideas denoting classes of objects. These general ideas are called *concepts*. After seeing a number of people, beggars, policemen, father, brothers, mother and sisters a child is able to say that they are all men, he has formed a general idea of "man" by mentally putting together characteristics in which all his mental pictures of men agree. This is the concept of man. The several words we use "station", "car", "fruit" and the like are all groups of qualities which are common to all stations, cars and fruits. A concept is a system of meaning.

The basis of concepts is sensory experience. The several sensory experiences or perceptions are compared, their common qualities are abstracted and a general idea which does not correspond to any one object but is the cumulative effect of many is formed. Concepts are the result of comparison, relation, abstraction and generalization. Since they ultimately depend on experience, the wider the experience the richer the concepts. A boy's conception of a soldier is very meagre, probably he has seen only an infantryman, later he sees a cavalryman, an artilleryman, an airforce man or a foreign soldier, and comes to know that in spite of differences they are all soldiers. Later he may see pictures of soldiers from many lands or from different periods of history. His general idea of a soldier becomes fuller and richer. It does not correspond to any one type of soldier but applies in a general way to all types of soldiers. This process is conception or concept formation.

It is obvious that concepts help to organize our experience into general heads and thus make for mental economy. We can think of many in one, and separate isolated experiences and facts are combined and retained under general heads. It is easier and more economical to use general ideas than individual objects. It is through the help of concepts that we can have abstract thought and reasoning and there is a system of general knowledge which we call science and which is applicable to all objects of a class, past, present and future. Though we have experience of only past events and objects, yet on its basis through the formation of concepts we are able to form ideas about those objects of that class which we are going to experience in future. The essential qualities of objects of that class are grouped together and summed up in concepts.

Concepts are formed with a purpose, an end in view. They are tools of thinking and because different individuals may have different purposes, the meaning of concepts differs from individual to individual. They involve essential qualities of objects and what is essential will depend on the purposes of an individual, what is essential from one point of view may not be so from another. Thus the selction of essential qualities will vary. Not only do concepts of general abstract things like honesty, wealth, virtue or duty vary from one individual to another but even concepts of concrete things like wood, book, food may vary. For example paper may mean different things to a student, examiner, booksellers or minister.

Concepts may be of objects, relations or qualities. House, book or pen are concepts of concrete things, honesty, obedience, sincerity are concepts of qualities, and higher, smaller or lower are concepts of relations. Too often young people acquire concepts through the use of language but have no experience of things they represent. When the charge of bookishness is made against present-day education all that is meant is that young people are taught concepts through words but have no real knowledge of actual things based on first hand experience. Words are important and useful, with their help we can fix ideas in our attention, and they help to make our thought clear and precise, but they are a poor substitute for things and events as presented in everyday experience.

## Judgment

To judge is to discover the relation between two ideas. "The train has come", "Crime does not pay" or "We need friends" are examples of judgment. The ideas related may be concrete or abstract and we decide about the relation by what we experience or perceive. Conception and judgment involve each other for in forming concepts we compare concrete things and comparison involves judgment. Most often judgments are not expressed but only understood. In comparing different kinds of soldiers the child does reach some relationship between qualities and types of soldiers. He does judge. On the other hand judgment involves conception. When ideas are related to other ideas, such ideas grow richer, more accurate and more definite. Fresh qualities and relations are recognized and new meanings are added. Making new judgments about war, education, food shortage does make our ideas about them richer and fuller.

Some judgments are made spontaneously and immediately as for example *the sun is very hot, this dog is not mad.* Some judgments are called intuitive. No effort of thought is involved. But some judgments are made after careful deliberation as *quarrelling does not do anybody any good, A morning walk is good for health.*

Judgments enter into every aspect of mental life. We are making judgments throughout our waking life and judging correctly is an asset in life. Correct judgments make a man confident, self-reliant and intellectually independent. But judgments often go wrong unintentionally. We may be honestly mistaken. Lack of experience, thoughtlessness, emotional prejudices like jealousy and the mental habit of depending on others may prevent us from making correct judgments for ourselves. Judge for yourself is a very helpful advice. Independent judgment is a sign of independent character.

**Reasoning**

Reasoning is the mental activity used in an argument, proof or demonstration. It consists in making a new judgment on the basis of judgment or judgments already formed and is commonly defined as perceiving relations among judgments or seeing agreement or disagreement among judgments already made. Reasoning is generally associated with rules and methods, formal laws of logic, but many people reason and argue without being consciously aware of it. When a dog comes back after seeing the master enter his car, when we expect a letter from a friend or turn to the gate on hearing a noise we are thinking and reasoning without realizing it.

Reasoning is a way of solving a problem or meeting a new situation. We have already described in detail the processes involved in problem-solving. Let us here take an example. The father on reaching home finds the servant missing. He is unable to account for his behaviour. The servant may have gone to the market, he may have fallen ill or he may have run away. This is the problem which he analyses carefully. He inquires from other members of the family if he has been sent to the market. Nobody has sent him out. He goes to his room and he is not there. Perhaps he has run away. If so he must have taken away his things or taken away some money. This hypothesis he proceeds to test. Going to his room he finds that his things have been removed. Later he may find money from his pocket missing. He concludes that the servant has run away. This final judgment has been reached through a careful analysis of facts.

Perception, imagination and memory are closely related to reasoning for they help in assessing the situation and finding out alternate solutions of the problem. Reasoning is not merely guessing for in guessing we do not have sufficient evidence. When we reason we are sure that we have enough material to reach a valid conclusion.

All reasoning involves two movements: one from particular facts observed to a generalization, hypothesis or theory, the other from generalization to particular consequences. When a universal judgment is arrived at on the basis of particular facts, the method of reasoning is called inductive, and when we start with a general truth and start applying it to particular instances, the method of reasoing is deductive. If after a number of particular experiences of taking food late at night I find that I have sleepless nights, I may draw the general conclusion that late dinners cause sleeplessness. This would be an inductive approach. But if I start with the general truth that heavy stomach causes loss of sleep and then proceed to apply it to my concrete experiences the approach is deductive.

The modern age is an age of science, numerous research workers have observed things in various fields, discovered some common elements in them, framed a hypothesis about their possible cause and verifying that hypothesis reached a general law as to how those things will behave and operate in future. Science proceeds inductively and reaches general laws on the observation of particular facts. But some people just borrow wisdom and knowledge from others and proceed to apply and demonstrate it by employing it on their own specific experiences. This is making use of the deductive method of reasoning. In actual practice these two methods are used together, we may apply the one or the other, and they are two aspects of the process of reasoning. In many attempts at problem-solving we may use both.

Though we have analysed reasoning and indicated its several steps, processes and methods, most people do not analyse their reasoning, have no knowledge of the several steps or processes involved and resent other people analysing their reasoning. They either jump at conclusions or reason unconsciously.

## The value and importance of reasoning

Reasoning is a valuable mental activity and in the solution of problems it is far superior to the method of trial and error. In the latter the material must be present but in the former the material need not be present. The administrator sitting in the capital can find out by reasoning the social changes that would come about by any legislation, the engineer can plan roads and canals without having to visit the actual places, the educationists can choose programmes and methods before putting them into practice; all this is done through reasoning. Reasoning solves problems by using the experience of others.

Reasoning has contributed largely to our cultural progress. Scientists and philosophers have liberated us from blind superstition, disease and ignorance, helped us to combat pain and suffering, given us machines of all kinds for large scale production of consumer goods by the use of reasoning. Our understanding of vital socia economic and political problems of today is largely dependent upon reasoning, and mankind's struggle against poverty, ignorance and disease, against war, racial prejudices and cruelty is being carried on through powerful reasoning.

Reasoning is a powerful source of individual efficiency and well-being. It is through reasoning that the individual is able to rise above the life of impulse and raw emotion, to foresee the effects of his course of action and to plan his conduct for personal and social benefit. But reasoning may also be a hindrance. There are people who go on reasoning without taking a single step toward the solution of their problems. They are obsessed and reason about everything thus lowering their efficiency and taking shelter in gross indecision. There are gems of wisdom inherited from our past and it is reasonable to accept them on faith. To reason about them is waste of time and energy.

What one reasons about and how much he reasons about it is a clue to his intelligence and personality. Individuals with superior intelligence create system out of chaos through reasoning and make problems and difficulties more intelligible and clear. Again some people are able to harness their reasoning to the service of values and ends we all cherish and to the promotion of interests which affect the well-being of a large number of people.

## Personality traits and reasoning

There are some qualities of character or traits of personality which promote reasoning. The foremost of them is self-reliance. A good reasoner is one who has a spirit of adventure and is prepared to try out new solutions of problems, He must not seek to run away from his difficulties and obstacles but meet them half way. This self-reliance should be supplemented by a steady nature in which violent emotions and passions of anger and fear have no place. He should not fall a victim to strong and uncontrollable feelings. Thirdly he should be free from prejudices. An open mind ready to follow a course which seems reasonable will reason out all possible solutions and follow the best. Exchange of ideas and frank discussion of issues will help reasoning. Fourthly he should have a reflective and critical approach to all issues and problems. Not that he should be given to too much thinking and deliberation but he should try to go deep into the question and assess things at their face value. For this he needs another very important quality, that is, active imagination. To guess how a problem can be solved and to anticipate its consequences requires a fertile imagination which may draw upon our own knowledge and experience and judge the merits of different solutions or courses of action.

## Creative thinking

Our civilization owes its richness and fullness to the dazzling progress made by scientific discoveries and inventions, by technology in industy and communication. Science is for ever discovering new relations and new solutions to problems, industry is devising new ways and methods of doing and producing things. Space and time have been conquered to an extent hardly ever anticipated by man. Literature, art and music are for ever exploring new fields for human enjoyment. The complex but glorious edifice of civilization is a testimony to the original and creative thinking of man.

Naturally, therefore, people endowed with the ability for creative thinking in any field of human endeavour are highly respected. Creative thinking in the sciences, in human relations, in industry, and in the arts is generally considered to be the highest form of mental activity for it is due to such new ideas, fresh insights and original creations that the human race has been able to record gains in history. Creative thinking also helps the individual to achieve a sense of personal dignity and esteem. It has, therefore, both social and personal advantages.

For too long people held that creative thinking is something rare and exceptional and is found only in a few favoured individuals. Recent researches and investigations have shown that it is a common characteristic found in greater or lesser degree in all individuals. It is associated with problem-solving and critical thinking. People who do creative thinking pass through essentially the same type of processes as are involved in reasoning or problem-solving with the possible difference that they break away from the old ways of thinking and reject systems of thought which were firmly established. The stress is on the new and different, the methods and ways are different and new. Some believe that creative thinking is involved in all types of problem-solving. The solution is new to the individual himself even though others do not accept it as original or creative. When a high school boy is called upon to write an essay on imaginary flight in an aeroplane his effort and achievement is creative even though by what has already been written his product may not be considered original and creative. Thus our approach to creativity or creative thinking has undergone a radical change. In the past people held that either a person is capable of creative thinking or he is not. Today modern psychology holds that everybody is capable of creative thinking, only some are more capable. When a child learns a new thing or improves upon what he has already learned he is taking part in creative behaviour and thinking.

Older psychology studies creative thinking by analysing the biographies of the accepted creative thinkers and their introspective statements they made about their effort and work. How they worked, what were their methods and habits, under what conditions they did their work and the like were described in detail, and in such descriptions terms like imagination, insight, inspiration and flashes of intuition were freely used. But modern psychology believes that everybody is capable of creative thinking and all that psychology is called upon to do is to analyse the process and indicate the several steps involved in it. The several processes involved in problem-solving are employed more meaningfully.

Let us outline the important processes involved in creative thinking. Generally stress is laid on four such processes as preparation, incubation, illumination and verification and these we shlall describe here in detail.

*Preparation* is the first stage in creative thinking in which the individual just collects facts and other relevant material bearing on the topic under investigation or problem under study. He may have to make a detailed study of what others have thought and written about it, what other evidence is at hand and what background material will be needed. He may have to discuss the problem with others who know or have experience about it or see other works in the same field and in the same direction. This means that the individual will need considerable patience and perseverance, and hardwork and application. That is why it is insisted that people do not succeed overnight and that there are no short-cuts to really great achievement in any area of human endeavour. Preparation means study and experience, hard work and application, intensive concentration of attention on the subject and work. An engineer can do creative thinking only in engineering as a doctor can do in medicine. A poet cannot do any creative thinking in engineering, for he lacks the preparatory adjustments necessary to achieve worthwhile success in that area of work. The first stage of preparation in creative thinking is really a stage of orientation and adjustment to the problem in hand. Research students call this stage as that of fact-finding and fact-collection. In several cases this stage takes much longer time and involves much greater work than any other stage. Preparation in research is really half the battle.

*Incubation* is the second stage. Here the individual after mastering all the knowledge and information and obtaining all the experience that is needed digests the problem in all its bearings and associations and his further effort at thinking things out is blocked. He has now to lie low, put aside his work and wait for the inspiration. He may have to just relax and forget about his work. The work is not really forgotten and thinking goes on at the unconscious level. He may often be indulging in daydreams. This is not anything uncommon. When we are unable to recall a name we turn it away and sooner than later the name turns up of its own. We often say that the name is on the tip of our tongue but we are unable to catch it. In sheer despair we give up the effort and get ourselves absorbed in some other work and then suddenly the name flashes across our mind. Daydreaming lets the mind go. While the mind is active it also relaxes a lot, discards old modes of thinking and reorganizes old material into new patterns or systems. Haste, impatience and tension are fatal to creative thinking.

In the third stage of *illumination* or *inspiration*, he begins t see light and there is sudden illumination about the possible soluti of the problem in hand. Illumination means insight when n ideas and suggestions, new solutions and inspirations flash acro our minds and make for new understanding. In this stage tl inspiration is sudden, the individual feels pleased that the long drawn period of incubation is going to end and the long awaited solution is in sight. The poet may have written a few lines and his further progress may have been blocked. He fumbles and lets the mind go. Then suddenly more ideas occur and the chain of thought appears in its complete form, he is extremely happy and now he has hope of completing his poem. What he was groping for is at hand.

The bright idea which flashes across our mind must be tested and applied so that it does not contradict known facts. This is *verification*. In scientific research the student has to see that the new idea works and is in harmony with facts already known, that its consequences are acceptable and fit in with our previous arrangement and that there is no contradiction between the new theory and the old theories which are accepted as true. This means that new ideas must be fully amplified and critically appraised, it may involve some trial-and-error examination before the new bright idea is accepted as workable.

**Conditions which stimulate thinking**

We have already dealt with such traits of personality which are helpful to thinking and now we may enumerate environmental conditions which are conducive to thinking. In a stimulating environment the individual is always confronted with problems, challenges and difficulties which he must solve, meet and overcome, there is a growing sense of mastery over our environment and the individual is encouraged to reflect and make changes in his environment to suit his needs, goals and purposes. Let us deal with conditions which will stimulate such an approach.

By far the most important thing favouring thinking is *social change*. In communities where everything continues in the same manner, where there is no growth and development, and where novelty and change are frowned upon there is little to think about. In extremely conservative and orthodox communities people follow courses and patterns of behaviour laid down by their ancestors. But in a rapidly changing society as is the case with present-day India we must chalk out new paths, take new steps to meet new situations, evolve new policies and programmes, solve problems which continue to rise and multiply. We have no option but to think, to apply our mind and intelligence to new tasks. Problems of production, security, defence, distribution of goods and the like are compelling us to think.

*Socical contacts* also oblige us to think. Meeting new people and living in new situations, going abroad and having experience of things, people and ways of behaviour different from our own make us compare and assess what is better, and we are compelled to think and reflect. There is a clash, often there is disagreement, and we have to make up our mind about certain issues and problems. How others are doing it compels us either to agree with them or to disagree and frame our own ways of doing and thinking. Social contacts also oblige us to express our thoughts and this makes them more explicit and definite.

Contacts with other cultures, travel abroad or receiving foreigners in our own country and home, is sure to make us think and deliberate about our modes of behaviour and living.

In the development of thought *language* is a necessary adjunct. Without language it is difficult to fix attention on our thoughts to communicate our thoughts to others and to organize them into a system. It is a commonplace to say that language makes our thoughts clear, definite and precise. When we express in words what we have in mind, it becomes more definite. Mastery of language indicates how rich and clear any individual's thinking is. Thought and language help each other and grow hand in hand. People deficient in the command of language may not be very clear and efficient thinkers.

Lastly modern world and life is full of stress and strain, we live [illegible] of anxiety and something is always being missed or upset as times are moving very fast. This stimulates thinking as nothing else does. We have to think and subject all our practices to clear logical analysis and to be guided by reason.

## Theories of thinking

Thinkers are not agreed as to what happens when we think. In explaining the manner and origin of thinking they have put forward several theories which we may discuss here. We have already referred to some of them but a more detailed treatment is called for.

We have already referred to J.B. Watson's view that introspective analysis of thinking is useless and that thought is nothing but talking to ourselves. It occurs mostly as a sub-vocal speech, that is, as imperceptible movements of the muscles of the tongue, throat and larynx. In support of this theory Watson cites the case of children who think out loud a process which is discouraged by social pressure, so that the child is compelled to think with closed lips. Watson holds that thinking might go on in terms of any muscle action. He cites deaf and dumb individuals who think just as they talk in terms of hand movements.

Psychologists in general do not accept Watson's views. Experiments have failed to show any correlation between thinking and movement of vocal muscles. There are other objections too. Woodworth argues that words sometimes cannot be found to express a meaning which is very clearly in mind. Or again a well-known poem can be recited while one thinks of things entirely different. Finally, objects Woodworth, thinking involves something new, the seeing of relationships; it is hard to account for this solely on the basis of muscular activity.

These days psychologists generally speak of two theories of thinking—the "central theory" and the "motor theory". According to the central theory thinking and reasoning depend on brain processes alone. But followers of the motor theory like Watson argue that thinking is a function, very largely at least, of muscular responses and of neural activity in outlying portions of the nervous system. But they have only shown that muscular activity accompanies thinking, not that it is in any way essential to or identical with, thinking.

Recently some research has been carried on to study brain waves or *encephalography* as it is called, by placing two electrodes on the surface of the skull. While this study has proved of some use in abnormal mental cases it has not yielded any data regarding characteristic brain processes accompanying various kinds of mental activity.

### Delusions

One of the greatest sources of error in thinking and reasoning is the tendency to believe what we wish to believe. This frequently leads to an effort to justify our beliefs even when there is not enough evidence and thus leads to distorted thinking. How often people eager to magnify their importance or to stimulate their feelings of self-regard begin to believe in grand things about themselves. Such groundless irrational beliefs or thoughts, particularly of grandeur or persecution are *delusions*. An intensely patriotic person distorts facts of history to believe that his country has always been doing the most honourable things. If others do not share his delusions he resents it and starts maligning them. To ensure that others accept his plea of jealousy he further distorts his thinking and believing. There is a type of mental disorder called *patranoia* in which the patient starts believing himself to be some great man like Napolean or Alexander. One cannot argue with such people as their thinking grows out of their emotional need to exaggerate and magnify their importance. What they need is medical treatment.

### Questions

1. Discuss how thinking differs from imagination and memory, and uses them.
2. What is the nature of thinking? Discuss problem-solving and the several processes involved in it.
3. Why do we think at all? Discuss the place of reasoning in life.

4. What conditions in the environment and personality traits stimulate reasoning?

5. What do you understand by creative thining? Describe the steps involved in the process.

6. What do you understand by reasoning? Describe the several steps in the process, and distinguish between inductive and deductive reasoning.

7. Discuss how reasoning is both a help and an obstacle to adjustment and efficiency.

8. Explain the several theories of reasoning? Is thinking a function of muscular activity?

9. What is a delusion How would you compare it with illusion and hallucination?

10. What is a concept? How is a concept related to image? Describe the process of conception.

## CHAPTER XIII

# INTELLIGENCE AND ITS MEASUREMENT

Some people are able to solve their problems easily, while others take much time and find it difficult. Some are able to adapt themselves to new situations readily while others need considerable time. Some quickly catch the idea, while others want something new to be explained to them again and again before they are able to grasp it. These are differences of intelligence which make people understand, learn or adjust to new situations at varying rates and with varying degrees of efficiency.

If one compares the behaviour of an individual with superior intelligence with the behaviour of an individual with inferior intelligence he is able to observe the characteristics of intelligent behaviour. Generally an intelligent person understands the situation readily, has very clear impressions, retains his experiences effectively, profits by his experiences, is able to manipulate ideas actively and has fertile imagination, has greater self-confidence and analyses even his own behaviour critically, he can readily see what is required of him, has strong motives and is able to respond to his environment with greater sensitiveness and efficiency. An intelligent person is alert, efficient, effective and resourceful, he has initiative and perseverance, and he knows what he wants and how to achieve what he wants. These factors or attributes of intelligent behaviour have been closely studied by psychologists. Many young people are considered dull and backward because their eyes or ears are defective, and when that defect is removed they work and behave very intelligently. Others are weighed down by their poor economic conditions and when they are transferred to more comfortable and prosperous environment they do better. In the study of intelligence such factors have to be very closely analysed, and in this chapter we shall try to study the nature of intelligence, how it can be tested and measured, what factors bear on it and what use is made of intelligence testing. Intelligence testing is an important service modern psychology is rendering to society in various areas of life and work like education, industry and army.

**The Measurement of intelligence**

That there are different levels or degrees of intelligence has always been recognized and the lay men have always classified people into bright and dull, into very dull and very bright, into geniuses and idiots, but it is only recently that attempts have been made to measure intelligence and to convert vague qualitative differences of intelligence into precise quantitative distinctions. To say that a person is very bright is not as helpful and reliable as to say that he is among the top ten percent of his group. Qualitative judgments are not as scientific as exact quantitative judgments.

The earliest attempt of test mental ability and activity was made by the German psychologist Wilhelm Wundt. He devised ment tests to gauge an individual's performance in sensory and motor activity. J.M. Cattell studied under him and on returning to Columbia University in America devised tests for measuring strength of grip, reaction time to sound, speed of naming colours and memory span for letters. This work was followed by Hugo Munsterberg devising and applying tests at Harvard University and Joseph Jastrow doing it at Wisconsin University. But all of them assumed that mental ability can be measured through sensory and motor activities, and the more sensitive an individual is the more intelligent he will be.

The father of intelligence testing is a Frenchman, Alfred Binet. Binet disagreed with those who sought to measure general ability by testing speed of reaction, rote memory, sensory acuity or muscular movements. Intelligence can be estimated, according to Binet, only by tests of higher faculties like reasoning, comprehension, judgment, adaptability, presistence and self-criticism.

In 1904 Binet was appointed to a national educators committee to investigate retardation in French schools and to devise a way of distinguishing the bright pupils from the dull who could not benefit from the ordinary teaching of the schools. Is it possible to find out what children cannot profit by common school education and should be taught in separate schools? This was the problem posed before Binet. He saw that in solving this problem he must find out some means of measuring intelligence, that no single test would do, and that children increase in ability as they grow up. In collaboration with Theophile Simon he devised a number of tests, graded in difficulty according to age and requiring information of a non-scholastic nature which every normal child of a particular age could be expected to possess. He had to try these tests on a large number of children of different ages to standardize them, that is to make sure that they suited children of a certain age level. Then these tests had to be tried again and again and revised frequently before they could be offered as an accurate measuring device. The scale of tests is known as the Binet-Simon scale.

In this scale there are thirty items arranged in order of difficulty. Among them are : following a moving object with the eyes, recognizing simple objects in a picture, comparing two lines of different lengths, repeating spoken sentences, memorizing things in a picture, finding rhymes for a given word, completing sentences, defining abstract terms. Binet tried out these tests on children and in 1908 published a revised scale which divided the tests into age groups from 3 to 11 years. At some age levels only three questions were asked; at others, 5 or 6. In 1911 shortly before he died, Binet published a second revision of his scale. It omitted certain test items previously included, added others, and brought the scale to the adult level. In this edition Binet included five tests for each age, except the 4-year level. The 1911-scale, validated and standardized, represented a great improvement over the earlier two series.

Binet observed that older children are, on the average, more intelligent than younger children. A five-year old is more intelligent than a four-year old. With this yard-stick he proceeded to find out what children of different ages can know and perform. As many as 200 children were studied in the first examination in order to get an idea of what children of a given age can do. Later these tests were given to a large number of children between the ages of three and twelve and a fairly satisfactory evidence was acquired about what the average child of Paris of any age could do. Now with a knowledge of the average it was easy to find out if a particular child was above or below it. The more widely these tests were applied, the more they were standardized.

H. H. Goddard, psychologist to the Vineleand Training School for the Feebleminded, began to use the Binet scale and found it useful in detecting mental deficiency in children and also in distinguishing between various degrees of feeblemindedness. But the tests had to be modified and adapted to the needs of American children, and this modification and adaptation Goddard accomplished by trying out the 1908 scale on several hundred children. But Goddard's revision was used mainly to detect mental deficiency rather than to test the intelligence of normal or suprerior children.

A tremendous advance in intelligence testing came with the work of Lewis M. Terman of the Stanford University. Terman tested 2000 school children to discover just what a normal child at any given age can do. He chose six tests for each year from 3 to 10, also for ages 12, 14, 16 and 18. His calculations indicated that an average adult has a mental age of 16 years while a superior adult has one of 18 years. By using six tests for each year he was able to give two months mental age credit for each test passed. He included many of Binet's items, though some were shifted to higher or lower age levels according to Terman's findings on normal children. Several new items were added so that the Stanford Revision as it was called, had a total of ninety tests compared with 54 of Binet's 1911 scale. In 1916 his monumental work *The Measurement of Intelligence* was first published.

**Intelligence tests**

A few samples of tests are given for the benefit of the reader.

**Binet Scale Tests**

*Three years*

1. Pointing out nose, eyes and mouth
2. Repeating two numbers

3. Enumerating the objects in a picture
4. Giving one's own surname
5. Repeating a sentence like: "It is hot, let me go."

*Five years*

1. Comparing two weights
2. Copying a figure, a square, for example.
3. Repeating a sentence of ten syllables
4. Forming a triangle from two triangles
5. Counting four coins

*Eight years*

1. Finding omissions in a picture
2. Counting backwards from 20 to 1
3. Giving differences from memory
4. Repeating five digits
5. Giving the date, month and year.

## Terman's Stanford Revision Test

*Three years*

1. Pointing to parts of the body
2. Naming familiar objects
3. Enumeration of objects in a picture
4. Repeating six to seven syllables
5. Giving the family name
6. Giving sex

*Five years*

1. Comparing weights
2. Naming colours
3. Aesthetic comparison
4. Giving definitions in terms of use
5. Putting 2 triangles together to make a rectangle
6. Performing a triple order : putting a key on the table, shutting the door, and bringing a book.

*Eight years*

1. The ball-and-field test
2. Counting backwards from 20 to 1
3. Comprehension e.g. what will you do if a playmate hits you without meaning to do so
4. Giving similarities
5. Definitions superior to use
6. Vocabulary, 20 words

The Stanford revision, first published in 1916, has been most popular. In 1936, Terman and Merill brought out an improved version of the scale. The new tests cover a wide range, provide a richer sampling of abilities, and include non-verbal test situations, particularly at the lower ages. Many more test items were included in the scale, tests were made suitable from the age 2 to the age 14, two forms of tests were devised so that each form could be a suitable check on the other and the tests could be repeated, and for each age test six to eight items were included.

**Mental age**

The usefulness of the method of intelligence testing is greatly enhanced by the concept of *mental age*. The tests were framed on the examination of a large number of children of different age levels, for example, tests devised for five-year-old children were those passed by a typical five-year-old child. If a test was passed by 60 to 90 per cent of the children of a given age level, Binet assigned that test to that age level. A child who passed all the tests designed for children of six years and did not pass any test for the seven was said to have a mental age of six years, no matter what his actual or chronological age might be. If he is six years of age he is normal, but if his age is five he is above normal having passed tests above his age, and if he is seven years he is sub-normal having passed tests much below his actual age and is judged backward. Thus an eight year old child may have the mental age of six or a six year old may have the mental age of eight. Mental age, often expressed symbolically as M.A., represents the level of mental development attained by a child, as expressed in terms of the average development of children of a given age. It is a relative measure of mental growth. If a child of 5 does as well on an intelligence test as an average child of 7, his mental age would be seven. It is the level of ability of a given child, expressed in terms of the age at which the *average* child attains that level of ability. The concept of mental age is an important contribution to the psychology of mental development and individual differences.

## Intelligence Quotient or I. Q.

Three children whose ages are eight, nine and ten may have the same mental age of nine, and yet the first one is bright, the second one is normal and average, and the third is backward. How are we to distinguish between the three having the same mental age? This is done by obtaining the ratio of the chronological age to the mental age of the individual, that is, by finding the socalled Intelligence Quotient or the I.Q. The mental age is divided by the chronological age or C.A. and the result is multiplied by 100 to avoid decimals and this gives us the I.Q. Thus the child who passed all the tests of the age group seven and two tests of the age group eight has a mental age of seven years and four months (two months for each of the six test items), that is, 88 months. If his chronological age is six years and three months, that is, 75 months his intelligence quotient would be

$$\frac{\text{Mental age M.A. } 88}{\text{Chronological age C.A. } 75} \times 100 = 117 \cdot 3 \text{ I.Q.}$$

The child whose chronological age is the same as his mental age has an I.Q. of 100. The child whose mental age is 9 but chronological age is 10 has an I.Q. of 90. As we shall see later, I.Q.'s below 75 are definitely inferior; those above 130 are quite superior.

The concept of Intelligence Quotient was devised by a German psychologist Stern, but its popularity is due mainly to its adoption by Terman. It is an index of an individual's intellectual development, determined by dividing his mental age by his chronological age and multiplying the result by 100.

For purposes of calculating mental age, if there are six tests to a given age level, each test score means two months added to the mental age as each failure means two months subtracted from the mental age. For the purpose of calculating the I.Q., 16 is treated as the highest chronological age and in testing the intelligence of an adult, his chronological age will be considered as 16 regardless of his actual age. The reason is that experimental studies have shown that basic intelligence does not increase appreciably after 16. This means mental ages of adults are not as meaningful as those of children.

From the above account it is quite clear that children of the same mental age may have different I.Q.s and children of the same I.Q. may have different chronological ages.

## The distribution of intelligence

Individual differences in intelligence are large but they are normally distributed, that is, there are more people of average ability than there are very bright ones or very dull ones.On the basis of studies made it has been found that 80 pe cent of the total population has an I.Q. ranging between 85 and 115. They are the average and normal people and the findings of the psychologists accord with the general statement that God must have loved the common people because he made so many of them. The lower I.Q. is as low as 25. These people are very inferior, of low intelligence such as morons, imbeciles and idiots; they cannot look after themselves nor are they able to learn a useful trade. The highest I.Q. is as high as 150. These people are very superior and make great success in life, their understanding and adjustments are of a high order. According to psychologists the following table indicates the distribution of intelligence in any randomly selected group of people. Of course these figures are based on studies made in the U.S.A.

| I.Q. | Percentage | Classification |
|---|---|---|
| 150 and above | 0.25 | Genius or near genius |
| 120 to 150 | 6.75 | Very superior |
| 110 to 120 | 13.00 | Superior |
| 90 to 110 | 60.00 | Average or normal |
| 80 to 90 | 13.00 | Dull (backward) |
| 70 to 80 | 6.00 | Dull, feebleminded |
| Below 70 | 1.00 | Definitely feeble minded |

| | | |
|---|---|---|
| 50 to 70 | ·75 | morons, mental age 8-10 years |
| 25 to 50 | .19 | imbeciles, mental age 3-7 years |
| below 25 | .06 | idiots, mental age 2 years |

The feeble-minded group, that is, those with I.Q.'s below 70, need special treatment and observation. Those with I.Q. between 50 and 70 may live by themselves as long as no emergency arises, but a person with I.Q. below 50 needs to be looked after in an institution, cannot avoid common dangers and needs constant supervision.

**Types of intelligence tests**

The following table shows the various types of intelligence tests at a glance:

- Intelligence tests
  - Verbal intelligence tests
    - Verbal individual intelligence tests
    - Verbal group intelligence tests
  - Non-verbal or performance intelligence tests
    - Non-verbal or performance individual intelligence tests
    - Non-verbal or performance group intelligence tests.

We shall describe and discuss these types of intelligence tests in detail.

**Verbal individual intelligence tests**

Binet-Simon scale and the Stanford Revised scale whose tests have been described above and whose historical development has been briefly indicated are examples of verbal individual tests of intelligence. They are verbal in so far as they make use of language and tests invariably consist of questions expressed in language spoken or written. They are individual tests because only one individual can be tested at a time:

As has already been indicated Terman and his associates at the Stanford university, in adapting Binet's scale to American children, found it necessary to shift the position of some of the tests, and in some instances, to substitute new ones. They also extended the scale to the adult level. Their scale was first published in 1916, and the revised version by Terman and Merill was published in 1937. This revision contains tests difficult enough to measure the superior adults as well as tests for infants as young as two years. There are two forms of the test, making it possible for the examiner to repeat the test if he so likes. Gesell and his associates at the Yale university extended the Binet's tests to include infancy.

These individual tests are very expensive. They take a lot of time, each individual is given about an hour. It obviously limits the number of individuals who can be tested by a single examiner. Because of the need of bringing out the best in the individual testee the examiner must be specially trained. He must have memorized thoroughly every detail of the test and must have a thorough knowledge of how to score the numerous responses made by a child in a test situation. Lastly these tests involve use of language and presuppose that individuals being tested are able to speak, read and understand the language of the test. This means that children who are retarded in language development will be handicapped in the test. Similarly children brought up in homes where some foreign language is being used or foreign students cannot easily take these tests. No test has eliminated these objections and though the Binet-Simon scale and its Stanford revision are not free from these drawbacks, they continue to be the best that is available so far.

**Verbal group tests of intelligence**

Several group tests, tests which may be given to many persons at the same time, have been devised. They are clearly more suitable than the Binet tests for measuring large groups of persons, as children in a public school system, applicants for jobs in industry or candidates for recruitment to the army.

Shortly after the publication of the Stanford revision of the Binet scale in 1916, the United States entered the World War I. Military authorities were at once faced by the problem of classifying hundreds of thousands of recruits into ordinary soldiers and commissioned and non-commissioned officers. The American Psychological Association placed their services at the disposal of the State and a committee of experts was appointed under the presidentship of Professor R.M. Yerkes of the Yale university to draw up a test that could be taken by a large number of people simultaneously. In framing the new group tests the committee took pains to reach innate ability, keeping the test as far as possible free from the effects of education or training. Two tests resulted, Army Alpha test for literates and Army Beta tests for illiterates or persons with meagre knowledge of English.

The Army Alpha test consists of eight sections, each containing 12 to 40 questions. Every section begins with easy questions and proceeds to more difficult ones, so that all persons can answer some questions, but few can answer all. Test one involves figures 1 to 9 placed in circles and the examiner says : "Attention. Look at question 2 where the circles have numbers in them. When I say 'go' draw a line from circle 2 to circle 5 that will pass under circle 3 and above circle 4.........GO".

Test Two has 20 questions such as "If an aeroplane goes 300 yards in 10 seconds, how many feet does it go in a fifth of a second?"

Test Three requires choice of the best answer from among three such as :

"Every soldier should be inoculated against typhoid fever because (1) many men have typhoid fever, (2) the doctors insist on it, and (3) it prevents epidemics."

In Test Four one is called upon to decide if 40 pairs of words are similar or opposite in meaning e.g. fault-virtue, excite-agitate.

In Test Five words of a sentence are jumbled together to be placed in order.

Test Six requires completion of the number series like 3-4-6-9-13-18.

Test Seven is verbal analogy test requiring seeing of relations as

Skirts : girl : : trousers: boy, hat, vest, coat

Mayor : city : : general : army, soldier, navy, private

Test Eight checks up on general information by requiring choice of correct word :

London is a city in England, Iran, Japan, America

The volt is used in measuring wind power, electricity, rainfall

Only 24 minutes, working time (excluding directions) is allowed for the eight tests.

Maximum score on Army Alpha is 212 points. Over 135 is excellent, 105-134 is good, and 45 to 104 is fair. Nearly all rated above 105; enlisted men averaged a little below 60.

Army Beta is a paper-and-pencil test, but directions are given by pantomime or demonstration. It includes tracing a line through mazes, counting blocks in given piles, completing patterns of X's and O's, substituting symbols for numbers, noting similarities and differences in two sets of figures, completing pictures by supplying parts omitted, and solving simple geometrical puzzles. While Army Beta did not test exactly the same abilities as the verbal Alpha test, it helped discover men of good intelligence whose Alpha performance was bad because they lacked schooling or command of the English language.

More than a million and a half recruits took the Alpha and several thousand took the Beta tests. The tests were very helpful in separating satisfactory from unsatisfactory soldiers. The experience with these tests demonstrated the practicality and the value of group intelligence testing and opened the way for dozens of tests of this design. They also yielded valuable information to the psychologists about intelligence and its testing. Shortly after the war many new tests were devised and began to be used on a large scale in schools, industry and business.

After the first world war several group tests were devised primarily for the selection of people for jobs in business and industry. Among the best-known intelligence tests for general adults is the Otis Self-Administering Test of Mental Ability (Otis S.A.). In this test the role of the examiner is reduced to a minimum since all necessary directions are printed on the test booklet. The examiner has only to see that the test is conducted under proper conditions and to give the signal for starting and closing the test.

A number of tests have been devised for new entrants to colleges and universities and the best known are those devised by the American Council on Education and the Scholastic Aptitude Test of the College Entrance Examination Board. They are most widely used in America.

In the World War II the army authorities took full advantage of the psychological research in intelligence testing and brought out a revised scale known as Army General Classification Test (AGCT). This was given to several million recruits to the army. It was in four different forms which could be exchanged with one another, each form required about an hour to give. Besides there were longer forms of the test which sought to find out scores on tests of (1) verbal ability, (2) spatial comprehension, (3) arithmetic computation, and (4) arithmetic reasoning. The Navy developed a similar test NGCT.

It is obvious that group tests take less time and are more convenient to administer when we have to deal with a very large number of people. But they are not as easy to manage as it appears. Conditions are very difficult to control and there is a chance of people copying from each other and feeling panicky or nervous about it. Besides these tests are group-centred rather than individual-centred. Their purpose is to select suitable individuals for certain objectives of the group. The main concern therefore is about the welfare and progress of the group, those who promote this are selected and those who hinder this are rejected. The concern is not for the individuals selected for special training or for promotion as officers but for the needs of the larger group, the army and the nation at war.

### Performance tests

We have seen that Binet's tests could be given to one person at a time and their validity depends on normal vision, hearing, muscular control, and comprehension of language. They are not suitable for testing blind or deaf persons, illiterates or those who speak very little English. Perfomance tests were devised to meet these special conditions.

About 1850 a French physician, Edouard Seguin, constructed a kind of test for feebleminded children. It consisted of fitting blocks of various shapes, such as a star, triangle, cross, square or circle, into corresponding cut-outs in a board. By pantomime the child could be shown how to put each block in its proper hole. Two psychologists, R. Pintner and D. Paterson, taking over the Seguin tests, prepared the first performance scale in 1917. In this series all the tests call for a motor response, such as putting together a puzzle, fitting blocks into a place or imitating the tester in tapping cubes. Verbal directions are unnecessary. Tests are scored in terms of time taken and moves or errors made. This scale included 15 tests and was meant for age levels four to fifteen. In picture completion tests the subject inserts irregularly shaped blocks into a board to complete a picture as we do in solving a jig-saw puzzle. In a form-board test variously shaped blocks are assembled and inserted into cut-out places in a board to make a complete picture. Some of these tests are designed for pre-school children and some will baffle even college students.

The Porteus Maze Test is a standardized performance test using a series of mazes of increasing complexity for children from three to fourteen years of age. The subject is given a pencil and begins at the maze entrance to trace the pathway to its end avoiding blind alleys. Maze tests are specially useful with illiterates, people of low or defective intelligence, and primitive people whose command of language is either nil or poor. These tests show that maze-tracing can test prudence, ability to plan and look ahead, and elementary foresight.

There are several other performance tests available and they all rely on movement of one kind or the other. It is possible to obtain mental ages on the basis of these tests and intelligence quotients can be calculated. Performance tests are a good supplement of the Binet-Simon scale but cannot be substituted for it.

Performance tests are mostly individual tests, though the Army Beta tests were used for groups very large in size.

**Wechsler-Bellevue Scale**

David Wechsler, a clinical psychologist at Bellevue Hospital, New York City, developed a scale for measuring intelligence of adults in 1939. In 1949 he developed the Wechsler Intelligence Scale for Children (age 5 to 15) commonly known as WISC and in 1955 he issued a revised version of his earlier scale. It was known as Wechsler Adult Intelligence Scale. The earlier scale for adult intelligence was very popular and the revised version began to be widely used. It could be used from the age of 10 to 60. Before this scale was devised there was no scale for testing the intelligence of adults. Psychologists have generally commended it.

The Wechsler Adult Intelligence Scale is an individual test. It consists of two parts, the *verbal* part has six tests and the non-verbal or *performance* part has five tests which require a minimum of language. The full scale is a combination of the two. The tests are outlined here :

**Verbal**

1. *Information* : 29 questions graded in difficulty.
2. *Comprehension :* fourteen questions requiring understanding.
3. *Arithmetical reasoning :* fourteen problems in mental arithmetic.
4. *Digits Forward and Backward :* memory span for digits of increasing length.

5. *Similarities :* thirteen pairs resembling each other in some way.
6. *Vocabulary :* a list of forty words of increasing difficulty to be defined.

**Performance**

1. *Picture-arrangement* which would make a story.
2. *Picture completion* : an important part of the picture is missing and has to be identified
3. *Bloc design :* cubes to be arranged so as to reproduce seven designs indicated.
4. *Object assembly :* jigsaw-puzzle type test.
5. *Digit-symbol* : a test of association learning in which digits have to be matched with symbols.

The Wechsler-Bellevue Scale does not provide for mental age as this concept is not applicable to adult intelligence but it does yield an I.Q. which is of value in comparing one adult with another. The I.Q. obtained in Binet scale indicates development ratio, that is, how a child stands with other children of the same age and what his mental status at present is. Wechsler-Bellevue Scale for children employs the same technique as the Binet-Simon scale.

**Standardization of Intelligence tests**

Tests are said to be standardized when they have *objectivity*, *validity* and *reliability*.

A test is objective when it is free from the personal bias of the examiner. With many people their wishes, desires, moods and whims affect their judgment. Our examination system is criticized for being a victim of this defect. Examiners mark answer-books according as they deem fit and it has been found that not only different examiners but the same examiner at different times marks the same answer differently. This shows that their judgment is subjective. Our tests should be such that whoever marks the answers judges the same way and gives the same score. This is possible if our tests are free from the factor of personal bias and function independently of the mental condition of the examiner.

In education new types of objective tests have been devised which try to eliminate this personal factor. The *multiple-choice* tests are of the type :

1. London is the capital of..............
   England, France, America, Germany
2. The river Nile falls into...........
   The Arabian sea, the Persian gulf, the Red sea, the Mediterranean sea

In *true-false* tests a number of statements are made and the subject is asked to indicate the true statements. In the *best-answer* tests three or four answers to a question are given and the subject is asked to indicate the best answer. In *matching-tests* some words and their definitions are given and the subject is asked to match definitions to correct words.

A test is said to be *valid* when it measures what it purports to measure. How are we to see that an intelligence test really measures intelligence and nothing else? This can be determined by finding how its scores correlate with scores obtained by some independent method or criterion. If a new test is devised its validity can be determined by comparing its scores with scores from the already recognized tests like that of the Binet-Simon scale or group tests. The validity of the Stanford Revision tests is so well established that it can be reasonably predicted that one who does well in these tests will do well in all tasks and areas of work which require intelligence. Tests given to new entrants to colleges have shown that certain students will do well in studies.

A test is said to be *reliable* when it consistently yields the same result on being repeated. If it yields different results every time it is given it is unreliable. Reliability of a test is measured by comparing its scores on different applications of the same test to the same children at different times. The bright child will continue to score high and the dull child will continue to score low. And the score of a child will not vary with different scales of tests. Generally well-standardized tests have a high coefficient of reliability of 1.00 but it may shift between .85 and .95.

**Constancy of the I.Q.**

The I.Q. is an index of the intellectual development or mental status of a child relative to other children of the same age; it is a measure of his brightness or dullness as compared with other children of the same age. Now the question is whether this measure or index remains constant. Even commonsense believes that a bright child in the class will continue to be bright and show promise and a dull child will continue to be dull, and we do not need intelligence tests to confirm that extreme cases of brightness and dullness tend to maintain their relative status. But this does not answer the question: how constant is the I.Q. and extensive research has been done on the question.

Testing is a human device and some error of measurement is bound to creep in, and it should not be surprising if there is a variation of two to five points in the I.Q. on subsequent measurements. This may be expressed by saying that the intelligence quotient is relatively constant and shifts only very slightly from the original. A number of studies reveal that bright children gain in I.Q. while dull children tend to lose in I.Q. This may be due to the fact that a bright child tried to do things beyond his age and these new experiences enrich and improve his approach and understanding and also subsequent achievement. A dull child on the other hand engages in inferior activities and thus his progress is retarded.

However there are many factors which affect a child's achievement in an intelligence test and thereby affect his score. Defects of eyes, hearing, illness, physical defects leading to poor health, direct coaching and the like do influence the I.Q. When these defects are removed children show better score just as children are shy to begin with and their I.Q. may be lower than what they score after a month's stay in the school. But more of it later.

**The nature of intelligence**

But what is intelligence? It is easier to measure intelligence than to provide an accurate definition of it. More time has been spent by psychologists in devising intelligence tests than in determining the real nature of intelligence. This should not discourage the reader. Scientists can measure electricity, heat and other forms of energy without being able to offer any hard and fast definition of them, and psychologists have done the same. But their definitions do not agree and here an attempt is made to discuss them and indicate the general nature of intelligence.

Binet was aware of the difficulty of definition and sought to develop a scale to measure the amount of intelligent behaviour shown by children. The more intelligently a given child behaved the more "intelligence" Binet ascribed to him. He thought of inteligence as comprising such qualities as comprehension, inventiveness, persistence and critical analysis; intelligence is "judgment or commonsense, initiative, the ability to adapt oneself, to judge well, understand well, reason well". It is the ability to take and maintain a definite direction, the ability to make adjustments for the attainment of a goal and the power of self-criticism. After trying to measure each one of these separately, he decided to test them in combination. He found that children who were best on judgment also did well on tests of attention, memory, vocabulary and so forth, thus demonstrating the inter-relation between the several capacities.

According to Terman, "An individual is intelligent in proportion as he is able to carry on abstract thinking". Stern thought of intelligence as "a general adaptability to new problems and conditions of life". Thorndike considers it "as the power of good responses from the point of view of truth or fact". Woodworth identifies it with general adaptability, "the ability to adjust means to ends and to reach a goal". Many psychologists have defined it as a general ability to learn, but most are agreed that it helps us to meet a new situation, to adapt ourselves to changing environments and to solve problems. It is a composite function of the mind and is innate. It is mental alertness. The concept of efficiency too has been put forward as indicating the real nature of intelligence, it is effectiveness in meeting the challenge of new situations or solving everyday problems. It is a good working definition of general intelligence.

But the concept of general intelligence does not find favour with psychologists and they usually speak of three areas or types of intelligence—the *abstract*, the *mechanical* and the *social* intelligence. Abstract intelligence is absent in animals and is found in our use of symbols, numbers, diagrams, formulas and the like. Persons with abstract intelligence are able to see relations among these symbols and to solve problems with their help. Lawyers, physicians, professors and literary men as also statesmen, business and generals owe their success to its effective use. Mechanical intelligence reveals itself in manual skill and co-ordination and manipulation activities. The engineer and the craftsman are able to use highly developed tools and control elaborate machines because of high mechanical intelligence, and this type of intelligence is necessary in entrants to highly trained industrial jobs. This means that students entering engineering colleges should be given tests of mechanical intelligence. Social intelligence is found in personal and social relations and behaviour. A good salesman, diplomat, political leader, social worker must have high degree of social intelligence to be able to cope with social situations successfully and control and manipulate the behaviour of his fellowmen. How to make friends, gain favour and popularity, impress others and get along with them depends largely on social intelligence.

Individual variations in different types of intelligence are very large. Often in the same individual wide variations in these aspects of intelligence are found. Some people may be high in abstract intelligence and just mediocre in mechanical intelligence. Very wide differences in different aspects of intelligence are exceptional.

With different aspects of intelligence we are saved the difficulty of comparing individuals as more intelligent or less intelligent than others. But the vast research carried on about intelligence deals mostly with abstract or conceptual intelligence, partly because it is easier to validate a test of abstract or conceptual intelligence than a test of social or mechanical intelligence and partly because such tests are more reliable. Learning situations in which abstract intelligence is required are more standardized and consistent, more "structured", than situations which call for the exercise of mechanical or social intelligence and this structured quality reduces the extent of variability, thus making prediction easier.

Or may be that learning skill is an ability which can be more readily identified.

Tests of mechanical and social intelligence are not as good, perhaps much attention has not been bestowed on them or perhaps in testing them there are several unidentified factors over which we have no control.

**Theories of intelligence**

Although these theories have only a historical importance they are discussed here for an understanding of the background of thinking about intelligence. *Spearman's Two-Factor theory* in its revised form appeared in his book: *The Abilities of Man.* According to it intellectual abilities on analysis reveal two factors—the general factor called *G* and the specific factor called *S*. The G factor is present in all mental activities but the S factor is present only in specific activities and for different specific mental activities different S factors are present, as for example, musical ability, mechanical ability, arithmetical ability. Musical ability includes some G factor and a powerful degree of S factors like musical memory, rhythm, pitch, and a great musician must have strong G factor plus powerful S factors of musical ability. The G factor is described as mental energy. Two individuals may have the same G factor but may differ in S factors. It is obvious that Spearman identified G factor with intelligence; though its influence is present in all activities, it is not equally present. People who show ability in one direction also show some ability in other directions as well. Spearman's two factor theory is called eclectic because it seeks to harmonize several other factors.

Thurstone, Thomson and Thorndike do not accept Spearman's theory. They question the existence of a "general intelligence" and argue that instead of a general ability there are several special abilities such as mathematical or mechanical ability. By analysing carefully whole batteries of test results they found clusters of abilities or "group factors". Thurstone isolated certain primary mental abilities, namely, visualizing, speed in perceiving, facility with numbers, memory, word fluency, verbal comprehension and two or three factors related to reasoning. The abilities are relatively independent; a person proficient in one is not necessarily so in another. In course of time we may not speak of any single index of ability like the I.Q. but will speak instead of separate abilities and there will be separate tests for each of them. When this is done we can determine which abilities are most closely related to success in school, and in the various vocations. An estimate of "general ability" can still be obtained, however, by averaging scores on the separate ability tests. This is the *multi-factor or synthetic theory of intelligence.*

Thurstone speaks of six factors : spatial, numerical, verbal relations, memory, word fluency and reasoning. But Kelly following the factorial analysis of intelligence put forward nine factors such as verbal ability, numerical ability, ability to deal with spatial relations, motor ability, musical ability, mechanical ability, social intelligence, interests and physical strength.

**Limitations of intelligence tests**

Intelligence tests have been severely criticized. Minor criticisms, as of certain test items and procedures, have often been met by revisions and improvements of the tests. We have already dealt with revisions of scales and shown how the Stanford Revision of 1937 was superior to the original Binet-Simon scale of 1917.

Other critcisms are more fundamental. It is said that intelligence tests fail to reach native inborn ability because a child's performance and the resulting I.Q. is greatly affected by his home environment and socio-economic factors. This is true, and therefore many comparisons between individuals or groups are invalid because they do not take into account differences of background and experiences. But on the other hand when children from a common or similar social background such as living in the same small town are tested, test scores of children offer a fair measure of the children's relative abilities.

Thorndike and Thurstone deny that there is any such thing general ability or general versatility of adjustment, and if that is what validity can tests of intelligence have. Instead of one general ability there are many special abilities, but as has already been pointed out even with many special abilities attempts are being made to correlate and combine their scores and obtain a collective picture of them by averaging scores on the separate ability tests.

Other critics rightly urge that intelligence tests leave untouched many important aspects of personality like interests, motives, attitudes or social adaptability. But these tests do not claim that they measure any such aspects of personality, and other tests have been devised to measure them.

It is also objected that tests measure intelligence only through language spoken or printed. Children from better homes are likely to score higher than those from poor ones. This is true but home conditions do not modify results to any serious degree. No doubt environment may discourage or stimulate intellectual activity, but tests can be slightly modified to suit different kinds of environment.

Intelligence tests are not adequately standardized and do not predict with absolute certainty success in school or industry. They are not a perfect measure of intelligence and in several areas of work intelligence alone does not make for success. One typist may be more intelligent than another, but may not be a good typist. There are other things like skills, attitudes and interests which also contribute to success. Happily tests are being devised for them also, and there is a growing feeling that intelligence tests must be supplemented by other tests to predict later success with certainty.

**Value of intelligence tests**

In the first place intelligence tests have contributed largely to our knowledge and understanding of human nature and behaviour. Even though no hard and fast definition of intelligence is available everybody is agreed that there is some intellective quality which is inborn and which determines the efficiency and effectiveness of our adjustments, learning and behaviour. Today on their basis we are able to draw some general and definite conclusions about human nature and its growth.

Intelligence tests were originally devised and used to measure the ability of school children to benefit by school teaching and for educational guidance, and there is no doubt that this purpose they have served fairly satisfactorily. Today we are able to predict the possibilities of children's success in learning and thereby direct their mental growth accordingly. If parents have a fair knowledge of what their children are capable of achieving they would not waste time and money on educating them to become what they never can become. Intelligence tests will also reveal to parents whether their children are doing their best in studies and making the best use of their opportunities. Many children are very intelligent but do not work hard or are not put to hard work, they develop bad habits of indifference. Many children are too slow and cannot keep pace with the programme of study in the school, and thus lose all interest in their work. If we have accurate knowledge and understanding of the intellectual capacity of every child we could plan his education better and not only eliminate failure but also the unhappines which accompanies it. With the help of intelligence tests the teacher can also check his work and methods of teaching. If the class is intelligent and their I.Q.'s are satisfactory but their examination scores are low this means that there is something wrong with the methods of teaching.

The chief value of determining a child's Intelligence Quotient is that we can classify him into a group to which he really belongs and then provide for his educational needs. If his I.Q. is low he may have to be placed in a group of feebleminded children and taught in a separate class to acquire intelligent behaviour. Those whose I.Q.'s are above normal have to be taught on a higher level and placed in special classes according to their capacity. And parents can be given vocational guidance so that they can prepare their children for the professions for which they are suitable.

Many colleges and universities in the West are using intelligence tests to select students for admission, and by weeding out those who are not capable of benefiting by higher education are able to reduce failure and wastage. In Indian universities and colleges all and sundry are admitted irrespective of the fact that they are capable of benefiting by the opportunities for education, and the result is appalling numbers of failures and wastage.

Business and industrial organizations can also employ intelligence tests in selecting new entrant to employment so that the unfit are weeded out. Intelligence tests are a great help in educational and vocational guidance and selection. What help the Army in America derived from intelligence tests in the two world wars can also be derived by all training and employment organizations.

**Intelligence and age**

Many people were shocked when Terman announced that the average adult intelligence is equal to that of a 16-year old. They forgot that psychologists define intelligence as capacity to learn, adaptability and alertness. In the tests, knowledge, experience, and information are kept at the minimum, though these factors are found to affect performance. Mental ability is at its highest between the age of 14 and 20, remains stationary till the age of 50 when it starts declining. Even then the decline is not marked. With superior persons the decline is slower. A number of studies indicate that mental alertness decreases very slowly till after middle age.

**The influence of heredity and environment on intelligence**

Individual differences in intelligence depend largely on heredity. Environment, however, has some effect. Because it can be changed more easily than heredity, it is important to know which environmental factors most influence intelligence, even though their influence is relatively small. Of these influences education is by far the largest and the most significant. Army tests show that soldiers with education score higher than the uneducated and some psychologists hold on the basis of studies made that good educational opportunities can raise the score by ten points or more. In general city children do better than rural children, perhaps because the test material is more familiar to city children, giving them the advantage.

**Intelligence and socio-economic factors**

Several studies have shown that children from better homes, with better economic status and social opportunities score higher in intelligence tests than children from backward, poor and depressed homes. The environment of the latter is unstimulating and there are no education facilities or social contacts. Children from isolated communities compare unfavourably with children from families and communities leading a busy social life and having rich cultural background. Social contacts with opportunities for communication affect the I.Q. When children from poor socio-economic conditions are transferred to more affluent homes they show improvement. Therefore psychologists insist that to have an accurate test of ability children must be drawn from uniform environment including home, school, socio-economic background and cultural experiences.

**Intelligence testing in India**

Attempts have been made to adapt intelligence tests for use in India. It is not merely a case of translating them from English to any of the Indian languages. Tests must be formulated on the basis of Indian environmental conditions and Indian subjects and must be validated and standardized with reference to Indian children and conditions.

The first attempt at standardization of mental tests in India was made by Dr. C. H. Rice of Lahore. It was an adaptation of the Binet scale and is described in his book *Hindustani Binet-Performance Point Scale*. The tests were meant primarily for Panjabi children and were in Urdu and Panjabi but with slight changes could be used in Hindi. The next notable attempt was made by V. V. Kamat in 1939. He issued a revision of the Binet tests for Marathi and Kanarese children. He examined more than 1000 children. Dr. Sohan Lal of U.P. constructed and standardized a verbal group test of intelligence for 11-plus school-going children of the U.P. Since then teachers' training colleges through their experimental psychology departments and psychological bureaus and institutes have undertaken the work of standardizing intelligence tests. Most of them are adaptations of the Stanford Revision. Pandit L. S. Jha, Dr. S. Jalota and Dr. S. M. Mohsin have done some useful work in this direction. Pandit Jha adapted the Simplex Mental Test by C.A. Richardson in Hindi, Dr. Jalota prepared a group verbal test for use among college students, and Dr. Mohsin has completed the standardization of a verbal group test of intelligence in Hindi.

## QUESTIONS

1. What do you understand by Intelligence? Discuss the several meanings given to Intelligence? Explain the several theories of Intelligence.
2. Describe briefly the history of the growth of intelligence testing.
3. What do you understand by Mental Age and Intelligence Quotient ? Illustrate your answer by an example how you would obtain the Intelligence Quotient of a child.
4. Explain what you mean by reliability, validity and objectivity of tests.
5. What do you understand by standardization of tests?
6. Explain the constancy of the I.Q. What are the limitations of intelligence tests?
7. What are the different types of intelligence tests? Give examples. Describe them briefly.
8. What are the important intelligence tests for individuals and groups? Describe them briefly? What are performance tests?
9. Briefly describe the Wechsler-Bellevue tests of intelligence? What peculiar advantage do they have over other tests?
10. What are the limitations and values of intelligence tests?
11. Discuss how far environmental factors influence intelligent behaviour. Is the I.Q. constant? If so, what is the meaning and influence of environmental influences? If not, what is the value of intelligence testing?

## CHAPTER XIV

# PERSONALITY

### The nature of personality

Personality is not easy to define. In popular language personality usually refers to the impression which an individual makes upon others, to those characteristic attributes which make an individual stand out from others, which make him attractive or unattractive or which strike others as unusual. This however is a very limited use of the term. There is much about the mental life of an individual which is seldom revealed to others and yet is of vital importance in understanding his behaviour. An individual's personality is not a surface phenomenon which may be seen at a glance, and when we talk of a person having "a fine personality", "no personality", "an aggressive or strong personality" or when tradesmen talk of items of dress, face cream or hair tonic adding to the personality of an individual they usually refer to the social effect which the appearance of an individual makes on others.

Psychologically speaking personality is the sum-total of all that an individual is, of everything that constitutes a person's physical, mental, emotional and temperamental make-up. Our experiences, memories, knowledge, daydreams, study, learning, habits, thoughts, attitudes, beliefs, sentiments, intelligence, goals and ideals, in fact all that we are and all that we hope and aspire to become constitutes our personality. Our taste, our understanding, our enthusiasms and ambitions, our principles of life and conduct and the like colour our personality. But these elements or items are not put together in a jumble, they are organized into a whole, they are merged or blended into a unity, these particular functions are integrated or organized into a system, and it is this whole system which we call personality. Personality is "the whole individual considered as a whole' as Munn puts it or it is "the dynamic organization within the individual of those psychophysical systems that determine his characteristic behaviour and thought" as Allport expresses it. With such a comprehensive definition of personality an individual's choice of particular style of shoes, the books he reads, the flowers he selects for his garden, his hobbies and the like, if made with deliberation, reveal some aspects of his personality, and in so far as these and his dress, digestion or lameness make a difference to his whole outlook on life and influence his total attitude towards his fellowmen, they are a part of his personality.

We have defined psychology as the study of behaviour as one whole or system. Now we may add that we have to study behaviour as expressing and revealing personality, the unique organization and integration of physical, mental and emotional qualities. If we have to understand and describe an individual we have to refer not to isolated acts of his life and behaviour but to the fundamental integration of his entire experience, attitudes and goals which is his personality.

Thus personality is made up of a number of elements. Our personal appearance, dress, manners, physical constitution, speech, gait, knowledge, intelligence, experience and the several mental functions mentioned above contribute to it. Secondly the concept of personality involves certain assumptions about its basic character. For example these elements are integrated into a unified whole. These we may describe as characteristics of personality, and these we shall outline in detail now.

Too many people identify personality and character, but they are different. Character implies moral worth, and when we talk of a person's character we inquire how good or bad his behaviour is and we pass a judgment of right or wrong on it. Now standards of right and wrong change from time to time as they have changed about slavery and prohibition, man's character may be good at one time and bad at another even though his behaviour remains the same. Nor is there any generally accepted definition of character and what traits are to be included in it may not be easy to decide. No doubt the importance of character in life and education cannot be denied but then character involves worth, idea of value, which is beyond the scope of a positive natural science like psychology. On the other hand there is no element of worth, goodness or badness, in the concept of personality. It only emphasizes the unity and integration of psychophysical functions.

**Characteristics of personality**

The chief characteristic of personality is *self-consciousness.* A person is a self-conscious being. We do not attribute personality to a dog or a child because they have no awareness of their own identity. It is only grown-up people who through success or failure, praise or blame begin to take an objective attitude toward themselves, to see themselves as others see them and to review and compare their different acts of behavour if they harmonize with each other and can be linked into one system.

Secondly personality is through and through *social.* It is only in relation to others that we are usually judged, and our consciousness of ourselves arises only in our interaction with other members of society. Our growth takes place through social experience, how other people react to our abilities, qualities and actions.

Thirdly a personality is continually *making adjustments to environment* and to inner life. Lack of adjustment means strain and tension and the individual is for ever acquiring new patterns of adjustment to meet the challenge of new situations. After adjustment our behaviour is smooth, easy and efficient.

Fourthly personality is always *striving for goals.* Our life and behaviour is purposive, and we are for ever seeking new ends and goals to meet our needs. Our needs define our goals, our interest and desires provide their basis, and our behaviour is directed toward their attainment. We have already described in a previous chapter some of the important drives, both biological and social, and have shown how our behaviour is motivated by them.

Lastly personality *functions as whole.* Different experiences and mental activities are joined together in a unity. The child is a creature of impulse, every passing fancy makes him act. But as he grows up there is a growing order and method in his behaviour, he exercises control and acts in a specific manner. There is now a growing unity and consistency in his behaviour. All his experiences and activities are now joined or integrated into one whole. Personalities differ in the degree of integration and some of the highly developed personalities like that of Mahatma Gandhi are highly integrated. The unifying force is provided by their ideals and standards of behaviour which they have acquired in the course of their life and experience.

**Elements of personality**

What elements are integrated into the unity called personality? What factors go to make up a personality? How are we to distinguish between one person and another? Now we see individuals in different ways, in different aspects or from different angles, these different facets are aspects are called "dimensions" of personality. In psychology these dimensions are spoken of as *traits*. They are the constituents of personality. Consulting a dictionary psychologists found that there are some eighteen thousand trait names but so many of them mean nearly the same thing that their number can be and has been considerably reduced. Many of these labels have overlapping definitions, some are very vague, and psychologists have tried to reduce their number by eliminating obvious synonyms. R. B. Cattell reduced them to 171. By applying them to several persons he found that a good many of them were related and found together. A further reduction to 35 and still a further reduction to 12 took place, and these Cattell regarded as the "primary source traits of personality". Some of them are discussed here. Only those which play the most important part in an individual's social adjustment have been selected.

*Personal appearance.* While some employees and friends place too much emphasis on "looks" and judge mental alertness from personal appearance it cannot be denied that to some extent success and failure is determined by personal appearance which includes not only height, weight, complexion but also voice, dress and other characteristics of personal nature. But often the lack of good looks is made up by good nature, by qualities like friendliness, good will, helpfulness. Not only do these traits bring success but they also contribute to personal and social happiness.

*Intelligence*, as we have seen, is the ability to solve problems and meet new situations. It is mental alertness, the ability to learn. All are not equally intelligent, some are much more intelligent than others. Without intelligence it is not possible to make much headway but a man may be very intelligent and yet lack the capacity to persist or work hard or get along with other people. Some crooks, cheats and criminals are highly intelligent. What is desired is a well-balanced personality in which intelligence is supplemented by healthy social feeling.

*Emotionality* has a powerful role to play in personality. The two extremes of emotionality are pleasantness and unpleasantness. Some people have a genial pleasant disposition, others are of a surly or gloomy type. These emotional states may be of varying degrees and generally we have four different types. The first is the *elated type*, overflowing with happiness, too active and cheerful. Such a person is usually of the silly superficial kind, he does not take anything seriously and is always getting into trouble. The *depressed type* is its opposite. Such a person is always seeing the dark gloomy side of things, is moody and depressed and cannot enjoy anything. The *irritable type* is always losing temper, picking up quarrels and staging fights. He is angry with the world. The *unstable type* is changing moods so often that one is not sure how to tackle him. He may be irritable at one time and elated at another. Such people are abnormal and our aim should be emotional stability and maturity. As has been stressed in a previous chapter training of the emotions is as important as that of the intellect.

*Sociability*. The young child is inclined to be extremely selfish and self-centred. He is not interested in others to begin with but gradually he learns to share his things and experiences with others, he plays with other children, lets them play with his toys, and such give-and-take co-operation in childhood lays the foundation of social solidarity at the adult level. This trait is present in varying degrees in different people, and at one end are those who are extremely interested only in themselves and at the other end are those whose interest in others is very strong. The self-centred type are called *introverts* and those deeply interested in others are called *extroverts.*

The distinction between introverts and extroverts was first made by a Swiss psychologist C. G. Jung. *Introvert* means turning inward and *extrovert* means turning outward. An introvert likes to be alone or with people he knows well, he keeps his feelings and thoughts much to himself, he is very much absorbed in values, ideas, imagination, dreams and feelings, and much of his activity takes place in his thinking, dreaming and imagining. He is given to meditation and reflection. The extrovert loves to be with people, lets others know of his thoughts and feelings, values things, active participation with others and prominence in social life. He is open and frank in his social relations. He is a go-getter and aggressive in everything.

Psychologists today do not believe that people can be typed into these two classes, but hold that all of us have both tendencies to introversion and extroversion at different times and are *ambiverts.*

In the next chapter we will be studying some of the maladjustments individuals develop in their relations with their fellowmen.

*Ascendance-submission.* This trait is essentially indicative of forcefulness of approach among individuals. Too often people are not able to succeed as well as they should by virtue of their intelligence and persistence because they lack the necessary aggressiveness or dominance. They do not assert themselves and meekly submit to others. But there are others who may be less intelligent but they have the spirit to take initiative, to dominate and rise above others, and to snatch leadership from others. A good many leaders in the social, political and economic spheres are not very able persons but they have the will to dominate and lead. Some become leaders, others remain followers; some are aggressive and active, others are submissive and passive; some protest against wrongs; others accept and submit to them. But very few individuals are completely dominant or submissive. Most of us try to dominate and lead people who are inferior and subordinate to us in social position, and submit to those who are superior to us.

*Moral character.* This trait of personality refers to social approval as to whether we have a balanced personality pursuing well-defined goals and purposes of benefit to the individual and society. There is one type of morality which is negative, not doing anything evil, but true morality lies in doing positive good to others and himself. Nor does moral character lie in being compelled to do what is good. A virtuous person behaves in a virtuous manner from habit.

This list of traits or elements of personality is not complete or exhaustive. There must be and are many more traits in personality, but if these traits are developed and integrated in a balanced manner they will make for a healthy and wholesome personality. Often one or two traits are developed in an exaggerated manner and others are neglected. A person with beautiful and smart looks may be deficient in intelligence or may lack sociability; or a person highly intelligent may not be able to get along with others; these are examples of lack of balance in the development and integration of human personality. Normal growth and development demands that the several traits of personality should be given proper and harmonious development.

**Determinants of personality**

What factors or influences determine anybody's personality? Individuals vary from each other and these individual differences indicate differences in personality integration. We may now discuss some of the important influences in the growth and development of personality.

Almost the first factor that crops up in our mind is that of heredity and environment. As to which is more powerful in determining the pattern of personality there may be differences of opinion and we have already discussed the question briefly. One view is that differences among individuals are all due to heredity, and the other view attributes them to environment. Both these views go to the extreme and take a partial view of human nature. Heredity cannot be ignored but it does not decide once and for all what the pattern of personality should be. It only lays down the broad lines of human potentialities for growth and development. How those potentialities will become actual and what shape and form human growth and development will take depends very largely on what stimulating or retarding influences environment will provide. An individual born with a musical talent may never become a musician till he gets opportunities for training and facilities for developing his talent. Economic backwardness is known to depress the development of individuals; social freedom, strict discipline and loss of parents in early childhood affects the growth of personality ; domestic tragedies, parental quarrels, war and famines have influenced human nature and left indelible marks on it.

Recently psychologists have studied the influence of the family pattern on personality. The only child is very much pampered by parents, he is the apple of their eyes, gets too much love and affection, and grows into a self-centred conceited individual. An only son in a family of daughters or an only daughter in a family of sons gets too much attention and tends to be spoilt. The eldest child and the youngest child cannot help being influenced by his position in the family.

Children brought up in slums differ in their personality pattern from children brought up in affluent homes, as children brought up by overstrict parents differ from those brought up by liberal parents.

Culture too makes a difference. An American child is encouraged to be aggressive, bold and dominant, while an Indian child is encouraged to acquire obedience, respect for parents and old people and humility. People living under an authoritarian rule will develop qualities of rigid discipline, obedience and loyalty but people in a democracy are sure to love freedom, to be more tolerant and to criticise and judge frankly and freely.

Geographical conditions of climate also make a difference to personality make-up. People living in the arctic regions differ from those living near the equator. Food, temperature, living conditions, and the like affect human personality.

Thus we find the environmental influences, physical, social, economic, political and cultural, affect personality.

*Physical constitution* also makes a differencc. A tall sturdy fellow will feel greater self-confidence, courage and strength. Shorter and weaker people will cringe to him and respect him. A weak thin fellow will develop feelings of inferiority. A handsome face is more attractive and popular, and an ugly appearance is likely to make a person less social. Individuals with physical defects are more often inclined to be seclusive, to shun society and to be bitter. They may seek other spheres of activity to compensate for their inferiority. Napolean was short in stature and sought military honours to compensate for his shortcoming. Physical giants dominate others.

We have already seen how *endocrine glands* make a difference to personality make-up. An over-active thyroid makes a man quick as under-active thyroid makes him slack and lazy. An over-active pituitary makes a man tall but if it is under-active it would leave him short-statured.

Intelligence and temperament also affect personality and their influence has already been discussed.

**Types of personality**

Popular thought has always indulged in classifying people into certain clear-cut types, and individuals are described as social, reserved, steady, emotional and the like. Such labels are many and varied, and the best plan would be to go over some of the attempts made by thinkers in the past to classify people into types.

The first classification into types was the work of Hippocrates, a famous Greek physician of the fifth century B.C. People are classified on the basis of temperaments which according to him are of four kinds: the *sanguine*, the *melancholic*, the *choleric* and the *phlegmatic* according to the bodily "humours": red blood, black bile, yellow bile or phlegm respectively. This theory seems to a be a forerunner of the modern attempt to explain personality on the basis of the working of endocrine glands.

Physiognomy interprets personality from physical features, particularly the face and dates back to the days of Aristotle. But it was J. Lavater who in the eighteenth century tried to describe the psychological significance of the height of forehead, shape of nose or jaw and other features. The Italian criminologist, C. Lambroso claimed to show that the criminals have prominent cheekbones and jaw, oblique eyes, receding forehead, and large ears. But English scientists C. Goring and K. Pearson repudiated physiognomy by showing that the criminals and Oxford men may have similar physical features, and many later writers took pains to discredit physiognomy altogether.

Williams James suggested that people can be classified into the "tenderminded" and the "toughminded" according as they are influenced by ideas or facts. Similarly W. Stern classified people into subjective and objective.

Probably the best known type theory is Jung's classification of people into introverts and extroverts. We have already discussed these labels in detail. The introvert lives mostly in an inner world of his own thoughts and feelings and for him subjective factors dominate. The extrovert lives mostly in an outer world of things and persons, and enjoys outside activity. Jung did not suggest that people should be classified either as introverts or extroverts. Unfortunately people assume that. He said that every one has both tendencies and may be an introvert at one time and extrovert at another.

E. Kretschmer, a German psychiatrist put forward three constitutional types. The "pyknik" is short, stout and thick-set, the "leptosome" or "asthenic" is tall and thin, and the "athletic" is muscular and well proportioned. But this classification applies more to psychotics and his study was based on his experiences in mental hospitals. Although his findings are confirmed by other psychiatrists as well there is no evidence that this relation between body form and personality type exists among normal individuals.

E. Spranger, a German psychologist, classified people according to what values they considered most important. He noted six types: theoretical, economic, social, political, religious, and aesthetic. He admitted that people do not fit exclusively into one or another category. Allport and Vernon devised a test based on Spranger's six values. The results showed that persons in various areas of life and work incline toward values predominant in their fields. Engineering and business students scored highest in economic values; students of languages and literature in aesthetic values and persons preparing for the church in religious values. Men ranked higher in theoretical, economic and political values, women in aesthetic, social and religious values. But people generally do not stress one value to the exclusion of other values. Spranger's classification is based on the social behaviour of individuals.

W. H. Sheldon a professor of the Columbia university has been working for some years past on classifying people on the basis of physique. This is known as *somato-typing* (*somato* meaning body). Dr. Sheldon holds that there is a relationship between a person's physique and those elements in personality which he believes are the most closely allied to the physique such as love of comfort, aggressiveness and so on. A person whose body is soft round and fat is called an *endomorph*. Such a person is likely to be comfort loving and to have a warm interest in people. A person whose body is square and hard is called a *mesomorph*. The temperament which goes with such a physique is one of active, energetic aggressiveness. A slender small-boned person is called an *ectomorph*. He loves solitude, does not let himself go, and is sensitive to noise and distraction. Of course few people fit into this classification exactly. Most people have some characteristic of each. So Sheldon uses a seven-point scale—1 meaning a little of the characteristic and 7 meaning the greatest amount. Thus if a person is classified 4-4-2 he would have an average amount of endomorphy and mesomorphy but only a slight amount of ectomorphy. From these data on the classification of a person's physique Sheldon believes that this temperament can be described.

Psychologists have learned the pitfalls of typing personality. The danger generally is that people tend to pigeonhole everybody into one type or the other. The author of the typing theory may warn people that it is not a case of either-or but still it does become a case of either-or—either an individual fits into one category or the other, and there is no middle course. Psychologists now regard types as extreme forms of personality traits. And these traits have so many varying shades and combine in such a large variety of proportions that to pigeonhole persons rigidly is neither practicable nor useful. These types have not in any way helped better understanding of the individual and his behaviour though they have provided a vocabulary in which to describe, people around us.

**Integration of personality**

To begin with the child is a creature of impulse and satisfies every need as it arises. At first the needs are mostly biological and primary but as it grows up it acquires more needs, as have been described in a previous chapter, and habits of meeting those needs. This cycle of activity of satisfying needs comes to be associated with other people and goals and purposes of life. Thus a large variety of responses are made to an equally large variety of environmental influences. In this complex process several habits, skills, knowledge, thoughts, interests and attitudes are acquired. Such traits and characteristics are the raw material out of which personality developes. They do not work separately, in isolation from each other. They react with one another and sooner or later harmonise with each other, gradually welding into a system. Such an organization has a certain degree of consistency and constancy of behaviour, and we can to some extent predict how a particular person will react and behave in a certain situation. This is the beginning of integration of personality.

With mental development needs and wishes are gradually transformed into goals and purposes, some of them are remote and require a long process of training and striving for their realization

These goals and purposes impart a unity to the reactions and behaviour of the individual. A few of them are general and comprehensive and embrace the entire life and activity of the individual, and to that extent they guide and direct his entire thought, feeling and activity integrating them into one integrated whole. A professor, a doctor or a businessman has his entire behaviour and activity influenced by his main pursuit in life and this imparts a consistency and unity to his life and striving. Higher up men with a mission see things only from one angle, the angle of their mission and their thinking, feeling and striving is directed toward the fulfilment of certain goals and the realization of definite ideals. They are highly integrated personalities. Mahatma Gandhi looked at every issue and programme from the point of view of Ahimsa, that is, non-violence and truth; ideals of peace and public good pervaded all his thinking, speaking and writing, and his entire life and activity was directed to the service of these ideals. Such a personality is surely most integrated. All attitudes, interests, goals and aspirations are so well harmonized that they eliminate conflict, and there is balance, maturity and harmony. Such a person may not be very highly intelligent or have a strong physical constitution, but his talents and abilities are reconciled to each other and he makes the most effective use of all that he is and that he has. He accepts himself and his world and is happy, successful and effective. A person lacking in integration is frustrated, he rejects himself and the world rejects him, and his problems for ever remain problems.

**Personality and the home**

We have already dealt with the influence of environment in the development of personality but we may consider in detail how environment in the home exercises a specific influence on the development of personality. This influence is all the more effective considering the fact that early years of childhood are the most formative years and the influence stamped at this stage is most significant as has been strongly stressed by psychoanalysts.

The child acquires the attitudes, habits and needs of the family. The peace, stability and happiness of the home is a powerful factor in the development of personality of the child. It is not necessary that parents should be highly educated or very rich. All that the child needs is that the home should provide him affection, care and security, that parents should accept each other and be mentally healthy. Researches have revealed that a large number of emotionally disturbed children come from homes where parents quarrel among themselves, quarrel with their neighbours and are not accepted by the community in which they live. Psychologists are not convinced that the family should be necessarily prosperous for healthy development of personality. All that is needed is that the daily needs of the child are met, the house is neat and tidy, he is given nutritious food and parents are satisfied with what they have. Rich but discontend parents, ignorant of what foods are good for the child, always quarrelling and complaining against fate, anxious and worried, provide a very poor home environment for the child.

The nature of discipline in the home is also significant. If parents are over-strict and cruel children may grow into submissive and cowardly, without any initiative and spirit of adventure, and if discipline is too lax they may grow into self-centred and wilful, resenting social control. Therefore discipline should be firm and benevolent, based on understanding and regard for social values.

The influence of the mother is very important, and many children losing their mother in early years develop many kinds of mal-adjustment. Deprived of maternal affection in the formative years of childhood they find it difficult to develop normal affectionate relations even in later years. Either they fall for the first affectionate response or distrust expressions of affection.

The number of children in the family also makes a difference to personality development. The only child is spoilt, selfish and domineering. He is less social and co-operative, and does not try to understand other people's viewpoint. In a large family children co-operate and compete with each other; they may always be quarrelling or living in harmonious adjustment with each other.

**Personality and the school**

The influence of the school in shaping and moulding the personality of the child has not been sufficiently recognized.

Children enter the school with some of the habits and attitudes already established in the home, but their contacts with children from other homes with different attitudes and habits and with teachers whose thoughts and attitudes may be different from parents are sure to influence them. They are no longer protected by family ties and stand on their own legs with their classmates. They are eager to win the approval of their classmates and teachers and therefore imbibe those interests, attitudes and ways which are commended and approved in the school community. They look up to the teacher for guidance, identify themselves with him, consider him wise and clever and imitate him as a model. Books, games, dramatics and social experiences widen the mental horizon of children and broaden their outlook. Making friends, choosing favourite teachers and following their interest in extra-curricular activities helps them to know themselves. He competes with some and co-operates with others, and his major interests and abilities find greater scope for expression and development.

In progressive schools the needs, interests and abilities are particularly kept in view in framing their educational programmes, procedures and activities, and children get much freedom to develop along lines laid down by their inheritance. Such atmosphere has a very healthy influence on the personality of the child. The type of discipline which prevails in the school, the type of teachers and children found in the school, and the contents of the curricula and activities influence children's social adjustments, their enthusiasm for group work and their independent thinking.

**Methods of measuring personality**

It would be better to speak of assessing or judging personality rather than of measuring it because our main concern is to find out the progress an individual has made in personality development the degree to which a particular personality trait is found in an individual, and these traits are always changing and growing. Our estimate and assessment of these traits cannot be accurate as our tools of measurement are not so quantitatively precise. An important advantage of personality measurement is to find out the extent of individual adjustment to environment and to help and improve it as far as possible.

The methods commonly used in testing and judging personality are :— Case history, Interview, Questionnaires, Rating scales, Situation tests, Psycho-analytical tests, and Projective techniques. These we shall now discuss in detail.

**Case history**

This method has already been discussed in detail in the chapter on methods of psychological study. Its aim is to get as much information as possible about the family history of the individual, the social environment in which he has been brought up and in which he now lives, his physical condition—constitutional make-up and health, his education and training, his habits, attitudes and interests, his social and economic status, his adjustments to things and people around him, and whatever else bears on his life and personality. In doing so the person compiling case history must seek the co-operation of all those who have dealt with the individual in an important way as parents, teachers, friends, colleagues, relations, doctors. The successful use of case history method calls for specialized training. The method can be employed to study both normal and abnormal people.

**Interview**

Interviews are a popular and handy method of judging personality and are largely used by staff selection boards and public service commissions. But an interview can be successful if the interviewer is trained and knows what he is looking for and testing. In the hands of a psychologist the interview means that the person to be interviewed is encouraged to talk freely without any hesitation about his past experiences, what he thinks of them, what are his problems, how he proposes to tackle them. The psychologist simply listens to him and accepts all that he says. If he makes any remarks it is only to encourage the person to speak out his mind more freely. All the time he keeps observing how the person behaves, what hesitations he has and what his emotional responses are. The interview and the observations made reveal a lot about the person. But the method of interview is not scientific, it is subjective and the most successful interviewers are not able to tell what makes the interview most successful. It is not quantitative either and the results of different interviewers cannot be compared. Again some of the problems of personality are very complex and may not be reached by even the most skilful interviewer. A successful interview depends on the intimate rapport which the interviewer is able to establish between the interviewed person and himself, but this is not always easy to secure.

**Questionnaires**

Personality is frequently measured by questionnaires or series of questions devised to test a particular trait. R.S. Woodworth was the first to use it and devised a "Personal Data Sheet" in 1918 to determine emotional instability or neurotic tendency among soldiers. It had 116 questions, each answered by yes or no. His questions related to fears, worries, feelings and physical symptoms of mental disorders. Some of the questions are : Do you usually feel well and strong? Do you have nightmares? Have you often fainted? Do you worry that people are watching you?

On the basis of questionnaires attempts have been made to test extroversion-introversion, ascendance-submission, and sociability-solitariness traits of personality. The *Allport Ascendance-Submission Reaction Study* is a recent questionnaire of this type.

There are a series of questions, and answers are required in the form of yes or no. It is a self-report type of instrument. By classifying answers, it is possible to find out the type of problem the subject is facing and what he is doing to face it. An important difficulty in this method is that subjects try to slant their answers in such a manner as to conceal some aspects of their personality. This method is more suitable for the study of groups.

**Rating scales**

By this method certain traits of personality are divided into several classes on the basis of varying degrees of a trait and the individuals are ranged into these classes by people who know them intimately. Usually these degrees are indicated by numbers 1 to 4, or 1 to 5 or 1 to 7, and then we have a four, five or seven-point scale. Generally a five-point scale is used indicating very superior 5, superior 4, average 3, inferior 2, and very inferior 1. And the question expressing varying degrees may be ranged as for example, Is he honest? may be divided into five point scale.

Very honest 5 Generally honest 4 Honest 3 Generally dishonest 2 Very dishonest 1

The rater places a mark on the suitable descriptive phrase, and his judgement or rating is converted into a numerical score on a scale of 1 to 5. Or rating may be done by arranging a number of persons in the order in which they show a particular trait like dominance, self-reliance or honesty. The most dominant, self-reliant or honest are placed at one end and the least dominant, self-reliant or honest at the other, with other persons arranged in between.

These rating scales can be used only by those who know the person very closely and have observed him in respect of the trait about which they are rating him. It is always possible for the judges to make rating favourable or unfavourable, and the validity of this method of measurement can be demonstrated only when ratings done independently by a number of judges tally.

**Situation tests**

In these tests the behaviour of an individual in a particular type of situation is judged. These tests are usually employed for children. The best situation study of personality is provided by M.A. May and H. Hartshorne. They gave children many natural situations wherein they could easily cheat. In writing meanings of a given list of words they could copy from a neighbour's paper, consult a forbidden dictionary, change answers when scoring their own tests. There were other situtations in which stealing and lying was tested. These situations tests are very much limited in scope and validity. For one thing they can be employed only on children. They cannot be used on adults who respond differently in different situations and whose personality cannot be assessed on the basis of their responses in any one type of situation. Nor is it possible to test the behaviour of an individual in every type of situation because life presents such a large variety of situations as to be almost inexhaustible.

**Psychoanalytic methods**

The method of psychoanalysis has already been described in brief in the second chapter of this book. Here its help in studying and judging personality is discussed. We have already seen that unconscious factors are very powerful in determining and influencing human behaviour and personality, and a large part of our behaviour and the hidden pattern of our personality can be understood and judged only when those unconscious factors — motives and wishes —can be revealed. There are two ways in which this can be done. One is the method of *free-association* in which the individual is called upon to put down every word that comes to his mind when another is spoken or read This is a talking-out method in which the person is told to relax, think about his troubles and say everything that comes to his mind. Freud preferred this method to hypnosis because the person remained in an active co-operative state while coping with his difficulty. The second is *dream-analysis*. It supplements free-association. During free-association the individual may fail to recall, or hesitate to express, certain painful and embarrassing items. These are repressed but they may be identified by interpreting the individual's dreams. During sleep the check is relaxed and repressed ideas and wishes may slip into consciousness in the form of dreams. But they are disguised and their real meaning is expressed symbolically. We have already described these symbols and how they are to be interpreted. Obviously these two methods of psychoanalysis are used to study and judge abnormal persons, particularly those who are suffering from some mental disorder. After these tests the psychoanalyst informs the patient of what is wrong with him and it is assumed that mere knowledge of the cause of his disorder proves beneficial to the patient.

Fig. 14. Ink-blot test similar to the Rorshach test. People see all sorts of things in an ink-blot what the ink-blot means to you will show what sort of personality you are,

Fig. 15. Ink-blot test similar to the Rorshach test. People see all sorts of things in an ink-blot what the ink-blot means to you will show what sort of personality you are.

**Projective techniques**

Projective techniques of judging personality are being increasingly used. In this kind of test, material which may be interpreted in any of the different ways is presented to the person for his interpretation. It is believed that the person tested will project his values, desires and feelings — his personality — upon this material, and thus reveal what he is like by what he says.

According to L. K. Frank of the Macy Foundation these new methods give a person a chance to express his "private world of meanings, significances, patterns and feelings". When a person tells what a cloud looks like to him, or gives his own interpretation of a picture containing people, he "projects" into it something of his own personality. If he interprets several items in the same general way, this may reveal important trends of thinking, attitude, interest and emotion. Of the many types of projective techniques we shall describe three.

*The Rorschach test* is also called the *ink-blot test*. It is named after the Swiss psychiatrist Hermann Rorschach, who invented it about fifty years ago. He died in 1922 at the age of thirty-seven but many other workers in the field of psychology have continued his work and made improvement in the test. To make readers understand what this test is like a sample of ink-blot is given on the opposite page. This ink-blot is similar to the ten that Rorschach perfected. The "ink-blot" test consists of ten cards, each containing a rather elaboate ink-blot. Five blots are in colour, five in grey and black. Subjects study one blot at a time and tell what each blot resembles. They can think about the ink-blot as long as they like over each card. The examiner records the responses, then shows the cards a second time asking the subject to deal in detail with ambiguous interpretations and explain which part of the blot led to their responses. There are three criteria of scoring. Do subjects react to a whole blot, to a part, or to a small detail? Do their responses involve movement, form, colour, or the three combined, and is the form clear or blurred? Do subjects see human or animal figures, or chiefly inanimate objects? The complete scoring is very complex, involving many factors beyond mere counting of responses.

Seeing whole figures shows high intelligence and ability to combine. Seeing forms in motion, particularly human forms, shows vivid imagination, responses to colour show impulsiveness, even emotional instability. Seeing animals suggests lower intelligence, and noting unusual details shows introversion and mental conflicts.

Psychologists are not agreed about the value of these Rorschach tests and projective techniques in general. One says that they may be valid with children but their value with adults is doubtful. Others say that they lack objectivity, that their interpretation is intuitive and lacks experimental verification. However they have helped in diagnosing mental disorders.

*The Thematic Apperception Test* is another kind of projective technique.[9] It uses twenty pictures, each to be shown to the person taking the test in order that he may tell a story about the picture, and tells what he thinks the feelings and thoughts of the people in the picture might be. One picture, for example, might be of an elderly woman standing at the door, looking out. In the room by a table sits a young woman, head buried in her arms. What you have to say about the picture, it is believed, will tell something about your own personality. What you would make the hero or the heroine of the picture say or think will probably reflect what you yourself would say or think in a similar situation. These tests were first devised and used by H.A. Murray of Harvard University.

***World Test*** is another projective technique in which there is a collection of toy houses, barns, fences, trees, cars, men, women, children and animals and the subject is asked to arrange these objects as he likes. The way he places these objects together will show how he pictures this world to be and what place he thinks he should have in this world.

**Interest tests**

"Vocational Interest Blank" developed by E. K. Strong of Stanford University is very popular. There are two forms of his test, one for men and one for women. Each form of the test is an eight-page leaflet listing some 400 items covering occupations, school subjects, amusements, peculiarities of people and self-estimates of personal abilities and characteristics. The average time needed for this test is forty minutes though no time limit is set. The subjects record the responses by commenting, Like, Indifferent or Dislike. Strong does not claim that his test will predict accurately a person's success in a given occupation. Psychologists report that it is the most useful test to direct students toward suitable occupations and what is more important—to keep them out of fields for which they are unfit. While interests are largely determined by training psychologists find them remarkably consistent over a long period of time. Strong notes however that noticeable changes of interest occur between 15 and 25 years of age.

Each test described above measures but a small aspect of personality but taken together they are capable of yielding an adequate picture of total personality pattern.

**Conclusion**

It must have become clear to the reader that personality development results from many influences which work on the child. His intelligence and physical constitution are inherited, his temperament, his underlying energy and emotional tone, are affected by his endocrine glands, his nervous system and physical and physiological conditions. But they are not the only factors determining the final picture of personality. An individual's personality consisting of his traits, habits, attitudes, ideas, interests, values and ideals is largely a product of the environment. The family in which he was brought up, its social climate, and relations obtaining among its members; his experiences in the school, the type of children he mixes with, the type of teachers he has; the community, socio-economic status and the whole culture-pattern — all these influences bear on his life and personality. It is very difficult for psychologists to measure adequately the importance of these factors in developing and moulding personality. What work has so far been done is just a small beginning, and it is promising enough.

## Questions

1. What is personality? How would you distinguish it from character. Describe some of the major factors determining its nature.
2. What are the characteristics of personality? Discuss the social and biological factors in the formation of personality.
3. What do you understand by personality "traits"? Discuss some of the main dimensions of personality, and illustrate your answer.
4. Discuss the importance of social factors in personality? What influence have the social factors on personality? Discuss the role of the home and the school in moulding the personality of an individual.
5. Describe the different types of personality. How far is it desirable to classify people into types?
6. Explain — Introversion-extroversion and Ascendance-submission and describe the characteristics of individuals having such traits in high degree.
7. Compare the popular and scientific notions of personality. Can we really measure personality? Describe some of the important methods of personality measurement.
8. Write short notes on:—case history, interview, questionnaire, rating scales and situations tests, and give their value.
9. What is a projective technique? Describe some of the important projective techniques and give details of their procedure.
10. What is the psychoanalytical method of understanding personality? Give details.
11. Describe the nature and value of interest tests.

CHAPTER XV

# VOLUNTARY ACTION, CONFLICT AND DEFENCE MECHANISMS

We have studied behaviour and activity motivated by needs both inborn and acquired. Needs create discontent and tension and the individual acts to satisfy his needs and remove tension. Often these cannot be readily and immediately satisfied and the individual has to do a lot of thinking as to how he should proceed to satisfy such needs. There may be obstacles from without and from within, and the individual takes lot of time and effort before acting. Such action in which the individual has full knowledge of what he is going to do and why he is going to do it is called *voluntary action, volition* or *will,* and will be discussed in this chapter.

## Voluntary action

All behaviour is purposive but while reflex, instinctive and habitual actions are performed automatically a voluntary act is preceded by a full pre-vision of what we are going to do. The outward bodily movements are the same, but they are accompanied by a desire and fore-knowledge of the nature of our activity as well as of the purpose going to be served by it. This future end is present from the beginning in the form of an idea, and this idea rouses a wish and suggests to thought means for the realization of the end. The idea of the means and the end along with a desire on the part of the individual distinguishes the voluntary action from other types of action. It is an action performed knowingly, deliberately, with desire, decision, precision, and free choice of both the means and the end.

A voluntary action is opposed to involuntary or impulsive action and should be distinguished from it. An impulsive action is isolated, not the type we usually perform and would have performed,

... is not accompanied by any pre-knowledge of the end and the ... to its achievement, as a person suddenly loses his temper and strikes somebody. Reflex, instinctive and habitual actions are involuntary because they are performed more or less automatically. In a voluntary action the means and the end are first considered in relation to the total system of tendencies included in the conception of the self. When two urgent needs leading to the opposite courses of action are present simultaneously, when two motives pull us in two opposite directions we have conflict followed by inaction temporary or permanent, but when two voluntary actions oppose each other we have deliberation and reflect on their respective advantages and disadvantages. Voluntary action does not follow either of the conflicting needs or motives as such; it follows our preference and choice of the one against the other. It is the conception of the self as an agent which makes the difference. The alternative is not "this" or "that" but whether "I shall do this" or "I shall do that". Each line or course of action is considered not in isolation but as part of the ideally constructed whole for which the word "I" stands.

Woodworth speaks of voluntary action as a special case of mental manipulation in which we imagine some change to be produced in the existing situation and then proceed to put our imagination into effect. James characterises voluntary actions as secondary and involuntary actions like the reflex, instinctive or impulsive action as primary. The former require an idea of the movement before the movement is performed, and we are not endowed with the prophetic vision of what movements lie in our power, we must have performed such movements impulsively or instinctively before we have an idea about them. It is only when a movement has once been performed in an involuntary, random way and has left an image of itself in memory, that the movement can be desired and deliberately willed. Hence it is that the voluntary action is always a secondary response.

**Ideomotor action**

When an action follows the bare presentation of an idea of that action we have ideomotor action. We think of a particular movement and our muscles carry it out, though we may not have meant to do it ourselves. Such ideomotor actions are very simple, the movement follows the mere thought of it. While talking I become conscious of a pin on the floor or of some dust on my sleeve. Without interrupting the conversation I pick up the pin or brush away the dust. I make no express resolve, but the mere perception of the object and the fleeting notion of the act seem of themselves to bring it about. A good example of ideomotor action is had in an athletic audience. You are watching your friend doing the high jump and so absorbed are you in his running and so desirous are you of his succeeding that when he rises to clear the bar your leg also rises as if to clear the bar. The movement performed by you is due to the fact that at the moment there was only one idea in your mind and there was nothing to inhibit it. No conflicting notion is present, preference or choice is absent and the monopolizing idea issues into action.

**Deliberation**

But often many thoughts are present, many motives demand action. The individual may choose one of them and act but others inhibit action. With some favouring and others opposing action the individual is in a state of unrest and *indecision*. Action is arrested and the mind is said to deliberate. Several objects and alternatives engage attention and the self reviews the merits of the opposing courses of action. Whenever any one of them issues into action we are said to decide or declare in favour of one of them.

The process of deliberation is capable of great complications. The alternatives may be very simple, doing a thing or not doing it: or they may be incompatible lines of action equally attractive. The mind hesitates and vacillates, there is a sort of mental see-saw. Now one alternative and then another is brought into consciousness. There is a conflict of motives. The two courses of action are weighed and considered in all their possible advantages, merits and drawbacks. This state of disturbed equilibrium may last for weeks and months, occupying the mind at intervals. Today one set of motives or reasons appears stronger and more attractive, tomorrow another set. The self is inclined sometimes to one and sometimes to another.

### Types of decision

The problem is how in cases of deliberation does decision arise? How is suspense and hesitation translated into resolution and action? One way is to decide on reason, let arguments for and against any course of action decide without any effort on our part. There are individuals who have fixed rules of conduct and they take their decisions in their light and according to them. In another type of decision the evidence for and against any course may have all been received and both may be equally attractive or unattractive, and we decide in favour of one because we are tired of a long state of indecision and think that any decision is better than no decision. In such cases we decide by accident, say by a toss of coin or by passion as we decide in a come-what-may mood. But there is one type of decision in which we feel as if we ourselves by our own effort have taken the decision. The course of action taken by us is clearly more reasonable but that is not enough because it is opposed by a course of action which is habitual and instinctive, and we have to add our own living effort to the reasonable course. This happens when a person represses his cries of pain under a surgeon's knife, exposes himself to social disapproval or follows a line which will force him to poverty, unemployment or suffering for the sake of some duty or ideal. He follows the "line of greatest resistance", and speaks of conquering and overcoming strong impulses and temptations. These temptations are emotionally very strong, the individual is in the habit of yielding to them but on this occasion he by his own strong resolve resists it, the voice of the ideal is weak but he adds his own living effort to it and thus overcomes the course of temptations, as a person in the habit of smoking or drinking resists the temptation.

Now where does this effort come from? Some psychologists describe it as the effort of will or will-power. Others hold that it springs from the *sentiment of self-regard.* It is a sentiment for myself, a system of impulses, emotions and desires which grows up and becomes organized about the idea of self and all that is related to it. Each one of us has formed a mental picture of what we consider ourselves to be in an ideal way and then have built up a sentiment for that picture so that all our actions and behaviour is consistent with that mental picture of ourselves. Mohan considers himself to be an educated man, son of a respectable person, member of a family considered high in social standing, one who does not go out in shabby dress, does not eat on the road, does not mix with low company, avoids using certain vulgar words and the like, and his course of conduct is affected by this picture. It is the sentiment for this idea of self which provides the effort to overcome temptations and behave in an ideal manner, to decide in favour of duty against easy, pleasant line of what most people do to avoid hardship. Modern psychology has stressed it in what they call the *self concept*.

Your *concept of self* plays a very important part in life. It may give you self-confidence or an inferiority feeling, it may make you brag and boast or it may make you modest and shy. Your behaviour is affected by what you consider yourself to be, and what concept you have formed about yourself is based on your experience of your self. You look yourself in the mirror, you hear people saying things about you, blaming you or praising you, you compare yourself with others, you note your success and failure, you read about the personality traits of others and compare yourself with them, you read biographies and novels with characters good and bad and you assess your own personality in the light of what you read about other people real or imaginary. All this gives you knowledge and thought about yourself, it helps you to form and develop a concept about yourself. It is this concept which re-inforces your choice or decision when you resist a pleasant course of action and follow a more difficult one.

Now it is very necessary that one should have a very correct and true concept of oneself, a very clear picture of what he can and cannot do, about his physique, intellect and personality. He should be aware of his flaws also, but ordinarily he should have a high opinion about himself so that he can go about doing the important things in life with confidence and courage.

**Conflict**

But it may not be always possible for us to reach a decision. We may continue to be torn by a feeling or desire for two or more courses of action which may be equally pleasant or equally unpleasant. It is this opposition or clash of desires which we call *conflict.* A conflict, when it is an even tug of war between two urgent and strong wants, keeps a person from acting one way or another, thus arousing painful emotions. This stirred-up emotional state is injurious to health and if it persists can do much harm. It is essential for a person's well-being that conflicts be overcome within a reasonable time by deciding on a definite course of action, fully accepted by the person. Conflicts vary from those that are comparatively short-lived and persist for a few days to those which are very serious and complicated and persist for weeks, months and years. The short-lived ones bring in only a brief period of tension, whereas the chronic ones may have serious emotional consequences.

A young lady may be torn between the desire to accept an offer of a job and the desire to get married into a rich family to a handsome youngman. Such an opportunity for marriage may not come again nor will there be an another offer of a job promising opportunities for promotion and advance. She is very unhappy and unable to decide. If she is wise she should understand that she cannot have the best of both the worlds and must decide early. Life is full of choices and conflicts. In every case we have moments when we are not able to decide and waver between two courses of action But few realize that to continue to waver and never make up one's mind is to invite serious mental trouble.

Violent conflicts may be caused by clashes between loyalty and desire between opposing ideas, and between right and wrong. Most of these conflicts cause trouble because the individual has no ideals, principles or goals of conduct and craves for self-indulgence and pleasure or has strong inferiority feelings and craves for independence. Some people are always wanting perfection and creating conflicts for themselves and others.

Conflicts are a great danger to mental health, and may be carried on at the unconscious level. The clash between urges, desires and motives may go on without our being fully aware of it, and ideas and wishes may disturb us without our knowing that a serious conflict is going on and causing mental turmoil. There is always an unconscious aspect of our interests, motives and mental processes, and of conflicts which prevent a solution and which keep the mental trouble stewing. The best thing to do is to keep analysing ourselves and to realize that decision and action are necessary to living.

**Frustrations**

People of all ages have needs which they try to satisfy. They need food and shelter, a feeling of worth, recognition and security. They need physical health, house and money, they need a job and friends. When they are unable to satisfy their needs and desires they feel *frustrated or thwarted.* Some frustration is normal and common and may often rouse the individual to higher and bigger effort. But if one is continually frustrated, if defeats and failures are more frequent than achievements and success, it may injure one's personality. Frustration is the blocking or thwarting of one's needs and desires. A student may feel frustrated because his parents do not send him enough money, his teachers neglect him, his classmates ignore him, he is unable to score high or get selected for the hockey team and in many other ways. Too many people in this world combine very high ambitions and dreams with very limited ability and resources and nurse feelings of frustration in their lives.

Sources of frustration may be physical obstacles such as distance, climate or social such as unemployment or lack of friends. Or they may be internal as lack of physical power, intellectual ability or health. So many people today are frustrated because they are not getting enough to feed their children, to give medical treatment to their kith and kin or to provide education and comfort to their families. Frustration is the blocking and unfulfilment of needs and wishes over a long period of time. Some people pitch their ambitions and aspirations too high for their abilities and powers; others have very high expectations far beyond their actual needs, and the cause of frustration is within them. But sometimes the source of frustration is outside. Unemployment, obstacles, defeats and failures due to political and economic changes over which we have no control may cause frustration.

The first reaction to frustration is that of anger, hostility, aggression and withdrawal but it may not lead to satisfactory adjustment. Or the individual may try to change and overcome the conditions which cause frustration or may avoid and bypass frustrating conditions, or the individual may change his goals. To overcome frustration we should act in such a manner as to promote growth and development.

**Adjustments and maladjustments**

On failing in the examination one student either works hard with greater application and diligence to pass next time or gives up studies and joins some job forgetting about his failure but another curses his examiners, develops a hatred for the college and the teachers, considers the whole organization corrupt and dishonest and blames teachers and examiners in every possible manner. The adjustment of the former student is healthy, he has got rid of any possibility of conflict in his mind and has overcome his frustrarion. The latter has only made his conflict and frustration more violent and worse, the type of activity in which he has sought shelter is unhealthy and his adjustments are false and wrong; he will not be able to achieve anything positive and he is only trying to deceive himself and his world that he is right, worthy and capable, and others with whom he is having to deal for his examination are wrong, unworthy and incapable. Such adjustments are called *mal-adjustments*, and may when more persistent and intense lead to disorders of the mind and behaviour.

Every normal persons needs recognition. He wants to be considered worthy in his own eyes and in the eyes of others. That is he wants self-acceptance and acceptance of himself by others. It is the most powerful force in every human being from an early age, and it is the mainspring of a large part of his behaviour. Our ambitions are greatly influenced by this need. If this need is not satisfied, that is, if the individual does not receive this acceptance because of his achievements and personality, he will try to obtain recognition and acceptance through other means. Such means, methods or devices which he employs to overcome his defeats, failures and difficulties are called *mechanisms*. Because they defend his esteem, prestige and dignity against defeats and failures they are called *defence mechanisms*. They are substitute or counterfeit methods and while they may for a short time pass for useful devices to boost and enhance one's prestige and save him from disgrace or humiliation, nothing positive or constructive can be achieved through their use. A healthy person will not use them for achieving health, happiness or success. One should try to achieve worth through true, straightforward and helpful attitude to men and situations around us.

We shall now discuss some of the important defence mechanisms like rationalization, negativism, compensation, projection, regression, respression, sublimation, indentification, malingering, daydreaming. We may classify them into two kinds, those in which the individual tries to hide his faults and weaknesses and those in which he tries to run away from his troubles and problems.

**Hiding one's faults**

We all hide our faults and weaknesses so that others may think well of us and we may have prestige with our friends, but the danger lies in allowing the tendency to do so habitually. When we feel inadequate and weak we try to give the impression that we are strong and capable. Let us describe some of the ways we do so. Maybe a knowledge of them helps us to avoid them.

The first mechanism by which we hide our faults and weaknesses is *rationalization*, in which we unconsciously give reasonable but untrue excuses or explanations of our behaviour. We do so in order to defend and justify our behaviour and to maintain our feelings of worth and self-esteem. When a father rebukes a son in college for unsatisfactory score, he may get a reply: "Marks do not mean much. I do not wish to be a bookworm". The son is defending and excusing himself for low score by giving plausible but untrue reasons. It is a face-saving device. When the fox in the famous story unable to reach grapes turns away that they are sour and it does not want them, it is rationalising. It had set its heart on it but unable to reach it says that they are not worth reaching. Thus it derives comfort and saves its esteem. Many poor people unable to provide better conditions for their children sing praises of poverty pleading that they do not have to worry about their wealth. They hide their lack of ambition and laziness and rationalize their poverty.

There is something good in rationalisation. When we cannot help or improve things rationalization will help us to bear them. Many leaders during war begin to sing praises of war so that people may accept the hardships it brings. But by rationalizing we are only deceiving ourselves and others and it creates further maladjustments. The best thing to do is to accept failure and weakness and try to correct or improve ourselves so that we can face reality, recognize the truth and try to solve the problem. One should think of solutions and not excuses.

Or we may throw the blame for our failures and weaknesses on others. The student may say "I do not get very good marks because the teacher does not like me", "There is so much favouritism in the college", "Even university examination results are cooked". All this is *projection*. Responsibility for our failures, defeats and weaknesses is shifted on to others, situations, tools, organizations or other persons—we are indulging in projection. A bad workman quarrels with his tools, a tennis player puts the ball in the net and then looks at the racket as if the racket has done it, the housewife blames the oven, the grocer or utensils for bad cooking. Or we may plead that others too have our faults, that the pass percentage this year is very low, that a large number of students have failed, that the university is going to the dogs and the like. In this way we not only try to push our weakness and failure away from us, but also gain a feeling of superiority over those to whom we attribute our faults.

Businessmen blame the times for bad trade conditions, or government for interference; many grown-up persons blame their early home conditions for their poor marks; a dishonest person criticizes others for dishonesty; modern China sees colonialism and imperialism in Indian and American policies and programmes. All of them are attributing to others their own motives, desires, qualities, defects or attitudes and thus using others as a screen on which are thrown out one's own mental states and processes. Literary critics are very ready victims of projection and through their comments and criticisms they reveal their own foibles and faults.

Projection, in a way, is a form of rationalization, because it excuses failure and places faults on others.

There are people who always answer "no" when they are asked to do something, to join in a game, or go out on a hike. This is *negativism.* Such people make negative responses to all situations and demands, they resent criticism, they usually do not accept invitations or cooperate with others. They are the contrary-type and build round themselves a fence of "no's". They hide their faults and weaknesses by not responding or doing just the opposite of what they are requested to do. Stubborn, hard and unrelenting, they rebel against every move. A good many of such people were unfairly treated in early life. This method of response is very common. Many people on reading "Stick no bills here", "keep off the grass", and the like deliberately violate such advice. Negativism is quite common among young children and women, and are they not often victims of unfair treatment?

Negative people sometimes expect to be asked a number of times. They get a feeling of worth if others have to ask them again and again. Some people are negative because they lack confidence, feel inadequate and insecure. They are afraid of not succeeding or doing well in the new situation, and others will find out thei limitations. In discussion they usually take the opposite view, do not welcome new ideas or people and are critical and fault-finding.

Many people use *compensation* to enhance their self-esteem and prestige. Compensation refers to more or less unconsciously motivated behaviour whose purpose is to make up for what the individual feels he lacks. A student not well up in studies may make up by distinguishing himself in games or dramatics or by putting on fine clothes and entertaining his friends. Compensation is good when we compensate for our inadequacies and failures with virtues and strength, with positive and constructive achievement. It is undesirable when we try to cover up our faults and weaknesses with unacceptable and useless behaviour. Many bullies, trouble-shooters and mischievous students in school are those who are trying to get into limelight, to earn a name for courage, hardiness and nerve, and to win applause from their school fellows. They may have an undesirable reputation but they are proud of it and brag about it.

Some people stand too much for their rights and are quick-tempered because of weakness in some other field. Those who are very stiff, do not invite conversation, are hard to talk to and dislike being questioned may be compensating for their lack of some quality or ability, for some inadequacy. Such behaviour helps to protect them and their formality and distant ways pass for loftiness. A really successful person is modest and does not need to put on airs. Many eminent persons have done remarkable things in life just to compensate for what they lacked in other directions. Compensation is very common in our modern competitive culture in which everybody is trying to excel and surpass others.

People may hide their faults and weaknesses by banishing them altogether from consciousness, that is, by *repressing* them. This process of forgetting of embarrassing thoughts and memories related to our faults and weeknesses takes place at the unconscious level. When we have conflicts we cannot handle, unpleasant thoughts we cannot face, and injuries to our prestige we will not acknowledge, repression occurs and for the time being they are avoided and banished from consciousness. Repression is burying our troubles but they are not destroyed, they smoulder in the unconscious and whenever there is an opportunity due to mental slackness they burst into conscious behaviour and cause trouble.

**Running away from troubles**

When situations and experiences are painful and shameful, when we are threatened with failure and defeat, we try to run away and escape them. We may pretend illness, take to drinking, daydreams, regression or displacement, identification or sublimation. They are *escape mechanisms.* Let us deal with them in detail.

When problems are hard to solve, when situations are fraught with failure and defeat, are unpleasant and embarrasing, we use illness, real or feigned, to escape them. Many students pretend illness or really fall ill on the approach of examinations. They have headache or nausea or may develop fever. They actually fall ill. This is a typical attempt to escape from the distasteful situation. They hope they would be excused because they cannot be blamed if they fall ill. The soldier who is afraid of the battle, and the housewife who dislikes housework, commonly make use of this escape mechanism.

Some people take to alcohol to escape difficulties, boredom and frustrations. *Drinking* transports them into a new world where worries, fears, humiliations, difficulties and problems do not bother them. Nowadays there is greater appreciation of the psychological aspect of alcoholism and psychological treatment is resorted to in helping alcoholics to get rid of this escape mechanism which in course of time becomes habitual.

We have already dealt with *daydreams* and *phantasy* in escaping from reality. Reading fiction, watching movies or listening to radio when excessively indulged in offer escape from the trials and tribulations of the real world, but they are a poor preparation to meet the problems and difficulties of life squarely and directly or to gain worth.

*Identification* is the unconscious placing of oneself in the situation of another person and assuming the characteristics of that person. It is the practice of feeling that you are in the role of someone else. When you look at a film, you may identify yourself with one of the actors in it and feel yourself in his position, thus obtaining the emotional experience of being that actor. Young people frequenting film shows identify themselves with actors to get rid of their troubles. In real life the young student may be struggling to keep his body and soul together but in the cinema hall he feels a millionaire or a lover. Hero-worship, declaring social and political leaders as our guiding stars, testimonial advertizing, and the like, help us to run away from our troubles and boost our prestige.

*Displacement* is the expression of our emotions in a situation other than the one which aroused it. Direct expression of such emotions is inhibited and it is transferred to a neutral idea or object. A man is snubbed by his superior but he cannot snub back. Soon reaching home he takes it out on his family and loses his temper with his wife. It is a kind of substitution, an escape from one situation and fixing one's blame on another situation or person. Many primitive people beat their breasts when they are helpless in expressing their hostility against their enemies. Self-torture and suicides are often cases of displaced aggression and anger.

*Regression* is a flight into childhood, and the individual retreats to an earlier and lower level of development. He adopts childish modes of adjustment. Very often instead of meeting difficulties and tragedies in the face people start weeping and sobbing like a child. In moments of anxiety they start biting their nails like children. Many women dash their heads against a wall when they are intensely frustrated. Many grown-up people shout and jump out of joy as young people do. All these are examples of regression in which adults go back to the childish level of behaviour and adjustment. In a way all maladjustments are regressive because the person withdraws from the situation and adopts too simple a solution of his difficulties.

*Reaction formation* is an unusual method of controlling undesirable or socially unacceprable urges, it is to deny their existence and to develop diametrically opposed traits that conceal and check the more basic motives. People who protest too much are really admitting their guilt, who pose as custodians of religion and morals are abnormally interested in sex and who go out of their way to impress you with their generosity are most miserly. Very often those who preach most aggressively are themselves guilty of not following what they preach.

*Sublimation* is "flight into creative work". Here primitive urges are re-directed into new channels which may be useful and enjoyable for both the individual and society. The term was originally employed by Freud and his followers for re-direction of sex urge into substitute behaviour like art, literature. The psychoanalysts believed that all our culture would not have developed into the complex pattern that it is today. Many young women to satisfy their needs of family and children of their own sublimate their desire by taking to teaching in a school or looking after patients as a nurse. Sublimation arises out of frustrarion of strong desires.

This long list of defence mechanisms describes different types of frustration reactions. The list is not complete, they are just modes of adjustment in conflict and frustration, and there are many more ways of adjustment. Some people take to back-biting in frustration, some withdraw and retreat from active life, others behave in such a manner as to attract attention. Such mechanisms are learned in social situations and lead to behaviour which is largely social. Social or group behaviour we will discuss in the next chapter.

## Behaviour disorders

There are certain disorders of mind, behaviour and personality which a student of psychology ought to be familiar with, and they are briefly described here.

*Psychoneuroses* or neuroses are minor disorders of behaviour and personality which are essentially mental. They are caused by inner struggles and unsatisfactory social relations. They are made worse by violent conflicts, emotional stresses and frustrarion, and since they are caused by psychological factors they can be treated only psychologically. No amount of medical treatment has any effect on them. They have physical symptoms but their treatment is mainly psychological. Although they disturb and weaken the person very badly, and are a source of great anxiety to the family and his friends compulsory treatment in a hospital is not necessary. The frequent psychological troubles are anxiety, depression, lack of concentration of attention, inability to decide or remember, doubts and fears of great intensity, compulsions, obsessions sleeplessness and bad social relations. Physical symptoms are indigestion, headache, fatigue, excitement of abnormal type, palpitation, temperature, pains all over the body and lack of control over sensory and motor functions. About 5 to 10 per cent people suffer from them. Some of the main kinds are *hysteria, neurasthenia, anxiety state, obsessions, phobias.*

Hysteria is marked by loss of function, limbs are paralysed, blindness, deafness, loss of memory and loss of feeling in the skin are present. But the causes of these ailments are essentially psychological.

In neurasthenia the individual is always extremely tired, he lacks energy, cannot concentrate, is irritable, there are pains in muscles and digestion is very much upset. Another form of this disorder is hypochondria in which the person is always worrying about his health, consulting doctors or reading books on health and disease.

In anxiety state the person suffers from tension, feels insecure, restless and dizzy, has fears, indigestion, palpitation and sweating, and is always expecting some calamity to happen to him.

In obsessions and compulsions the person feels persistent and irresistable urge to touch and handle things, to count steps or to wash his hands again and again. Phobias are abnormal fears without any reason or ground. The person may be terror-stricken by a feather, open spaces, high places or crowds.

Then there are psychoneuroses produced by such situations as sad tragedies in the family or a battle-field.

*Psychoses* are very serious conditions; a person's maladjustment is so severe that he cannot associate with other people, look after himself or carry on any work; he is so disturbed that he cannot judge between the real and the unreal and his personality is highly disorganized; we call him *psychotic*. A psychosis is considered organic when it can be explained in terms of infection, brain damage, alcohol, aging of brain, tumours and the like. When no such cause is found it is functional.

Functional psychoses are paranoia, schizophrenia and manic-depressive reactions. A patient of paranoia has persistent delusions either of persecution or grandeur. He may believe that the whole world is against him and is trying to do him harm or he may believe himself to be some big man. Schizophrenia is marked by retreat from reality, delusions, silly behaviour, stupor, excitement and the like. A manic-depressive patient has spells of prolonged elation or prolonged depression. When he is elated he is over-talkative, most active and agile even without reason; when he is depressed he is silent and withdrawn.

Organic psychoses are general paresis due to syphilis in which personality and intelligence are impaired, senile psychosis in which brain degenerates due to old age and there is loss of memory, confusion and depression, hardening of cerebral arteries with the same symptoms as occur in old age, or delerium tremens due to excessive drinking over a long period of time in which the person has hallucinations, no awareness of time and place, and strong fears.

Psychoses need hospital treatment and go by the general name of insanity though this term is avoided by psychologists. Often more than one mental disorder is present. Psychological treatment or psychotherapy has no effect on such patients. The causes are organic and the diseases need medical treatment, while psychoneuroses are purely psychological and respond to psychotherapy.

## Questions

1. What do you understand by voluntary activity? Compare it with reflex, instinctive and habitual actions.

2. How do we decide in a case of clash of motives? Discuss the role of self-regarding sentiment and self-concept in deciding choice of behaviour.

3. Explain conflict and frustration. What is their effect on our behaviour and how do we react to them?

4. What is a defence mechanism? Illustrate your answer.

5. What defence mechanisms do people employ to hide their faults and weaknesses? Give examples.

6. What defence mechanisms do people employ so as to run away from their troubles?

7. Explain : Displacement, projection, rationalization, compensation, regression and sublimation.

8. Distinguish between psychoneurosis and psychosis, and mention examples of each giving their symptoms.

9. Give a few examples of unhealthy behaviour and show how it can be treated.

CHAPTER XVI

# SOCIAL BEHAVIOUR

So far we have been discussing the behaviour of the individual, but man is essentially a social being. He is tremendously affected by the people he meets and talks to daily, and they in turn are affected by him. He is born in a particular culture made up of institutions, laws, customs, fashions, language and objects of many kinds which are peculiar to it and his behaviour is influenced by it. We have already pointed out how culture and our social patterns influence personality and behaviour. What distinguishes an American from a Bengali to a large extent sums up differences in influences of culture on personality and behaviour. Therefore a study of human behaviour would be incomplete without understanding the social situations and forces which influence, shape and mould it. To this aspect of behaviour we now turn our attention.

**Social behaviour**

Social behaviour is behaviour in a social situation which is marked by the presence of other people and which involves social interaction. Other people may be directly and immediately present or they may be present in thought, as we meet a friend and smile or remember a person who injured us and frown. Other people are sensitive, that is, they perceive us and react to us. They communicate with us by gestures or language, spoken or written, and they adjust to us in the light of our role and status in society. They may respect and obey us if they are junior to us or command and control us if they are our superior.

Social behaviour is described as interaction with the social environment which consists of inter-personal relations, inter-group relations, customs, ideals and institutions, language, art, literature, crafts, science and technology. They all act on the individual and influence his responses. His needs are modified his habits and traits are influenced and his entire personality undergoes change under its influence. He develops etiquette, follows the fashions prevailing in his group, learns their language and lives and behaves like them. His joys and sorrows, his taste and hobbies, his aims and ideals are all products of social interaction. He works for the group, community or state in which he lives and is in turn influenced and moulded by them.

Social interaction may take place between one person and another, between one person and a group, and between one group and another. The individual learns many things from his father and teacher, enjoys the company of his best friend, and shares domestic life with his wife. This is person-to-person interaction. He follows the traditions of his community, he captains the college team, obeys the college rules and does in a crowd what others do. This is person-to-group interaction. His caste does not permit marriages with certain castes, his nation is at war with a neighbouring country, his college is playing a hockey match against another college; this is group-to-group interaction.

Such interaction may be one of opposition, clash and conflict or it may be one of co-operation and mutual helpfulness. In social life differences, irritations and quarrels are as common as agreements, joys of working together and affectionate ties. Social psychology which studies social behaviour has to study all those relations and processes which are involved in social interaction, which change social behaviour and which stabilize and direct social behaviour.

**Socialization**

We have described man as a social being, but he is not social to begin with. In fact every child is very much self-centred and unsocial but through interaction and learning becomes social. Socialization is a process of social growth. The individual through social interaction and social learning comes to acquire and adapt patterns of behaviour prevalent in adult society to which he belongs, and is accepted as a member of the adult community. Every culture has its own ways of satisfying biological needs, of responding to and behaving toward, other members of the group, of meeting social situations, of communicating with others through language spoken and written, of expressing feelings and emotions, of improvement in conduct and the like. Unless the individual conforms to such conduct he cannot play any effective role in society. He learns to eat, dress, talk and behave in the same manner as other members of his community do, and to cherish the same ideas and ideals as they do. Of course there are individual differences but the general pattern of life and behaviour among members of the same group is similar. He develops the same habits, traits, needs, attitudes and the like, as are tolerated and approved by society in which he is born and brought up.

Obviously the process of socialization is not a simple process. Many types of influences contribute to it. The family and parents are most effective in moulding and shaping his behaviour. The influence of the mother in teaching children habits of cleanliness, eating, dressing, speaking and behaving in a manner acceptable to their group is very important. The home training and discipline lays the foundation of his moral and social growth, and he learns the primary lessons of sharing things with others, co-operating with them, treating them with consideration, postponing the gratification of his desires.

The process is further carried by the school, his play groups, neighbours and the street. Direct and frank criticism of his conduct and achievement gives him a knowledge about himself and the world around him. He learns to give and take, to discover his abilities and weak points, to adjust himself to a large variety of people, young and old. His knowledge of the world grows, his command of the language improves and he is more and more effectively introduced to the social heritage. The school and the college, together with the newspapers, the radio, the cinema, social experiences in several areas of life and work, contact with great men and their thoughts, and books, friends and relations, all subject him to the culture of the group, and community and race and make [illegible] man of him. Social interaction converts the biological organis[illegible] into human, social and moral. Conformity makes him res[illegible] his fellowmen, and though individual differences persist, the individual is socialized.

### Some factors in socialization

*Imitation*, *suggestion* and *sympathy* play a very effective role in socialization and social interaction. Some psychologists like McDougall have called them general tendencies. We will discuss them here in some detail.

In a popular sense *imitation* means anything from following the leader to copying a design. Psychologists have tried to explain similarities of behaviour by imitation but the modern view is that similarities of behaviour may occur for several reasons, including pure chance, and even when imitation does take place, it does not occur blindly. The individual imitates those acts which have a meaning for him and which harmonize with his desires. Boys follow the hair-cut of their favourite film hero and girls follow the coiffure of their favourite actress because they think it makes them look like him or her.

There are two types of imitation. Children smile or cry because others are smiling or crying. This is primary imitation. Children learn to speak and use a language by primary imitation. But they learn to write or multiply by deliberately and consciously imitating how others do it. This is deliberate imitation.

Many people believe that imitation is a low order of learning and behaviour, something lavish and unworthy, and is characteristic of the raw and the immature. Others think that it kills originality and creativeness, but in the first place imitation is never an exact reproduction and in the second it is always those who can imitate who are more educable.

There are certain conditions in which people imitate and there are other conditions in which they do not imitate. It seems that people imitate only when imitation satisfies some need or helps them to reach a goal. Young people imitate hair-cuts, gait or dress but not the art, skill or diligence of their favourite stars. Some imitate one thing and some another. All this shows that imitation is not as powerful a force as some psychologists used to claim some years back.

*Suggestion* is accepting other people's ideas without reason or criticism and a person who is inclined to accept uncritically a statement made by another is called "suggestible". When film stars, champion athletes or statesmen recommend a certain brand of soap, many suggestions are carried along with their statements. It is suggested that the soap is good for complexion and helps to acquire qualities of leadership. Many experiments show how effective suggestion is. How a dead wire gives a shock when the button is pressed, how a chemistry student reports smell from an odourless liquid, or how children are frightened by a striking picture of a cat.

People differ very widely in their readiness to accept suggestions from others. Children from the age of five to twelve are more suggestible than boys and men, ignorance makes people more suggestible. Crowds are more suggestible than individuals comprising them. Suggestibility is not a personality trait because it is often greatly affected by changes in environment and mental and bodily states.

Suggestions may work directly or indirectly. Parents, teachers, leaders and salesmen make direct suggestions and call upon them to behave in a particular way. But in indirect suggestion the aim is concealed: "It is better than the best", "A good boy speaks the truth", "Millions have found relief by using this medicine" are indirect suggestions.

We usually speak of three kinds of suggestion: ideomotor suggestion, prestige suggestion, and auto-suggestion. Ideo-motor suggestion is what is called empathy, as for example a spectator watching a high jump lifts his leg when the jumper takes the jump. Prestige suggestion is illustrated by advice given by great names in public life, film stars recommending soap and face creams, athletes recommending a tonic and the like. In auto-suggestion the suggestion comes from within, we accept our own ideas uncritically. We stick to our opinions, ideals and beliefs, it is auto-suggestion.

Suggestion plays a powerful role in social life and interaction and is an important way of modifying and controlling social behaviour. It underlies all processes of socialization.

*Sympathy* is feeling with others, experiencing emotions which are being experienced by our fellowmen. Seeing other people in grief, joy or anger we tend to feel the same emotion. During riots people are carried away by the emotions of others. Sympathy binds people together and is a source of strengthening social ties. Leaders make appeals to the sympathy of people to arouse them to action. Social unity is often based on sympathy.

**Co-operation and competition**

Co-operation is working together for a common end which cannot be achieved by individual effort. Modern civilised life is largely a co-operative affair. Schools and colleges, religious institutions, business houses, industrial plants or government work cannot go on without active co-operation between those associated with them. Co-operation is working together without conflict, and human society depends on people working together. Competition is mutual rivalry. It is trying to equal or surpass the speed, quality or amount of work done by another person or group. Modern society is very competitive and everybody seems to be running a race to get ahead of others. Our educational system encourages competition and students are always trying to beat and surpass other students. Examinations and tournaments are based on competition.

For psychologists the question often posed is: which motive is more powerful, co-operation or competition? There are certain communities in the world which have no spirit of competition and if anybody tries to excel others he is looked down upon. Americans are far more competitive than Indians for example. But generally speaking both co-operation and competition are found in all social life and interaction. A game of cricket, a business house, work in the classroom and other areas of life and work involve both competition and co-operation. Usually individuals take to competition when co-operation fails as they jump a queue when standing in the queue does not help. Some experimental studies have been made taking two similar groups one of which worked in co-operation and the other in competition, and it has been found that the co-operative group produced better and greater results.

With greater trend toward socialism all over the world co-operation is being encouraged and stimulated in all areas of life and work.

### Personality and Culture

Personality varies with the kind of culture in which it develops. The cultural and social environment in which an individual is brought up has a powerful influence on personality traits. Broadly speaking an American is different from a Hindu as is a Chinese from an Arab. Primitive peoples are different from civilized people, an orthodox Hindu brought up in hills is different from one who has returned after spending ten years in England. Such differences are due to cultural and social background which have affected their ways of doing and behaving.

Even within the same culture are seen personality differences between people living in affluent rich quarters and those living in slums, between people of high castes and of low castes, between intellectuals and low labourers. Hindu personality did undergo changes in different periods of history. A Hindu of the Mogul times is different from a Hindu of the British days or ancient Hindu days. Cultural influences make a difference to personality make-up.

### Social Norms

The characteristics of each culture are expressed in customs, traditions and values. They represent their *social standards* or *norms* of behaviour. Hindu widows shave their heads in some communities, in others they only cover their heads. Hindus take off their shoes while eating, Englishmen take off their hats on entering a room or on meeting a lady. Certain standards of living and behaving are expected of a Brahamin, a soldier, a doctor or a state governor. Muslim ladies have different social norms from American ladies. A man should have only one wife, we should work only six days in a week, women should not go to the cremation ground and the like are social norms which regulate the behaviour of people in different communities, societies and cultures.

Social norms are changed and reconstructed. After Independence Indians have been changing social norms in dress, greeting, language, ceremonies and the like.

Again every individual plays several roles in society. He is a father, brother, friend, a boss, subordinate, member of a club, community or nation. All these roles affect his attitudes and traits and influence his everyday behaviour. His status in social life makes him live and behave according to the expectations of his colleagues.

**Ego-involvement**

Accepting social norms, playing certain roles and acting according to his status makes an individual conscious of his identity and self. It is only through social experiences that he develops the idea of self, and when his attitudes toward himself get involved in his activities we call him *ego-involved*. Bringing up children he gets deeply interested in their progress and welfare. He provides them with food, clothes, medical aid and education. If they make progress and prosper he feels proud, if they fail he feels humiliated. We say he is now deeply involved in them. This ego-involvement is highly selective and the entire behaviour of the individual is directed only toward certain things and situations, those which affect the persons with whom he is so involved. Some individuals identify themselves with certain causes, ideals and objects, they work and live for them with consistency and single-mindedness. They do not attend to other things. Tolstoi. Gandhi and Lenin were intensely pre-occupied with their missions and this ego-involvement pervaded their whole behaviour.

**Social attitudes**

As a result of social learning and interaction each one of us acquires certain attitudes toward persons, things, situations and issues. They are more or less permanent ways of adjusting and behaving. We do not experience or feel them but we infer them from what people say and do. These attitudes make a considerable difference in the life of almost everybody and our success and failure depend on our attitude to our abilities and work and we are anxious to create favourable attitudes in all those with whom we come in contact. Officers must know the attitudes of thier subordinates toward themselves and work, business managers must know what the attitudes of workers are toward work, things produced and management, statesmen must know what attitudes people have toward their policies, programmes and administrative measures. Our attitudes largely determine our behaviour, thoughts and effort, with regard to any situation or issue and therefore knowledge and study of attitudes is most important in any programme of controlling and changing other peoples' behaviour.

During the last few decades extensive studies have been made of attitudes, their measurement and changes, and social psychology has now become largely a study of attitudes.

Social attitudes are those which are shared by others. My attitude to socialism, prohibition, widow re-marriage, disarmament and other social problems may be shared by a large number of my countrymen. They concern a large number of other individuals and are social attitudes.

Leaders in political life must know how widely and strongly these attitudes are held by the people because it is not possible for them to work against them. They must either change them or go by them. In any democratic government people's attitudes are a matter of vital concern to people in authority, not only they may vote against them but they may also not co-operate in any new measures of social change that are taken in hand from time to time.

Several scales of attitude measurement have been devised. They help us in finding out how stable are our attitudes, and what has been the effect of education and propaganda in influencing and changing our attitudes. Scales have been used before and after the use of such influences. These studies have revealed the influence of factors like religion, parents, education and film shows in modifying our attitudes. A knowledge of what social conditions change our attitudes will help us in controlling social behaviour.

Secondly surveys of attitudes and opinions have been used by business men to find out in advance whether a particular commodity which they are going to produce will be accepted by the public or not. When they produce any new commodity they take a financial risk and must make sure that it will sell and be used by the public. If they can know in advance what people's reactions will be they can plan their production accordingly. They may also know the attitudes of their employees and thus improve mutual understandings and relations.

Thirdly attitude scales and measurements have helped vocational guidance and counselling immensely. The attitudes of successful people in several vocations are studied, their attitudes are considered characteristic of the vocational group and subjects are advised on the basis of tests whether to enter that vocation or not. Vocational guidance can be greatly helped by attitude measurement.

Lastly they help in finding out what the public likes and prefers, how our education and propaganda is affecting such preferences and in making sure that people co-operate in government measures and policies. If people are against any measure the government can take steps to change that opposition in time.

Attitudes are largely the result of social influences and are always being formed and re-formed. In fact all social change and reconstruction turns on the change and reconstruction in attitudes. By controlling social influences and exposing groups of people to them attempts have been successfully made to change and modify people's attitudes. How the atmosphere and attitudes prevailing in an educational institution affect new students admitted to them has been experimentally studied. Group discussion of new measures is very effective in changing attitudes and has been experimentally shown. It is a pointer to our government who are keen to change peoples' food habits.

## Public opinion

With the rise of democratic forms of government public opinion has become a great force in determining and influencing individual and social behaviour. That is why statesmen are very keen both to feel the pulse of public opinion and to create and change public opinion in their favour, and that is why social psychologists are greatly interested in the nature and function of public opinion, its psychological characteristics and measurement. Recently the public opinion in India has compelled the government to take a number of anti-corruption measures. The press, the radio, the cinema and other media of mass communication greatly help to form, strengthen and clarify public opinion.

Psychologists consider opinion an expression of attitude though in common language opinions are considered more variable compared with attitudes which are considered more enduring. Public opinion arises from public discussion of a problem affecting the interests and values of people. Public opinion is not the unanimous will of the people. It does involve disagreement which promotes its growth and development. In fact if all people were agreed there would be no public opinion. In some countries public opinion polls are frequently held to find out in which direction people are thinking.

## Propaganda

Propaganda is a powerful means of controlling and influencing public opinion, it is a technique of changing attitudes in a desirable direction. It has to be distinguished from education. Education tries to produce an open mind, propaganda strives for a closed mind-closed to everything except the object of propaganda.

Several experiments have been made about the nature and effects of propaganda. In one experiment it was shown that emotional propaganda is much more effective than rational propaganda The Institute of Propaganda Analysis at the Columbia University trains people to analyse, evaluate and understand the many kinds of propaganda and thus protect themselves against dangerous and undemocratic appeals. Its report contained a number of devices used by propaganda. During the last World War the Institute was closed down because it was risky analysing home propaganda.

Successful propaganda is rooted in human motives, desires, needs, frustrations and anxieties. If it works through frustrated desires and offers satisfaction of those desires it can influence behaviour in any direction. The desire to improve one's appearance, health and lot in life is universal, it is rarely fully satisfied and all those goods whose advertisement promises these are readily bought, all those policies which promise opportunities for free, happy and comfortable living are readily adopted. During war such frustrations are greater and stronger than those in peace and that is why propaganda during war is far more effective.

Successful propaganda should appeal to as many motives as possible. It must respect social norms and sentiments of the group at which it is directed. Propaganda should be repeated again and again to be most effective, and must be done indirectly in a concealed manner.

Too many people fall victims to propaganda and the best defence against it is to be wide-awake and check whatever one hears or reads.

Propaganda makes use of suggestion on a large scale and names of eminent people in different areas of life and work are used to give prestige to suggestions.

**Prejudice**

In social relations and behaviour prejudices play a very powerful role. They are based on preferences and are simple but irrational judgments of pleasantness and unpleasantness. Some are favourable others unfavourable. Often the individual is unable to explain his prejudices and they are acquired in the course of social experience, from groups in which one moves and lives. Prejudice means pre-judgment, that is judging before and without sufficient evidence. They are not inherited as is commonly supposed but are acquired as a part of our social heritage. Some of them are produced by very pleasant or unpleasant experiences. Although modern life is much more rational and free yet prejudices abound. The reason is that modern life is full of frustrations, frustrations lead to hostility and aggression which find expressions in prejudice. The desire for prestige and security is very strong and with competition and rivalry widespread in modern life most people are not able to satisfy them. And then they feel angry and frustrated and develop prejudices.

Psychologists have made several studies to inquire if there is any relation between personality traits and prejudice and they have found that conservative or reactionary people have racial prejudices. Those who are emotional, conventional and attached to traditions and those who are self-centred are inclined to blame others for their faults and nurse prejudices. And prejudices feed themselves and continue.

Education and propaganda and better ethnic relations promote understanding and reduce prejudice. A number of international organizations are promoting international co-operation in several areas and indirectly serving to fight down racial and national prejudices.

**Groups**

We live in a highly organized society, there are families, clubs offices, institutions, associations, departments, army, postal service, educational institutions, hospitals, markets, and it is through membership of such organizations that we satisfy our basic needs and desires. Psychologists have studied such social organizations and found that before a collection of people can be called a group its members must be stimulating and interacting with each other, they must have a common purpose so that they interact more with members of their own group than with others, they must be conscious of belonging to a group and they must have developed social norms of behaviour.

C. H. Cooley divided groups into primary and secondary, the family is a primary group and the tax-payers association is a secondary group. In a primary group there are only a few members and they have intimate face-to-face contacts with each other. Interaction is direct and they have warm intimate emotional relationships. Members meet each other very frequently. They think and act together and make willing sacrifices for each other. The family is the universal primary group. Play group for children and neighbourhood are other primary groups. In small villages and in primitive society groups are small and primary. In large towns people are woven into several types of groups and associations and one may be a member of several recreational, social, professional groups. In secondary groups relations are less personal and intimate, they are casual, abstract and intellectual. In modern society secondary groups express the cultural pattern of life in any community. They satisfy only partial and secondary needs, and face-to-face contact may not be present.

Groups are also divided into *in-groups* and *out-groups*. My group to which I belong is an in-group for me and an out-group for those who do not belong to it. Our relations with members of our in-group are very cordial, we are loyal to them and co-operate with them. But we are not so inclined to out-groups, in fact we are hostile to them.

Some groups are formal as a college staff or a syndicate and some groups are informal as a picnic party.

The organization of some groups is democratic but of others is very autocratic ruled by one or more individuals.

Groups work together and have definite programmes and objectives. Often their members think, feel and act together. Some psychologists argue that such groups have a group mind which expresses the unity of and solidarity of group behaviour. But the concept is no longer in use.

**Leadership**

Leadership expresses very clearly the fact of social interaction among members of a group. Leaders are responsible for the quality of group effort and the morale of the people in a group.

Psychologists have been studying numerous leaders to find out what personality traits qualified them for leadership. One found that leaders are dominant persons, yet leadership and domination are not the same thing. Another stressed the quality of guiding people in pursuit of a common purpose. Terman studied the characteristics of leaders among children, as rated by their companions, and found that leaders are either very good or very bad in appearance, health, social status, school work, boldness and fluency of speech. They stood out from others. Partridge studied leaders among Boy Scouts and found that they were taller, heavier, better looking, more athletic, more intelligent, and more independent than the other boys. He also found that boys chosen as leaders remained leaders.

Many psychologists like Allport and Bernard have tried to list the personality traits of leaders in good appearance, high intelligence, strong physique, energy, initiative, courage, self-confidence, persistence and the ability to deal with people. Besides he must identify himself with the group. And then educationists have sought to cultivate such qualities among students to make them leaders. Public schools are supposed to produce leaders. Some psychologists plead that leaders are extroverts, of higher socio-economic status.

But all of them seem to believe that leaders' personality is what makes him a leader. There is another view that it is the social situation which produces leaders. It is argued that qualities necessary for leadership depend on the structure of the group. When a problem has to be solved theoretically a clear thinker and a forceful speaker will become a leader. In a gang, leader will have to be dominant and powerful. In a society suffering from too many parties persons with flexible views and loyalties become ready leaders. Leaders arise when there is need for action and there are a number of people who are ready to accept a person's leadership. It may be the followers who influence and rouse a leader. Leaders are creatures of the times and the circumstances in which they arise.

A number of studies and experiments have been made to find out what type of leadership is more helpful to group work and behaviour. Groups of boys have been placed under three types of leadership democratic, authoritarian and *laissez-faire*. In the first boys decided their own programme, helped and guided by their leader, in the second the adult leader dictated policies and programmes and in the third the leader did not care and let them do what they liked. The boys preferred the first type of leadership.

**Mass behaviour**

Mass behaviour is behaviour of a large mass of people in which interaction is altogether impersonal as nobody knows others such as is found in a *kumbh mela*, crowds or mobs. Large streams of men and women gather in a procession or to welcome a leader. There is no intimacy among them, they treat each other formally.

A crowd has no organization, no leader and no division of labour. It is a temporary assembly and has no past or future. It is casual and anonymous, though it may have a common object of attention. There is shoulder to shoulder relation between members of a crowd and they may act together. There is pushing and shouting together but no further interaction.

Mobs are crowds in action. People in a mob have similar thoughts, feelings and actions, and are aware that others in the mob share them. They are highly emotional and excited, do not pause to think and reason. Fear makes them panicky, anger makes them violent. Suggestion and imitation are all powerful and people act irrationally and irresponsibly. They believe whatever they are told, they are fickle and they do not tolerate any opposition or criticism. Psychologists are of opinion that crowds are generally less intelligent than individuals and their behaviour is intellectually lower than that of some individuals. People behave irresponsibly because they are highly excited and there is little chance of their being called to account. An agitated mob of students breaks their own college library and laboratory equipment and they are easily exploited by any leader that comes forward. At this time they are highly suggestible and credulous. They feel all powerful and safe because they cannot be found out. Individuals are not held responsible for their actions and therefore they behave freely and with no responsibility.

According to William McDougall mob behaviour has three characteristics : (1) intellectual processes are inhibited in a crowd, (2) emotions become very intense, and (3) there is regression or relapse into instinctive activity.

Mobs are of several kinds. Aggressive mobs try to do injury to some person as in riots; mob violence may take a very serious turn as many students agitations do. Escape mobs are panic driven as when there is a sudden fire or shooting. Acquisitive mobs rush to acquire a particular object as in food riots. Lastly there are expressive mobs in which people assemble to give expression to their common emotions such as religious congregations.

People may collect at a street corner to listen to a flute-player. Such a collection is an *audience*. Casual audiences assemble by accident, have no programme and are not organized. Formal audiences are arranged, their time and place is pre-determined, and they have certain standards of behaviour. The leader in an audience is active and the followers listen or watch. Some audiences seek information as in a lecture, some seek entertainment and some seek to be persuaded and converted to a new way of thinking.

**Fashions**

The term fashion is commonly used to indicate changes in modes of dress but psychologists have extended the usage to the current or prevailing usage, mode, manner or characteristic expression of cultural traits which custom allows to be changed. Fashions represent a short-lived, superficial, rapid departures from the customary behaviour. They are a modern phenomenon, and flourish in a progressive dynamic society. When customs are rigid leaving no room for change fashions have no place.

Fashions have a wide range and they affect every class of society. In our days society has become so democratic that fashions of the rich and the high are soon followed by the poor and the low.

Sometime fashions are started by lower classes and the rich follow them, as the backless *choli* has spread from the poorer classes to the higher classes. Now-a-days due to quick means of communication and transport, fashions spread to all countries of the world in no time, as the bush shirt has done.

Psychology is interested in knowing what motives control fashions and changes in fashions. Perhaps one of the most obvious fact is that fashions make an individual both unique and like others of his class. If a person is dressed in the latest style he breathes greater self-confidence, is admired by others and is delighted with himself. And if a person is dressed in outworn style he feels shy and diffident. The desire to change fashions may be rooted in the desire for the new and the different. Every individual wishes to conform to what is popular in his social circle as well as wishes to be different from the rest. Both motives find ample scope in fashions and their changes. Some people take to latest fashions to compensate their feelings of inferiority.

**Social change and progress**

Psychology is mostly interested in people's attitude to social change and tries to study psychological processes involved in individual adjustment and resistance to social change. Our culture influences our attitudes, and changes in society modify our attitudes. But changes in social relations and standards are not possible unless people's attitudes change. Therefore the problem for the social psychologist is to study and analyse factors which bring about change or resistance to change. Generally we have four types of attitude.

Reactionary people glorify the past and do not want any change. Conservative people want things as they are. Liberals want gradual change. They speak of evolution of society. Radicals are thoroughly dissatisfied with the present and would like to change things completely, even violently. But it is difficult to say that these attitudes are generalized. Psychology has also studied the influence of home and school on our attitudes to social change.

In another study psychologists have shown that conservative attitudes go with religious ideas and social conformity, and radicals are not very keen about religion or social customs.

Some personality traits favour social change. Intelligent people with knowledge and understanding are sensitive to the needs and difficulties of others and are liberal toward social change. The factor of age is also important. Youth is inclined to change things while old people do not favour social change. Many people want social change because conditions as they are do not suit them, and they agitate for change.

But social change should be a harmonious adjustment between culture, group, man and nature, so that disease, ignorance, famine, poverty, crime, slums or depressions are eliminated. This is the content and aim of social progress.

## QUESTIONS

1. What is social behaviour? What do you understand by socialization.
2. How is an individual socialized? Describe some of the factors and processes involved.
3. Discuss the role of imitation, suggestion and sympathy in making a man social.
4. Discuss the role of co-operation and competition in social life. Which is more powerful?
5. Personality differs from culture to culture, explain the truth of this statement by giving examples.
6. What do you understand by social norms? Give examples and discuss their role in socializing an individual.
7. What is an attitude? Give examples of social attitudes. What are the advantages of measuring attitudes?
8. Discuss the role of public opinion and propaganda in a democratic society.

9. What is prejudice? Is there any relation between personality traits and prejudice?

10. Distinguish between several types of groups, and describe the characteristic of groups which exercise most effective influence on group behaviour. What are the characteristics of mob behaviour?

11. Write a short note on the psychology of fashions.

## Suggestions for Further Reading

1. MORGAN, C. T. : *Introduction to Psychology*, McGraw - Hill Book Co.

2. BORING, LANGFELD AND WELD : *Foundations of Psychology*, John Wiley & Sons.

3. H. E. GARRET : *General Psychology*, Eurasia Publishing House.

4. ADCOCK, C. J. : *Fundamentals of Psychology*, Penguin Books.

5. LINDGREN AND LINDGREN : *Psychology, An Introduction to the Study of Human Behaviour*, John Wiley and Sons.

6. WOODWORTH, R. S. : *Psychology, A Study of Mental Life*, Methuen.

7. EYSENCK, H. J. : *Uses and Abuses of Psychology*, Penguin Books

8. EYSENCK, H. J. : *Sense and Nonsense in Psychology*, Penguin Books.

9. BHATIA, H. R. : *A Textbook of Educational Psychology*, A [illegible] Publishing House.

10. BHATIA, H. R. : *Elements of Social Psychology*, Somaiya Publications.

11. HEPNER, H. W. : *Psychology : Applied to Life and Work*, Prentice-Hall.

12. STORR, A. : *The Integrity of the Personality*, Pelican Books

# INDEX